DATABUSTING FOR SCHOOLS

Sara Miller McCune founded SAGE Publishing in 1965 to support the dissemination of usable knowledge and educate a global community. SAGE publishes more than 1000 journals and over 800 new books each year, spanning a wide range of subject areas. Our growing selection of library products includes archives, data, case studies and video. SAGE remains majority owned by our founder and after her lifetime will become owned by a charitable trust that secures the company's continued independence.

Los Angeles | London | New Delhi | Singapore | Washington DC | Melbourne

RICHARD SELFRIDGE

DATABUSTING FOR SCHOOLS

HOW TO USE AND
INTERPRET EDUCATION DATA

SAGE

Los Angeles | London | New Delhi
Singapore | Washington DC | Melbourne

Los Angeles | London | New Delhi
Singapore | Washington DC | Melbourne

SAGE Publications Ltd
1 Oliver's Yard
55 City Road
London EC1Y 1SP

SAGE Publications Inc.
2455 Teller Road
Thousand Oaks, California 91320

SAGE Publications India Pvt Ltd
B 1/I 1 Mohan Cooperative Industrial Area
Mathura Road
New Delhi 110 044

SAGE Publications Asia-Pacific Pte Ltd
3 Church Street
#10-04 Samsung Hub
Singapore 049483

Editor: James Clark
Editorial assistant: Diana Alves
Production editor: Nicola Carrier
Copyeditor: Sharon Cawood
Proofreader: Thea Watson
Indexer: Gary Kirby
Marketing manager: Dilhara Attygalle
Cover design: Sheila Tong
Typeset by: C&M Digitals (P) Ltd, Chennai, India
Printed in the UK

Library of Congress Control Number: 2017961390

British Library Cataloguing in Publication data

A catalogue record for this book is available from
the British Library

ISBN 978-1-4739-6349-8
ISBN 978-1-4739-6350-4 (pbk)

At SAGE we take sustainability seriously. Most of our products are printed in the UK using responsibly sourced
papers and boards. When we print overseas we ensure sustainable papers are used as measured by the PREPS
grading system. We undertake an annual audit to monitor our sustainability

Contents

About the author

Richard Selfridge is a primary school teacher and writer on education. He has written about the use of education data for *The Guardian*, *The Times Educational Supplement* and *Schools Week*, and is a regular speaker at national teaching conferences, including researchED, Northern Rocks and the Festival of Education.

He contributed a chapter on the use of education data to David Didau's 2015 book *What if Everything You Knew About Education Was Wrong?*, and he has been a regular contributor to national discussions about the use of numbers in education. This is his first book for SAGE Publications.

About the website

DATABUSTING FOR SCHOOLS

HOME   ABOUT   BLOG   CONTACT   OVERVIEW

LOOKING BEHIND THE NUMBERS IN EDUCATION
Not all numbers are the same,
and they don't always mean what you might think

www.databustingforschools.co.uk accompanies Richard Selfridge's *Databusting for Schools*, providing up-to-the minute information about data use in schools. In the fast-evolving world of education data, it provides valuable information on national testing frameworks and the latest developments in the use of numbers in education.

DATABUSTING FOR SCHOOLS

AN INTRODUCTION TO USING AND INTERPRETING EDUCATION DATA

1

What you will learn from this chapter:

What databusting means
What databusting means for schools
How to become a databusting educator

1.1 Databusting

In *The Tipping Point*, first published in 2000, Malcolm Gladwell explores ways in which complex systems suddenly change. Gladwell makes extensive use of data to show that changes have taken place, and then explores why this might have happened. In his opening chapter, he considers a sudden and dramatic change in crime statistics in New York City:

> New York City in the 1980s (was) a city in the grip of one of the worst crime epidemics in its history. But then, suddenly and without warning, the epidemic tipped. From a high in 1990, the crime rate went into precipitous decline. Murders dropped by two-thirds. Felonies were cut by half. Other cities saw their crime drop in the same period. But in no place did the level of violence fall further or faster. (Gladwell, 2000: 137)

Why did this happen? Gladwell looks at the data which was available and comes to a number of conclusions:

> During the 1990s violent crime declined for a number of fairly straightforward reasons. The illegal trade in crack cocaine … began to decline. The economy's drastic recovery meant that people who might have been lured into crime got legitimate jobs instead, and the general aging of the population meant that there were fewer people in the age range … that is responsible for the majority of violence. (2000: 140)

After these initial observations, Gladwell notes that the situation in New York was, however, 'a little more complicated'. The city's economy hadn't improved in the early 1990s, and if anything welfare cuts had hit the city hard. The crack cocaine epidemic was in long-term decline and lots of immigration meant that the city's population was actually getting younger. And the reduction in violent crime which was being recorded was dramatic. As Gladwell says, 'One would expect (these trends) to have gradual effects. In New York, the decline was anything but gradual. Something else clearly played a role in reversing New York's crime epidemic' (2000: 140–1).

Gladwell then looks at what that something else might have been. He suggests that it might have been what has become known as the 'broken windows' theory of crime: when a window is broken and left in an unrepaired state, it signals to the community at large that the rule of law has broken down, which leads to a declining spiral in the community with unrepaired broken windows. Because many negative aspects of life in New York City were not being addressed, from graffiti and fare-dodging on the subway to tacit complicity in low-level criminal disorder, the city's criminals were acting with impunity.

Gladwell charts the clean-up of the New York City Transit System between 1984 and 1990, as a widespread problem with graffiti was tackled head on. This was followed by a concentrated focus on fare-dodging from 1990 onwards, and then a policy of 'zero-tolerance' policing following the election of mayor Rudy Giuliani in 1994. All of this activity coincided with the dramatic fall in the rate of violent crime, all of which was explained neatly – as far as Gladwell is concerned – by the actions of those in authority.

As with almost any neat explanation of complicated human interaction, with a bit of lateral thinking, someone somewhere will be able to find an entirely plausible alternative hypothesis which casts doubt on the original theory. Suddenly, what seems to be a clear explanation often turns out to be simply one of many possible simple explanations. In the case of the drop in crime in New York, one alternative hypothesis came from Steven Levitt and Stephen Dubner, who popularised their ideas in their book *Freakonomics*, published in 2007.

Donohue agreed with Gladwell up to a point. In an original 2001 academic paper, which was drawn on for the above 2007 book, Levitt and his co-author John Donohue had looked at similar crime statistics to those Gladwell had considered. Their initial findings were similar to Gladwell's:

> Since 1991, the United States has experienced the sharpest drop in murder rates since the end of Prohibition in 1933. Homicide rates have fallen more than 40 per cent. Violent crime and property crime have each declined more than 30 percent. Hundreds of articles discussing this change have appeared in the academic literature and popular press. (Donohue and Levitt, 2001: 379)

Their alternative hypothesis was that, rather than the efforts of the Transit Authority and the effects of zero-tolerance policing, the real reason for the fall in crime was that 'legalised abortion has contributed significantly to recent crime reductions. Crime began to fall roughly eighteen years after abortion legalisation' (Donohue and Levitt, 2001: 379). They stated their hypothesis that 'Legalised abortion appears to account for as much as 50 percent of the recent drop in crime' (2001: 379).

Donohue and Levitt argued that, following the nationwide legalisation of abortion in 1973, poor mothers were much less likely to have children who they would have struggled to raise to become law-abiding citizens. They explored the links between the kinds of crime which had ravaged New York City and the deprived, unstable backgrounds of those who had been contributing to the high crime statistics. They also looked at the effects in different cities and states of changes to allow localised legalised abortion before the national change brought about by the famous Supreme Court decision in the case of Roe v Wade in 1973.

Donohue and Levitt didn't entirely dismiss the argument made by Gladwell, but they suggested that the effects of legalised abortion were much greater than the alternative theory put forward in *The Tipping Point*. Was Gladwell wrong? Gladwell himself responded to Donohue and Levitt's interpretation of the data, poking holes in their argument by, for example, questioning why the widespread availability – and use – of contraceptive pills from the mid-1960s did not have the same effect as the much less prevalent use of abortion as a form of birth control from the 1970s onwards.

Gladwell, Donohue and Levitt were not the only prominent voices trying to find an explanation for the situation in New York. Steven Pinker, leading academic and writer of books on popular science, wrote about the issue in his 2011 book *The Better Angels of Our Nature.* Pinker noted that the Freakonomics theory seemed 'too cute to be true' and noted that, 'any hypothesis that comes out of left field to explain a massive social trend with a single overlooked event will almost certainly turn out to be wrong, even if it has some data supporting it at the time' (Pinker, 2011: 143).

In Pinker's book, which was about broader declines in rates of violence in human society over time, he explored the Freakonomics theory, drawing on other data to support his arguments. Pinker noted, for example, that the proportion of children born to mothers in the categories Donohue and Levitt had identified as vulnerable should have decreased according to Donohue and Levitt's theory, whereas it had actually substantially increased.

Pinker also suggested that there were compelling arguments to suggest that mothers who avoided having unwanted children were likely to be more responsible citizens than those in similar circumstances who did not, and that therefore the opposite to the Freakonomics claim should have occurred, leaving a generation *more* likely to commit crime. Pinker put forward his alternative theory, based on the same data utilised by Donohue, Levitt and Gladwell. In Pinker's view, the violent crime decline happened because older criminals had laid down their weapons and younger cohorts simply did not follow in their footsteps.

So what did happen to cause the decline in violent crime in New York City in the 1990s? It rather depends on the point at which you enter the debate, whether you have any strong desire to disagree with the general consensus, and your need to question the views of others. The most obvious truth is that, using virtually the same data, different people are likely to come to different conclusions. One explanation may eventually become the accepted narrative, but human actions are complicated and alternative theories may explain the same or similar facts in contrary but logically plausible ways.

A more recent example of this phenomenon, this time in education, is the thorny issue of what has become known as the London Effect. At a point in the early 2000s, pupils in Inner London's state schools began to record better and better examination results at the age of 16. Starting from a point which was noticeably lower than the average for children across England, GCSE results in Inner London rose inexorably into the 2010s, leaving other regions of the country behind. By 2016, the typical child in an Inner London state secondary school was attaining qualifications at 16 which were 10% higher than the national average. In 1998, Inner London had been the worst-performing region in the country, with results 18.5% lower than the average measure.

The first major theory which attempted to explain this 'London Effect' was put forward by Ofsted, the government's school inspection agency, in 2010. Ofsted explained that an initiative called the London Challenge had:

> continued to improve outcomes for pupils in London's primary and secondary schools at a faster rate than nationally. Excellent system leadership and pan-London networks of schools allow effective partnerships to be established between schools, enabling needs to be tackled quickly and progress to be accelerated. (Ofsted, 2010: 1)

The London Challenge was an initiative introduced into London secondary schools in 2002, and extended to primary schools in 2008. It used outside advisers to support schools which were deemed to be underperforming. Ofsted identified four areas which it suggested had been the cause of the rise in pupil outcomes: clear leadership, experienced external advisers, work to improve the quality of teaching and learning, and the development of robust tracking systems in schools.

This narrative held sway until 2014, when the Institute for Fiscal Studies (IFS) considered the issue, and added some new data, and a new theory, to the conversation. The IFS's conclusion was that, rather than the London Effect being the result of anything which happened in secondary schools, the reason for it was a change in the prior attainment of students who began to enter Inner London secondary schools 15 years earlier.

Key Stage 2 scores had improved in the late 1990s and early 2000s, but the IFS report was unsure why this had happened:

> What caused the improvement in Key Stage 2 test scores that led to the 'London effect' at Key Stage 4 is not clear. However, the explanation will be related to changes in London's primary schools in the late 1990s and early 2000s. This means that programmes and initiatives such as the London Challenge, the Academies Programme, Teach First or differences in resources are unlikely to be the major explanation. (Institute for Fiscal Studies and Institute of Education, 2014: 8)

The IFS then went on to suggest that, since the national literacy and numeracy strategies had rolled out at the right time, these might have been the cause of the rise in GCSE pass rates seen in Inner London a few years later. Even if this was not exactly the case, the IFS suggested that the theory that the London Challenge, structural changes such as the academies programme, or initiatives such as Teach First were responsible for the London Effect, was unlikely to be true.

A further report was issued at the same time as the IFS report, this time claiming that the improvements were due to efforts being made in secondary schools. This report offered no additional data and relied on narratives generated by those who believed themselves to be responsible for the successes of the schools for which they were responsible (CfBT Education Trust, 2014).

Following these two alternative explanations, a further theory was added to the mix, as the Centre for Market and Public Organisation (CMPO) at the University of Bristol published a report which noted that the improvements in London schools were 'entirely accounted for by ethnic composition'. The CMPO report introduced some further numerical data to the mix, using some detailed statistical analysis which enabled it to suggest that 'if London had the same ethnic composition as the rest of England, there would be no "London Effect"' (Burgess, 2014: 3). In essence, this theory suggested that London was simply becoming increasingly different to the rest of the country, and therefore that like was not being compared with like. The London Effect was interesting, but didn't offer any particular insight into implementing any particular policy initiatives at school level which would improve GCSE outcomes across the country.

As with the various theories about violent crime in New York City, the different theories about what caused the dramatic increase in GCSE results in Inner London are all plausible to some extent. Those who have developed their theories have done so with the best of intentions – we all want to try to explain the phenomena that we observe in a way which fits the data which we have available. We do this to try to decide how to act in future: should we clean up problematic neighbourhoods and introduce zero-tolerance policing, or seek structural changes which allow citizens to make difficult decisions which might be good for society? Or should we simply recognise that longer-term socio-economic factors might be at play?

In the case of the London Effect, what does it tell us about decisions which schools and governments should make about improving exam results? Should we implement policy initiatives similar to the London Challenge in other parts of the country? Or should we recognise that the effects that school-level change might have are minimal compared to wider underlying factors related to educational attainment?

This whole process – gathering data, analysing the data, developing and testing theories, debating and developing ideas, finding ways to act in future – is common to many walks of life, including education. This book is about data and its use and interpretation in educational contexts.

Schools have, of course, gathered data for a long time. The use of numerical data in schools has, however, increased massively in the last 40 years. There are a number of reasons for this, from the increase in affordable computing power to ever-increasing external involvement in the internal workings of schools. Whatever the explanation for the rise in the use of numbers in schools, teachers, senior managers, governors and others working in and with schools are finding that they are being required to gather, analyse, interpret and act on numerical-based data as part of their role in education.

For many working in and with schools, this has required a level of understanding of numbers, and of statistics based on those numbers, which asks a great deal of busy professionals whose main focus is on education, not data. This book aims to give you a readable grounding in the use and interpretation of educational data throughout the education system. Aimed at the general reader, the book takes as its starting point those teachers, middle leaders and governors who are getting to grips with data. Those senior leaders who entered teaching before the current data-focused era will also find the ideas set out here invaluable in understanding many common misconceptions about numbers, as well as the many ways in which numbers can provide valuable insight into effective (and ineffective) practice in schools.

In the cases of New York's violent crime and London's GCSE results, the gathering, analysis and interpretation of numerical data are key to making sensible decisions about future courses of action. Since the decisions we make in school have an impact not just on our students, but on the whole school community, we need to understand the new educational data landscape so that we can decide how to move forward. In the modern world, databusting has become essential.

1.2 Databusting for schools

Teachers, senior leaders and governors will be only too aware of the amount of data which those working in school work with on a regular basis. We all want to know how our students are progressing in their learning, and to ensure that we are not setting our sights too low or missing areas where children are not making the progress which they should be making. We use data extensively to monitor and evaluate what we are doing to help the children in our care to get the most out of their time at school.

Databusting for Schools begins by introducing two fictional school governors who are attempting to understand the data which is available to them to help them to understand their schools. A great deal of the data they have been given is generated in school, from attendance data, pupil performance data, which is usually based on some sort of written test, to other data which identifies particular groups of children within their school. They have also been given data that is generated by government agencies, and used as part of the accountability system which holds schools to account for the educational progress of the pupils in their care.

As people relatively new to schools, governors often find the sheer amount of data overwhelming, but it is important to understand what is available, before going on to be able to critically assess what the data might be able to indicate about a school. It is also useful to understand how centrally generated data has evolved since it began to be used in schools, particularly as many of those leading schools, and those holding them to account, have often built up their understanding of data through practices which have developed in ways which are frequently haphazard, un-evidenced and somewhat questionable.

For those in the classroom, the use of data has become an essential aspect of teachers' roles. The 2011 Teacher Standards, which apply to all teachers in English schools, set a clear expectation that teachers should use 'relevant data to monitor progress, set targets, and plan subsequent lessons' (DfE, 2011: 1). As we note in Chapter 3, as with so many things in education, the term 'data' is somewhat unclear. Whilst the word is commonly used to mean 'a collection of information', much of the data teachers are required to use to 'monitor progress, set targets, and plan subsequent lessons' is numerical data rather than narrative information in the more general sense of the word 'data'. Understanding the use of numbers is therefore the main thrust of this book.

Much of the data used in school is a summary of raw numbers. In order to understand what numerical data can tell them about their classes, teachers need to have a good working knowledge of the considerations which have to be made when looking at these summaries. Confusingly, the summaries themselves are often numbers which describe larger sets of numbers. And even more confusingly, not all numbers are the same, and the ways in which numbers can be manipulated depend on the type of number which is being used. Describing differences in numbers is particularly fraught with pitfalls. Many readers with non-mathematical backgrounds may be surprised what they learn as they begin to discover that there is more to numerical data than meets the eye.

Databusting for Schools introduces two fictional teachers to explore numbers in depth, beginning by looking at simple uses of numbers before exploring how equations work and the way in which graphs can bring light – and shade – to numbers. Much of the early part of the book is essential reading for those whose understanding of higher-level mathematics is a little rusty, or those who have not had cause to consider the ways in which more advanced summary data is generated and presented.

Those who have explored basic statistics in some depth will find the main section useful as a refresher in the use of measures of central tendency, and the use of samples to shed light on wider populations. As many of those working in schools will be aware, some understanding of more advanced statistics has become an essential aspect of many roles in teaching, and in the management and oversight of schools. Those working in school leadership and governance need to be able to interpret data which is presented with confidence intervals, for example, and this requires a good understanding of the assumptions and calculations required to create these kinds of data.

Of course, numbers themselves are only one part of the picture. Being able to appraise information in numerical form critically has become a large part of the work both of those leading schools and those holding them to account. The latter part of *Databusting for Schools* explores in depth the ways in which the use of numbers has evolved in our ongoing efforts to understand and change education, and looks at some of the criticisms which have been levelled at the increasingly data-driven nature of school management and education policy.

1.3 Becoming a databusting educator

The very fact that you are holding this book in your hands indicates that you have questions about the use of numbers in education. This increasing engagement with the how and why of teaching policy and practice has been fuelled by a number of parallel developments. The modern interconnected world has enabled those working in schools to reach out and connect with other likeminded people beyond their classrooms, offices and schools much more easily than was the case just a few short years ago.

Until relatively recently, most of those in school were simply not in a position to explore the wider issues which arise from the use of numbers in education. Teachers, school leaders and governors were presented with complex analysis which many struggled to understand. Those who wanted to investigate education research which relied on regression analysis and sampling theory, to take one example, found that they came up against ideas and terminology far beyond the crowded syllabus of their teacher training.

The rise of social media, and the ability for educators to connect with each other and to share ideas and experience, has enabled an increasing number of us to evaluate critically many of the accepted explanations of complex processes in education. Educators have begun to use services such as Twitter to discuss their experiences and opinions, and to begin to ask questions about the way in which numbers are used and interpreted in education.

At the same time, the growth of the internet has meant that enormous amounts of previously difficult-to-access research into education has become available at the click of a button. The increasing demand for access to educational research has seen more channels opening up, with new bodies such as the Chartered College for Teaching enabling much wider availability and discussion of educational research. Those who popularise research into education, such as Dan Willingham in the USA, Tom Bennett in the UK and Dylan Wiliam across both countries, have become significant figures at the forefront of promoting discussion and understanding of education.

Teachers have come together at grassroots educational conferences such as ResearchEd, founded by Tom Bennett and others, Northern Rocks, Beyond Levels, Primary Rocks Live and Women Ed, with more teacher-led conferences appearing each year. At the same time, Teach Meets – in which teachers gather together to share ideas and practice out of school hours, independent of their schools – have grown exponentially in the last five years.

Each of these events features educators sharing ideas, many of which involve the use of numbers to a greater or lesser extent. As educators look for ways to improve their practice or their schools, they naturally consider ways to assess the impact of changes to children's educational experiences. Much of this assessment uses numerical data generated by testing or assessing children. As teachers have looked more closely at the issue of assessment, they have discovered that in the rush to generate numbers, important considerations have often been ignored, hidden from view or simply overlooked through ignorance.

Influential voices such as those of Daisy Christodoulou – former secondary teacher and until 2017 Head of Assessment at Ark Schools, and author of *Making Good Progress?* – and Daniel Koretz, Professor of Education at Harvard University, have attempted to increase teachers' awareness of the issues surrounding testing and assessment.

All of these disparate factors indicate an increasing desire for knowledge and understanding of the numbers being used in education, as we move into the age of the databusting teacher.

1.4 The pressing need for databusting teachers and leaders

As the different interpretations of the reduction of New York's violent crime and the increase in London's GCSE results show, the more we consider and discuss ideas, the more we explore the data which is available, the more nuanced the general picture becomes. But, ultimately, we need to decide on a course of action based on the evidence which we have considered.

Simply fixing the broken windows in future, literally and metaphorically, may not in itself reduce violent crime in cities seriously affected by the problem. Similarly, passing legislation now in the hope of improvements in future may not have the intended outcome many years down the line. The factors which caused the decline in violent crime in New York City – which had become the 10th most safe city of 50 cities ranked by *The Economist* magazine in 2015, with crime far below the US average – appear to be complex, and the theories explaining the causes of the decline may not help in planning for the future.

Those shaping policy in a high-crime city like Baltimore, for example, have a difficult task on their hands. Baltimore has crime rates which are far higher than the US average, and has done for a long time (City Data, 2017). Viewers of *The Wire*, a crime drama series based in the city, were left in no doubt of the extent and effects of the crime epidemic in the city. With almost four times the national average level of crime, policy makers have to decide how best to tackle the problem. Those reflecting on what actions should be taken to reduce crime in Baltimore would certainly be well advised to take New York City's experience into consideration, whilst exercising caution given the differing views which have been put forward. Databusting becomes increasingly important in a data-immersed world.

Likewise, to those looking to improve educational outcomes in England, setting up city 'challenges' similar to the London Challenge may have seemed to be a sensible way to boost the GCSE results of cities such as Birmingham and Manchester. Yet, when the UK government set up 'City Challenges' in Greater Manchester and the Black Country, the results were nowhere near as dramatic as those seen in the capital (Kidson and Norris, 2014). This may be because the underlying factors which led to the significant increase in GCSE results in Inner London were, as researchers such as Simon Burgess of Bristol University have suggested, related to changes in demographics and the attainment of children entering the capital's secondary schools a few years earlier.

As with the case of those seeking to develop policy in Baltimore, those responsible for public policy would do well to draw on the perceived lessons from elsewhere. Similarly, those responsible for schools outside the UK's capital should bear in mind what happened in Inner London in the early 21st century when deciding how best to proceed in future. In both cases, the ability to critically evaluate earlier research and experience is vital. Those working in and with schools need to be able to rigorously interrogate the use of numbers in any procedure which attempts to shed light on educational processes and outcomes.

At a local level, teachers and school leaders need to understand the limitations, as well as the benefits, of the numbers generated in school. The rise and fall of the system of *levels* in English schools, as discussed in Chapter 2, is illustrative of this point. In summary, levels were introduced as part of the National Curriculum when it was rolled out in the 1990s. As children progressed through school, they were expected to progress through a series of levels of learning.

Whilst there was much discussion prior to the introduction of the system of levels (Wiliam, 2001), what was introduced was, on the surface, fairly simple to understand. Children were expected to achieve one level of progress every two years, with most starting at Level 1 at age 5, Level 2 at age 7, and so on, until they achieved Level 6 at age 15. Of course, some children start and end at higher levels, and therefore there were actually 8 levels.

A further complication arose as schools began to segment the National Curriculum into a series of 'sub-levels', which split each level into three tiered sections. These sub-levels were then allocated a numerical value, as discussed in Chapter 2. Schools began to develop a series of 'Expected Levels of Progress', with many children (and their teachers) being set targets framed as 'Levels of Progress' or, worse still, 'Points of Progress'. More worryingly, teachers were largely required to assess children they taught using written criteria for each sub-level, creating powerful incentives for assessments to become distorted by the myriad of pressures being placed upon them.

At this point, the problems with this kind of 'datafication' of learning should become clear to a databusting teacher. Unfortunately, it took a long time between the point when more data-and-assessment-literate teachers and school leaders began to highlight the many problems with the levels system, and the point in 2014 when the system of levels was abandoned. When the government eventually published the final report from its *Commission on Assessment without Levels* in 2015, it reiterated comments made in the Carter Review of Initial Teacher Training, which had said that, 'of all areas of ITT content, we believe the most significant improvements are needed on training for assessment' (Carter, 2015: 9).

The Carter Review had identified that teachers should receive training in:

important concepts in assessment (such as validity, reliability, norm and criterion referencing). New teachers should also be taught theories of assessment – for example, why, when and how to assess. Trainees also need to be taught how to use pupil data, including training in basic statistics. (Carter, 2015: 9)

There is a pressing need for those working in school to develop their knowledge and understanding of each of these areas, which are all covered in *Databusting for Schools*.

1.5 Databusting in practice

The rapid rise of the use of numerical information in education has introduced a number of issues which databusting schools have to address. First, and possibly most importantly, is the rise in the use of numbers to inform systems used to hold schools to account for the education which they provide. School governors and leaders need to have a good knowledge and understanding, for example, of the processes involved in creating standardised tests and the important ways these differ to the types of non-standardised tests routinely used in school to assess and develop learning.

Understanding external standardised tests, such as those which are administered each year in Years 6, 11 and 13, and taken by entire cohorts each year, has become an essential part of school leadership. Understanding the way in which these tests are used to create measures of Value Added, for example, is a vital part of understanding the summary measures created for accountability purposes by external agencies. Databusting schools learn to interrogate these measures to ensure that they present an accurate picture of the learning which takes place in their classrooms, and to ensure that decisions for the future are made using justifiable conclusions based on the data which is available.

Primary schools have particular issues to consider, from the difficulty of creating accurate measures of the learning of very young children, to the problem of ensuring that measuring 11-year-olds does not become an end in itself. Understanding the pressures and distortions to which tests are subjected helps those responsible for managing the use and interpretation of test results to make the best decisions they can for the children they educate.

Databusting schools look beyond test results to understand how numbers can help to ensure that every child gets the most out of the educational opportunities in school. In these schools, useful but often neglected data is used to understand how children are progressing. Age within cohort data, for example, is often neglected. The differences in children's physical development across a single year group, particularly in primary school, can be enormous. Too often, those in higher prior attainment groups are simply the autumn-born children, for example. Even in secondary schools, younger children are often at a disadvantage within their cohort; databusting schools work to ensure that all of those in school take into account crucial age data when planning for, teaching and assessing children.

One legacy of levels in school is the all-too-frequent mixing of formative and summative assessment, leading to a situation whereby neither type of assessment is used effectively. The differences between norm-referenced and criterion-referenced tests, likewise, are often glossed over in school, resulting in test preparation which does not work as intended. Databusting assessment enables schools to fully understand the purposes of each type of assessment, and to understand the best ways in which to prepare – and not to prepare – children for end-of-key-stage tests.

For those who are held accountable for school outcome data, the need to understand the complexities involved in creating national comparison measures is crucially important. The use of tests of significance and of confidence intervals in comparative data is controversial, for example, and databusting schools should understand the differing views which are held by those in the academic community about the validity of these measures. This requires some in-depth exploration of the mathematics which underpins this area, and Chapters 5 and 6, in particular, may present a challenge to some readers. This is because the concepts involved are extremely complex, however, and there is no getting around the fact that these ideas are difficult to master. Databusting is, at times, a highly complex task.

Critically appraising data is crucial when looking at analyses of education which use numbers, and Chapter 8 provides a clear outline of the processes required to ensure that you are not mislead by data. *Databusting for Schools* concludes by looking at the history of data use in education, which has been complicated and controversial in equal measure.

1.6 Databusting for schools

The key message of this book is that those working in and with schools need to be extremely cautious when using numbers in education. Used carefully, with due consideration for the many potential pitfalls which occur all to frequently, numbers can help teachers, schools and outside agencies to identify potential strengths and weaknesses within the schooling system. But as the examples of New York and

London demonstrate, numbers are simply the start of any discussion. Databusting is becoming an indispensable skill in the modern world, and the time for *Databusting for Schools* has come.

References

Burgess, S. (2014) *Understanding the Success of London's Schools*. Bristol: The Centre for Market and Public Organisation.

Carter, A. (2015) *Carter Review of Initial Teacher Training (ITT)*. London: Department for Education.

CfBT Education Trust (2014) *Lessons from London Schools: Investigating the Success*. London: CfBT Education Trust.

City Data (2017) Crime rate in Baltimore, Maryland. Available at: www.city-data.com/crime/crime-Baltimore-Maryland.html. Accessed 20/2/18.

Department for Education (DfE) (2011) *Teachers' Standards*. London: DfE.

Donohue, J.J. and Levitt, S.D. (2001) 'The impact of legalised abortion on crime', *Quarterly Journal of Economics*, 116(2): 379–420.

Economist, The (2015) *Safe Cities Index 2015*. London: The Economist.

Gladwell, M. (2000) *The Tipping Point*. New York: Little, Brown.

Institute for Fiscal Studies and Institute of Education (2014) *Lessons from London Schools for Attainment Gaps and Social Mobility*. London: Institute for Fiscal Studies and Institute of Education.

Kidson, M. and Norris, E. (2014) *Implementing the London Challenge*. London: Joseph Rowntree Foundation/Institute for Government.

Levitt, S.D. and Dubner, S.J. (2007) *Freakonomics*. New York: William Morrow.

Office for Standards in Education, Children's Services and Skills (Ofsted) (2010) *London Challenge*. London: Ofsted.

Pinker, S. (2011) *The Better Angels of our Nature*. New York: Viking.

Wiliam, D. (2001) *Level Best? Levels of Attainment in National Curriculum Assessment*. London: Association of Teachers and Lecturers.

2

GATHERING EDUCATION DATA

WHERE DOES IT COME FROM?

Case study 2.1

Getting up to speed with education data

Andrew and Samaya are newly appointed school governors. Andrew is a governor at his child's primary school and has taken an interest in the educational attainment oversight on his governing body. Samaya is a secondary school governor with a similar interest.

Both Andrew and Samaya have been given large files of data for their schools, and have been asked to read the information before their induction meetings with their governor mentors. As governors with non-educational backgrounds – Andrew works for a bank and Samaya is a solicitor – they are both new to the schools sector.

The data which they have been given is generated both by the school and by local and national bodies which provide data to schools. As with so much technical information, the files are awash with acronyms, terminology and concepts which are new to Andrew and Samaya. The more they read, the more confusing the information becomes, as they struggle to interpret what they have been given. Neither Andrew nor Samaya find it easy to understand the sheer complexity of the data generated and used in contemporary education, and both need guidance to help them to support and challenge their school in their role as governors.

2.1 Where does education data come from?

Schools are awash with data, generated both within the institutions themselves and by numerous external bodies supplying data via government agencies and departments, or via third-party companies contracted by schools themselves. Whilst individual teachers have always collected information about the children they teach, much of school-generated data, particularly in school years not subject to external examination, was not collected or analysed centrally until relatively recently. Prior to the 1980s, schools in the UK mostly collected data about those working in school, the numbers of children they taught and what might be thought of as the administration of schools, rather than the education within them.

In England and Wales, this changed as a result of education reform and computing power from the mid-1980s onwards. Reform led to a system of national assessments at age 7, 11 and 14 (since disbanded), which, along with revised assessments at age 16, provided central government with large amounts of data designed (in theory at least) to facilitate accountability and improvement in schools. Increased computational power and technology have made previously laborious analysis and collection of data much more feasible.

Schools now collect, analyse and store significant amounts of data.

2.2 In-school data

Teachers generate tremendous amounts of information about their classes every school day. From primary school teachers, who develop comprehensive knowledge of the 30 or so children they work with each school year, to secondary school subject specialists working with multiple classes, teaching requires adults to spend significant amounts of time analysing and understanding what children already know, and what they need to know in future.

Much of the information generated is not written down, of course, and much is held in the heads of the professionals working in school. For the effective administration of schools, however, a certain amount of data is generated and held centrally in the school.

2.2.1 Daily attendance data

Teachers must complete a daily attendance record, which has to be collated centrally via each school's administration team. By law, every child's attendance record must be completed twice daily, once at the beginning of the school day and again after the lunch break. Each half day of a child's schooling is referred to as a *session*, and children must be recorded as being present (or not) for each session a school provides.

Where a child is not present for a session, the school must record whether the child is attending an approved educational activity, is absent, or is unable to attend due to exceptional circumstances. Whilst there is no legal requirement for schools to use any particular codes to record absence and attendance, the government provides a list of recommended codes which are, in practice, used by the vast majority of schools.

Some of the codes used are clearly phase-specific. Primary school children rarely attend work experience, for example, and do not need to attend interviews with prospective employers.

The codes the government uses are as follows:

L	Late arrival	After the start time, but within a given margin.
U	Arrival after the register has closed	After the 'late arrival' cut-off.
B	Off-site educational activity	Usually provided by another educational facility.
D	Dual registration	Regular attendance at another educational facility.
J	At an interview with a prospective employer	
P	Participating at a supervised sporting activity	
V	Educational visit or trip	Usually a school trip supervised by school staff.
W	Work experience	
C	Authorised leave of absence	Schools can agree to a leave of absence.
E	Excluded with no provision	
F	Extended family holiday	Holidays over 10 days in length.
H	Family holiday	Holidays less than 10 days in length.
I	Illness	Not medical or dental appointments.
M	Medical or dental appointments	
R	Religious observance	
S	Study leave	For Year 11 pupils.
T	Gypsy, Roma and Traveller absence	When families are travelling.
G	Unauthorised family holiday	
N	Not yet known	
O	Unauthorised absence	
X	Not required to be in school	Used for non-compulsory school-age absence.
Y	Exceptional circumstance	School is closed, transport fails or there is another emergency.
Z	Not on admission register	Used prior to child joining school.
#	Planned or partial school closure	Inset days, school holidays, weekends, etc.

Many school management information systems go further than this, allowing schools to record attendance in each lesson, which can be particularly useful at secondary level when children move between classes during the school day. Some systems generate text messages and emails which can be sent to children's parents and carers, and some allow selected teachers to be alerted when children are not attending classes they would be expected to attend. Systems such as Capita's SIMS and Class Charts allow schools to give children's parents and carers access to their child's attendance and behaviour records.

Whilst much of this kind of information is used within school, as governors, Andrew and Samaya may find it useful to talk to their school data managers to establish what attendance information is shared over the course of a given period, and with whom.

2.2.2 Assessment data

Schools use a number of different methods to assess children's learning. Andrew and Samaya will need to find out how their schools choose to measure both children's raw attainment and their progress over time. In the majority of cases, schools use a system which is based on a combination of teacher assessment (whereby teachers use standardised criteria to assess children, although this can be subject to bias) and test data (which is, theoretically at least, free from potential bias).

One reason for this hybrid assessment system is that, from the introduction of the National Curriculum in the 1990s up to 2014–16, the majority of schools used a system of 'levels' to assess children from Year 1 through to Year 9, as introduced in Chapter 1. This system was designed to enable children to progress through different 'levels' of learning, from Level 1 through to Level 8. As schools began to develop their computerised tracking of pupils using levels, levels were split into three 'sublevels', with a level c, b and a within each level.

Levels were then allocated numerical 'points' values, with Level 4B, for example, being arbitrarily allocated 27 points. Each sub-level was separated by two points, so that Level 4A was allocated 29 points, two more than Level 4B.

> ## Box 2.1 | National Curriculum levels – point scores and fine grades
>
> Following the introduction of the National Curriculum in the period from 1992 to 1996, a series of levels of attainment were introduced. These were intended to provide an overview of progression from the start of schooling in Key Stage 1 through to the end of Key Stage 3. There were eight levels of attainment, from Level 1 to Level 8.

Most children were expected to attain Level 2 in Year 2, Level 4 in Year 6 and Level 5 or 6 in Year 9. In the Key Stage 3 tests used from 1992 to 2008, children could attain a maximum of Level 8 in Maths and Level 7 in English and science tests.

Levels were split into three sub-levels, A, B and C, where A was the highest sub-level and C was the lowest. These sub-levels were then allocated point scores in the mid-1990s following the pattern in Table 2.1, which was used in Key Stage 2.

Table 2.1 Sub-levels and their point scores

Level	Points
2C	13
2B	15
2A	17
3C	19
3B	21
3A	23
4C	25
4B	27
4A	29
5C	31
5B	33
5A	35

Oddly, Level 1 was not split into sub-levels, and all assessed at Level 1 were allocated a point score of 9. Level 6, which began to be used in primary school in 2012, was not split into sub-levels and was allocated a point score of 39. Those who were working below Level 1 were allocated 3 points.

In some government analysis, children were put into level 'buckets', whereby all of the sub-levels in Level 4 were allocated 27 points, for example. In other analyses, children were allocated 'fine grades', which converted marks on Key Stage 2 tests into level scores with two decimal places, such as 'Level 4.8', for example.

Moving from levels to point scores and fine grades enabled complicated statistical analysis to be undertaken, which was then distributed to schools and school inspectors. This isn't without its problems, as discussed below and in Chapter 10.

The levels system was abandoned over the period 2014–16 as a new National Curriculum was introduced. The legacy of levels remains however, as many schools have embedded tracking systems based on using numerical values to record progressive stages of learning. Whilst the coming years will see further change, currently many children in Year 1 to 8 are allocated one of four possible bandings of development, with children now graded as either 'emerging', 'working at', 'exceeding' or 'mastery' levels. Different systems use different values for these bandings and there is no longer a national system which all schools have to employ.

Many primary schools have begun to use the terminology of 'age-related expectations' (ARE) to track children, although the range of terminology is quite wide, with some schools making creative use of the freedoms offered by the changes which were made post-levels. Whilst tracking systems vary from school to school, the majority of schools continue to administer tests to enable the tracking of children as they progress through their education. This is, once again, not without its problems, which are discussed in Chapter 10.

For children entering primary education, attainment and progress are tracked using Early Years Foundation Stage (EYFS) profiles. The EYFS was introduced in 2006 and became statutory in 2008. The basic structure of the EYFS assessment includes 17 early learning goals for each child, which must be submitted to the Department of Education at the end of the Reception year. Attainment for each goal is recorded as either 'expected', 'exceeding' or 'emerging', and this has influenced the way in which the majority of schools assess and track children in their early years in education.

Tracking progress and attainment for children with special educational needs has largely used a set of 'performance scales', or p-scales. These are performance descriptors for each subject and were developed alongside the system of levels described above. From 2017, these were made non-statutory following the Rochford Review, which recommended that p-scales should be replaced by seven areas of cognition and learning. Governors such as Andrew and Samaya will need to discuss their school's approach to assessing children with special educational needs and disabilities, with their special educational needs coordinator.

In Key Stage 1 (KS1; Years 1 and 2), children generally sit tests in reading and mathematics at the end of Year 1, with mandated testing in Year 2. Some schools undertake formal testing more frequently than this, although this is rare. Since 2012, those in Year 1 are required to undertake a 'phonics screen check', in which children are asked to read aloud a list of 40 decodable words. Twenty of the words are 'phonically plausible', in that they can be decoded even though they are not words used in English, such as 'strom'. The check is designed this way so that children are neither unduly advantaged nor disadvantaged by their prior vocabulary knowledge.

Children sit mandated Key Stage 1 tests at the end of Year 2. Schools must administer these tests and are expected to use the results of the tests to inform teacher assessments of children's current academic attainment. This is not without controversy, as discussed in Chapter 10. Since 2016, KS1 tests have included an assessment of spelling, grammar and punctuation, as well as tests of reading and mathematics, although as a result of mistakes in administration in 2016, schools did not have to formally submit results for spelling, grammar and punctuation that year, and these tests have subsequently become optional.

Current government proposals indicate that Key Stage 1 SATs will be withdrawn in 2023, as a new reception baseline check is planned for 2020. This follows an aborted attempt to introduce reception baseline assessments in 2016, and therefore there is some degree of uncertainty about the statutory framework in the future.

Whilst it is rare to conduct formal testing in other subject areas in Key Stage 1, some schools do administer tests supplied by various outside bodies. Durham's Centre for Evaluation and Monitoring (CEM), for example, offers a suite of tests for KS1 which include assessments of ability, and of attitudes towards reading, maths and school.

Children in Key Stage 2 (KS2; Years 3–6) generally sit tests in reading, mathematics and spelling, grammar and punctuation (SPaG) at the end of each school year, with mandated statutory testing in Year 6. In-school tests are usually administrated either three or six times a year, i.e. either at the end of each term or half term. Some schools test at different times during the year, although this is fairly unusual. Tests in other subjects are rare in Key Stage 2, although once again some outside organisations offer a variety of assessments which can be used by schools.

Secondary schools test children in a number of ways which are markedly different to primary schools. On entry in Year 7, for example, most children sit standardised tests measuring ability. Known within education as cognitive abilities tests, or CATs, these are usually split into three parts; verbal (thinking with words); quantitative (thinking with numbers); and non-verbal (thinking with shapes and space). These scores are standardised (i.e. placed on a standard scale, usually with 100 as the mean score) and results are given for each part alongside an overall score.

Box 2.2   Standardised tests and standardised scores

Standardised test is the generic term for a particular type of summative test. A standardised test is uniform, in that all those who take the test undertake the same tasks, which are administered in the same way, and tests are scored in the same way for all who take them. Ensuring that the test has been standardised should mean that every candidate taking the test is treated in exactly the same way.

This has advantages, in that no candidate is given unfair support, or is treated differently when taking the test. Standardised tests were developed to remove the potential pitfalls which can affect examiners who, being human, inadvertently and unconsciously treat test takers differently. A child's handwriting or spelling, for example, may affect an examiner's

(Continued)

(Continued)

impression of their proficiency in a subject. Where examinations are taken face to face, a candidate's accent, manner of speaking or some other trait may influence an examiner's conclusions about the candidate's proficiency.

Teacher assessment, for example, has been consistently shown to be biased against certain groups of children, as those assessing children frequently make unconscious assumptions about children's capacity and capability to learn. Those children with wider vocabularies, or particular ways of talking, are often assumed to be more able than they actually are; likewise, those who lack vocabulary and speak in particular ways are often marked down.

Standardised tests have been shown to have disadvantages. Some students, particularly those with disabilities or limited proficiency in the language of the test, are less able to access the test and are therefore likely to be given scores which do not reflect their learning. Those who lack the maturity to do their best in formal situations may also be disadvantaged by standardised tests. Standardised tests are prone to distortion, in that they frequently have high stakes attached to them. Where these high stakes encourage those who prepare children for and administer the tests to focus their efforts on maximising scores on the tests rather than on deepening knowledge and understanding of the whole domain being assessed, extensive evidence suggests that a substantial proportion of the resulting scores reflects preparation and support rather than wider learning.

Standardised tests should also, in theory, have been developed so that every mark awarded represents an equivalent degree of difficulty for each student. This is surprisingly difficult when creating tests, and assessing whether questions represent equivalent demands on a student is laborious and complicated. Where standardised tests are held to have marks which represent equivalent difficulty, they are held to produce interval data rather than the ordinal data which most tests produce (see Chapter 3 for further information on this).

Scores from standardised tests are often converted into Standardised Scores. Standardised Scores represent the deviation from the mean of a set of data, and these are usually transformed into having a mean of 100 and a standard deviation of 15 (see Chapter 5 for more about means and standard deviations). Standardised scores make it easier to compare scores across a number of different standardised tests a child might have taken.

In Key Stage 3 (KS3; Years 7–9), schools generally administer tests in reading and mathematics at the end of each school year. As well as these tests, schools will often administer tests either termly or half-termly for other subjects. As a new governor, Samaya will have to discuss her school's approach with a member of staff to understand exactly what testing is used in Key Stage 3 at her school.

As children approach their GCSEs in Year 11, most schools collect test scores at the end of Year 10 at a minimum, and the vast majority administer regular testing throughout the two-year GCSE period. Once again, Samaya will need to discuss her school's approach to testing with a member of staff. Students studying for post-16 qualifications take regular tests leading up to their external examinations.

2.2.3 Other non-academic data

As well as academic tests, schools collate and record personal data about each child. The government uses eligibility for free school meals (FSM) as an indicator of educational disadvantage, and the collection and recording of FSM status has become an important data point for schools. Following the election of the Coalition government in 2010, a new measure of 'Ever 6' was introduced, which records whether a child has been eligible for FSM at any point in the previous six years. Ever 6, which became known as 'disadvantaged' in 2015, is used to allocate a substantial premium (the 'pupil premium' carrying in the region of £1000 additional funding for each eligible child) to educational funding for children who qualify.

An increased focus on the attainment gaps between 'disadvantaged' and 'non-disadvantaged' children has meant that schools are much more likely than previously to consider free school meal history when exploring the performance of groups across the school.

Schools also record details of those children who have special educational needs over and above the educational provision provided for a typical child in school. The way in which children are assessed and allocated the status of having special educational needs (SEN) is beyond the scope of this book; all schools have staff who are responsible for managing SEN issues and provision. The addition of 'disability' to the SEN acronym saw 'SEN' become SEND in 2014, and 'education, health and care' (EHC) plans began to replace statements of special educational needs.

Children who have English as an additional language are generally also tracked in school. This data is largely based on family self-reporting, and as such is often subject to substantial error. Governors such as Andrew and Samaya should ask whoever is responsible for collecting the information how they ensure that the data which they hold is valid.

Teachers are frequently asked to record occasions when children's behaviour has breached the school's behaviour guidelines. In primary school, a system for the written recording of incidents is often in place, although this is heavily dependent on the school's context and the extent to which the school chooses to actively manage behaviour which is judged to be dangerous or disruptive. Generally, behaviour issues are managed by teachers in classrooms in the majority of primary schools; incidents which require formal recording often happen outside class when adult supervision is more dispersed, although some schools have regular classroom-based behaviour incidents which have to be formally recorded.

Many secondary schools collect behaviour data for their pupils in lessons as a matter of course. This may be collected for every lesson, for every school session or for each school day, depending on the circumstance and requirements of the school. In addition, secondaries generally record behavioural issues outside of the classroom in a similar way to primaries.

Schools have substantial responsibilities when it comes to vulnerable children, and they must record and notify various outside agencies of any concerns which they might have about any child's well-being. Children who are looked after by the state qualify for additional funding and are tracked closely in school.

Beyond these categories, schools may collect and record data for a wide variety of sub-populations within the school, depending on the specific context in which they work. These subgroups may include children of Gypsies, Roma and Travellers, military personnel, asylum seekers, refugees and new migrants, amongst others.

2.3 Government-provided data analysis

A great deal of information about schools is now generated and published by the government, for both the general public and for those in school themselves.

> ### Box 2.3
>
> ## Understanding 20 years of government-provided data analysis

As newly appointed school governors, Andrew and Samaya are new to the often complex world of school data. Both have taken an interest in education for some time, and they are aware of some of the history of RAISEonline, PANDA reports, school performance tables, CVA-based accountability data, and so on. As newcomers to their role, they will find the following history of government-provided data useful background reading.

Information regarding secondary schools' examination results at GCSE began to be published in 1992, when secondary school performance tables were first introduced. These initial performance tables listed the percentage of pupils who had been awarded five or more GCSEs with grades from A to C. From 1994, the tables listed the percentages of children awarded five A* to C grade GCSEs, when the A* grade was introduced.

Whilst these early performance tables were published with schools listed in alphabetical order, newspapers soon began to publish them in a 'league table' format with schools ranked by their percentage of 5+ GCSE A*–C grades. These crude tables were not popular with schools and teachers, who expressed concern that raw results failed to take into account the contexts and starting points of children in different schools, and thus gave a distorted picture of state education. Even before the publication of the initial school performance tables, academics had been warning that the analysis they offered was extremely crude and would be prone to misinterpretation. They argued that more sophisticated statistical models should be used to account for both context and the clustered nature of school data (students are 'nested' within schools, so that students in a given school are more similar to each other than they are to the general student population).

As a result, in 1995 the Department for Education began to develop 'value-added' models (as discussed in Chapter 9), which led to the publication of value-added measures in secondary school performance tables in 2002.

Primary school performance tables were first published in 1997, based on the results of the first Key Stage 2 tests introduced in 1996. These suffered from the same issues identified in secondary school performance tables, taking no account of context and prior attainment, and value-added measures for primary schools were first published in 2003.

Following the creation of Ofsted in 1992 (originally the Ofsted for Standards in Education, although the exact title has changed on several occasions subsequently), schools and local authorities were sent performance and assessment reports, known colloquially as PANDA reports, by Ofsted. These reports were not available to the general public.

PANDA reports included complex statistical analysis and interpretation of schools' outcomes in end-of-key-stage assessments and tests, comparing schools both to the national data set and subsets of schools deemed to be operating in similar contexts. An electronic tool known as the Pupil Achievement Tracker (PAT) was developed and made available to schools to allow them to undertake their own in-house analyses of their data using the DfE's value-added model.

From 2002, the Department for Education and Skills began collecting data in what was known as the Pupil Level Annual School Census (PLASC). PLASC gathered a wide range of demographic data, including date of birth, sex, ethnic background, special educational needs, whether students had English as an additional language (EAL), were in local authority care or had joined the school late in a particular Key Stage (a 'mobility' indicator). The data for each individual student included their free school meal (FSM) status as well as an IDACI (Income Deprivation Affecting Children Index) score.

This data was gathered for use in contextual value-added (CVA) models, which were being developed in response to criticism of the lack of contextual data used in school performance tables and PANDA reports. Following the release of data from a pilot study in 2005, CVA scores were published alongside the existing value-added analyses for all secondary schools.

A further innovation was the introduction of 'confidence intervals' in both the PANDA reports and in the school performance tables published by the government (confidence intervals are discussed in Chapter 6, and a further discussion about using confidence intervals in this way appears in Chapter 10). This presented value-added scores as being within a range of values, rather than as a single definitive number. In the school performance tables, schools were divided into those with 'significantly above average CVA', those 'in line with the national average CVA' and those with 'significantly below average CVA'.

(Continued)

(Continued)

In 2006–7, secondary school data for the PLASC began to be collected via a school census. Whereas previously data was collected once each academic year, data for the school census is gathered three times a year (in the spring, summer and autumn terms), with slightly different data being collected each term. The main census is taken in January, providing much of the information previously gathered once a year. Secondary schools were required to provide information on fixed period exclusions, including the reasons for exclusions, as well as the standard information they provided on permanent exclusions previously. Primary, nursery and special schools changed from PLASC to termly school census collection in 2007.

In 2007, PANDA evolved into Reporting Analysis for Improvement through School Self-Evaluation, known as RAISEonline, and RAISEonline provided schools, local authorities and other public bodies with information about the performance of schools until it, in turn, was superseded by Analyse School Performance (ASP) in 2017. ASP and RAISEonline are similar, with ASP clearly having evolved from RAISEonline.

2.3.1 ASP, RAISEonline and PANDA

Each academic year, schools are issued with external analysis based on their end-of-key-stage data and school census information. What is now ASP, and was previously known as RAISEonline and PANDA, has changed a great deal since it was introduced in 2007, largely in response to changes to the National Curriculum testing structure and ongoing feedback from those in school and elsewhere. 2016 saw a wholesale change to RAISEonline reports at primary level, as reforms to Key Stage 1 and 2 tests came into effect.

From 2016, governors and school staff had to use two different types of RAISEonline reports, as the attainment data post 2016 was not comparable with earlier attainment data. RAISEonline was superseded by ASP in 2017, which made yet more changes to the way in which schools' summary data was presented. This makes the interpretation of government-provided data over time somewhat complicated, and, for the foreseeable future, Andrew will need to understand both types of RAISE reports and ASP to gain an overview of primary attainment data.

The situation has been further complicated by attempts by the DfE to provide simplified data for governors and inspectors in the form of 'inspection dashboards', which were first introduced in 2014. These were a development of the 'Ofsted data dashboards' which were produced previously.

It is worth looking at each of these data sets in turn, to explore the evolution of data available to schools and governors and to build up an understanding of the ways in which government data has helped, and potentially hindered, those attempting to make sense of school performance.

Much of the data in government provided data sets is described using substantial amounts of context-specific jargon. Where appropriate, specific terms are expanded on, but for any terms which are not clear or are unfamiliar, it is best to ask someone in school to provide an explanation.

2.3.1.1 Primary RAISEonline

Primary RAISEonline reports contain a huge amount of information in six main categories. These are:

1. Context
2. Absence and Exclusions
3. Prior Attainment and Early Years Foundation Stage Profile
4. Attainment in Key Stages 1 and 2
5. Progress (Value Added then Expected progress, for schools with Key Stage 2)
6. Closing the Gaps

The context section includes information about the number of children on roll, the split between girls and boys, the number of children known to be eligible for free school meals, the percentages of children from ethnic minority groups, with English as an additional language and with special educational needs. It also contains a school stability percentage (essentially, the number of children who stay in school, without interruption, from the usual school starting point) and a school deprivation indicator.

This information is provided for the three academic years prior to the report itself, although governors like Andrew should be careful not to over-interpret this relatively limited indication of change over time.

Absence and exclusion data is recorded in RAISEonline reports, showing the percentage of school sessions missed each academic year and, of those who have recorded absences, the percentage of children who have been persistent absentees (classified as those who have been absent for 15% or more of all sessions).

As with most measures of school performance including RAISEonline, prior attainment in Key Stage 1 will be recorded using the 1996–2015 National Curriculum system of levels until 2020, when the new scaled scores (recorded from 2016 onwards) will be used for all cohorts. Levels are converted into point scores, and average point scores are calculated to indicate prior attainment in Key Stage 1 for those in each cohort in Key Stage 2. Children are split into low, middle and high prior attainment bands based on their KS1 APS.

RAISEonline reports provide detailed breakdowns of the outcomes of the Early Years Foundation Profile assessments in Reception, as well as detailed information about attainment in the Year 1 Phonics Screening Check.

From 2016, children's Key Stage 1 assessments resulted in single scaled scores for mathematics, reading and spelling, punctuation and grammar (although the 2016 spelling, punctuation and grammar tests had to be abandoned due to maladministration in the Department for Education). Thresholds are set to separate children into those 'working at least at the expected standard' (split into those 'working at the expected standard +' and those 'working in greater depth') and those 'working below the expected standard' (split into 'working below pre-Key Stage 1', at 'foundations', and those 'working towards the expected standard'). RAISEonline reports document the percentage of children working at least at the expected standard within their school and at national level.

Older RAISE reports used National Curriculum levels to report attainment, in which Level 2 was the expected level at Key Stage 1. Level 2b was allocated a point score of 15 points. (Further details of the levels and points system can be found in section 2.2.2 above.)

Primary schools, which generally have small cohorts, should be careful not to over-interpret this data, since each child is likely to represent a relatively high percentage in the school reporting. In a school with 25 children in Year 2, for example, each child represents 4% of a school's results. Thus, the difference between a school's percentages and the national percentage of 20 percentage points represents just five children out of 25 working at a different standard from the national picture (which is based on results from around 500,000 children for whom SATs scores are recorded each year).

Primary RAISEonline presents data for groups of children in the following categories at Key Stage 1:

- male/female
- disadvantaged (those in receipt of FSM in any of the past six years)/other/free school meals/Looked After children
- SEN with statement or educational health (EHC) plan/SEN support/no SEN
- English as a first language/English as an additional language
- autumn/spring/summer birth
- good level of development in the EYFS yes/no
- reading/writing/mathematics emerging/expected/exceeding in the EYFS.

Children's ethnic background and the percentage of children reaching the expected standard are also recorded in the following categories:

- White, British, Irish, Traveller, Gypsy/Roma, any other White background
- mixed, White and Black Caribbean, White and Black African, White and Asian, any other mixed background
- Asian or Asian British, Indian, Pakistani, Bangladeshi, any other Asian background
- Black or Black British, Black Caribbean, Black African, any other Black background
- Chinese, any other ethnic group
- unclassified, refused/not obtained.

Primary RAISEonline uses the categories of emerging, expected and exceeding in the Early Years Foundation Stage, and shows how children in each EYFS category have progressed in Key Stage 1 in each of reading, mathematics and writing using the following categories of attainment in Key Stage 1:

- below pre-Key Stage 1 standards (BLW)
- foundations for the expected standard (PKF)
- working towards the expected standard (WTS)
- working at the expected standard (EXS)
- working at greater depth within the expected standard (GDS).

Children assessed using p-scales are shown compared to the Early Years Foundation Stage categories of emerging, expected and exceeding.

This information is separated into disadvantaged and non-disadvantaged groups.

Primary RAISEonline also includes a pupil list at Key Stage 1, which includes all of the information used to create the overview tables above. The pupil list also includes children's date of birth.

At Key Stage 2, Primary RAISEonline uses more complicated measures of progress and attainment. Academic progress from Key Stage 1 to Key Stage 2 is presented using value-added analysis (see Chapters 9 and 10 for commentary on these types of measures). Cohorts are scored, and scores are presented with confidence intervals (see Chapter 6). RAISEonline uses colours to indicate statistical significance, with green indicating scores which are above the national average and red indicating those which are below the national average. Where data is flagged as statistically significant, it is also marked as being (or not being) in the top 10% or bottom 10% nationally.

Box 2.4   Significant confusion

Those who work with data have long lamented the confusion which the term 'statistical significance' causes. To a statistician, a significance test result is said to be 'statistically significant' at the 95% level, for example, if the sample mean is calculated to have a less than 1 in 20 chance of being drawn from the same population as another sample. There are other levels which can be used, and the process for creating this kind of test is explained in Chapter 6.

What statistical significance does *not* mean – in stark contrast to the colloquial use of the word 'significant' both outside and within education – is *important*. A data point which is significant is simply unusual. It *might* be important, but equally it might not. It is important to note that statisticians caution that results may contain different types of

(Continued)

(Continued)

errors, which can occur either when a result is calculated to be unusual, but was not actually different to the norm, or when a result is unusual, but the calculations do not indicate this to be the case. Where a result is deemed to be 'statistically significant', this suggests the result needs careful examination, which may give some indication as to why a data point has been flagged up.

In a class with a large number of September-born children, for example, a significant result might be explained by the unusual average age of the cohort compared to the national population. A cohort with many summer-born children might be flagged as significant for a similar reason.

Somewhat unfortunately, ASP/RAISEonline present data which has been deemed significant as 'Sig+' and 'Sig−', where 'Sig+' means a data point is higher than a national average and statistically significant, and 'Sig−' means a data point is lower than a national average and statistically significant.

'Sig+' and 'Sig−', as used in ASP/RAISEonline and in other government reports, are both highly misleading if the impression which is given is simply that 'green is good' and 'red is bad'. They are neither. They are merely statistically significant, i.e. not likely to be the result of chance. They are *not* 'significantly good' or 'significantly bad'. They are simply unusually high or low and are therefore worth exploring. For more on this point, see Chapter 8, and for criticism of the use of statistical significance in this way, see Chapter 10.

RAISEonline reports have a particular focus on children who are flagged as 'disadvantaged', and Key Stage 2 reports include progress scores for those who are disadvantaged alongside the scores for all children in a Year 6 cohort. Schools are asked to consider the differences between scores for these groups within the school and scores for the national averages for each group.

Academic attainment in writing, reading, mathematics, spelling, punctuation and grammar, and a combined reading, writing and mathematics score are presented for the most recent Year 6 cohort, split into 'all' and 'disadvantaged', alongside national percentages. From 2016, children's KS2 scores have been reported as a scaled score index, where a scaled score of 100 is the 'expected level' and above 110 is 'high attainment'. These are similar to, but not the same as, the previous Level 4 and Level 5, as used from 1996 to 2015.

Children at Key Stage 2 are split into three bands of prior attainment – low, middle and high. These used to be based on National Curriculum levels, as used until 2015, where Level 1 and below at Key Stage 1 was 'low', KS1 Level 2 was 'middle', and KS1 Level 3 and above was 'high'. From 2016, the methods of allocating children to low, middle and high categories of prior attainment at KS1 became considerably more complicated, but, in essence, children are split into three categories based on KS1 results. Once again, both school and national percentages attaining the expected standard and a high standard are presented.

At KS2, RAISEonline flags attainment percentages as representing 0, 1 or 2+ children above or below national percentages, once again using green for above and red for below.

Primary RAISEonline presents percentages for those reaching at least the expected standard for groups of children in the following categories at Key Stage 2:

- male/female
- disadvantaged (those in receipt of FSM in any of the past six years)/other/free school meals/Looked After children
- SEN with statement or educational health (EHC) plan/SEN support/no SEN
- children who have been on roll in Years 5 and 6
- English as a first language/English as an additional language
- overall, reading, writing and mathematics split into low, middle and high attainment at KS1.

These attainment breakdowns are presented for reading and mathematics.

In addition, progress for each group is presented graphically using a bespoke visual representation indicating confidence intervals around the calculated progress score.

KS2 RAISEonline presents progress in reading, writing and mathematics in scatterplots (see Chapter 4) for both the disadvantaged and non-disadvantaged groups of children in Year 6. These scatterplots are very flexible in their electronic form, allowing differences between groups to be explored.

Box 2.5 — Sifting through the RAISEonline data mountain

RAISEonline reports present an enormous amount of data, making it somewhat unwieldy and difficult to summarise and comprehend. As a primary school governor, Andrew is likely to be overwhelmed by the sheer volume of data within a RAISEonline report. The KS2 scatterplots offer an at-a-glance summary of the most recent Year 6 cohort, and can provide a quick overview of the insights RAISEonline offers.

First, however, as with most similar reports, Andrew should note that a RAISEonline report offers a snapshot of one cohort of children, rather than an overview of the achievement and progress within school as a whole. On a different day, with a slightly different group of children, the figures which appear would likely show a very different picture.

Second, the scatterplots give a clear indication of the spread of attainment and progress within the Year 6 class, and most schools will have a wide range of both. A consistent finding of education research is that the spread of achievement and progress *within* schools is much greater than the differences in average progress and attainment *between* schools.

Andrew should be extremely careful to draw any firm conclusions based on the data, and to use the data in RAISEonline reports to inform questions he can ask the school about, relating to specific points which the scatterplots reveal.

Primary RAISEonline shows 'transition matrices' for reading and mathematics. These grids show the numbers of children with each combined prior attainment level at KS1 (W, 1, 2a, 2b, 2c, 3+) and KS2 standard, coded BLW, PKF, PKE, PKG for those working below the standards measured by KS2 SATs, and those with low, middle and high test scores at KS2 (defined as scaled scores of less than 100, from 100 to 110, and from 110 to 120). Transition matrices are also presented for children who are assessed using p-scales.

There is a transition matrix for writing which codes children as working towards, at or above the expected standard at Key Stage 2, as well as a transition matrix for those assessed using p-scales.

The final section of Primary RAISEonline presents a pupil list similar to that shown for Key Stage 1. This includes all of the information used to create the overview tables, scatterplots and matrices above, as well as children's date of birth, unique pupil number (UPN), date of entry to the school, and teacher-assessed standard of attainment in KS2 Science.

2.3.1.2 Secondary RAISEonline

Secondary RAISEonline reports contain a similar amount of information as Primary RAISEonline, this time in seven main categories. These are:

1. Context
2. Absence and Exclusions, Destinations
3. Prior Attainment
4. Attainment
5. Progress (Value Added then Expected progress)
6. Closing the Gaps
7. Progress 8 and Attainment 8.

The context section once again includes information about the number of children on roll, the split between girls and boys, the number of children known to be eligible for free school meals, the percentages of children from ethnic minority groups, with English as an additional language and with special educational needs. It also contains a school stability percentage (essentially, the number of children who have stayed at school, without interruption, from the usual school starting point) and a school deprivation indicator.

Attendance and exclusion data is presented over three years. As ever, it is important to bear in mind that each figure represents a slightly different group of children, and a small number of children in one particular school year can have a considerable effect on these figures. Around 5% of all sessions are missed due to illness and most school absence is not a cause of concern. RAISEonline provides a breakdown of persistent absence, which is defined as the percentage of absentees who are absent for more than 15% of the sessions they should attend.

Schools report the number of times children have been excluded from school. Exclusions are defined as any period a child has been required to stay away from school due to a contravention of a school's behaviour policy. Most exclusions are fixed term, often a fixed number of days, rather than permanent (when children are required to find a school elsewhere).

Absences and exclusions are reported by gender, FSM, EAL and SEN status, as well as by ethnic group. Secondary schools report destination data for their children at 16.

Until 2016, secondary RAISEonline reported prior attainment using average point scores (APS) at Key Stage 2. Children are split into one of three prior attainment groups – low, middle, high – based on Levels 3, 4 and 5 in the National Curriculum levels system. From 2016, the scaled scores produced at Key Stage 2 have meant that children are split into low, medium and high using scaled scores rather than National Curriculum levels.

Attainment was, until 2016, reported with a focus on the percentage of students achieving five or more A* to C grades, as well as an average capped points score in the 'best 8 subjects'. Since 2016, attainment has been reported using a measure known as Attainment 8, which groups together eight separate subjects to create a single Attainment 8 score.

Attainment 8 is made up of English, mathematics (both of which have double weighting in the calculation of an Attainment 8 score), three other English Baccalaureate (EBacc) subjects (sciences, computer science, geography, history and languages, amongst others) and three further subjects.

Attainment is presented by subject, and split into attainment by groups including gender, FSM, EAL, SEN status, prior attainment and ethnicity. Value Added scores are created and these are presented by the best eight subjects – English, mathematics, science, languages and humanities – as well as by ethnic background and pupil characteristics (gender, FSM, EAL, SEN status, prior attainment, and so on).

Secondary RAISEonline also presents tables of pupils achieving 'expected progress' between Key Stages 2 and 4, which are based on the outcomes of pupils at Key Stage 2 (a child who was recorded as attaining Level 4 in KS2, for example, would be 'expected' to achieve at least a C grade at GCSE). Expected progress tables are presented for English and maths, both for all students and for disadvantaged students.

The percentage of students making expected progress is also presented for English and maths by the usual categories.

RAISEonline reports are primarily a tool for school improvement, and are used both by Ofsted inspectors and schools to identify areas for further investigation. As such, it has a section on 'Closing the Gaps' which was a particular focus of the DfE from 2010 onwards. The gaps are those between disadvantaged pupils within a school and all pupils nationally, and these are shown in tables with data for the previous three years.

RAISEonline summary reports conclude with breakdowns of Attainment 8 and Progress 8 measures, shown for the usual categories.

As of 2017, RAISEonline was superseded by Analyse School Performance (ASP), which is similar to RAISEonline. (For details of what is available within the government data currently available to schools, visit www.databustingforschools.co.uk.)

2.3.1.3 Inspection dashboards

Inspection dashboards were introduced in the autumn of 2015 partly due to changes in government accountability measures and partly due to criticism of 'data dashboards', the previous attempt to simplify data for governors, which were withdrawn in September 2016 following pressure from schools and others. Those responsible for inspection dashboards took on board criticism that previous reports focused too heavily on a single year's results, and widened reporting to include the previous three years' data where possible.

The inspection dashboards were superseded, in turn, by a new Inspection Data Summary Dashboard made available from October 2017. Given the pace of change in this area, describing what is available in the inspection dashboards will give new school governors such as Andrew and Samaya an indication of what government-supplied data is likely to be available to them. (For information on the current data for governors, visit www.databustingforschools.co.uk.)

2.3.1.3.1 Primary inspection dashboards

These reports begin with an overview indicating a school's strengths and weaknesses, as well as summarising a school's expected progress in reading, writing and mathematics, and reading, writing and mathematics combined. These four measures are compared to National Floor Standards set by the DfE, and a school is flagged as either having met, or not having met, Floor Standards.

Children in Year 6 are split into three prior attainment categories, as per the methodology used in RAISEonline. Results are then presented showing whether children recorded the expected progress in reading, writing and mathematics. Results are also presented for disadvantaged children, showing gaps both within school and nationally. Unusual results are flagged using red and yellow dots, which indicate whether any such result represents more than one pupil.

Inspection dashboards include a KS1–KS2 Value Added measure, which is shown including a confidence interval indicating the spread of possible results any given value is held to represent. Reading, writing and mathematics are shown, with separate indicators for disadvantaged and non-disadvantaged, girls and boys, SEN with and without statements and without SEN. These measures are all shown for the previous three years.

The percentages of Year 6 children attaining Level 4+ and Level 5+ (split into all pupils and disadvantaged children only) are shown for the previous three years in reading, writing and mathematics. KS2 average point scores are also shown for all pupils, disadvantaged pupils, non-disadvantaged pupils, boys, girls, SEN with and without statements and without SEN; these are all shown for the previous three years.

KS1 average point scores are shown indicating whether any data is deemed to be statistically significant, with gaps both within school and against national data shown and flagged where there is a difference between disadvantaged children and non-disadvantaged children. KS1 children are compared to national thresholds for reading, writing and mathematics, with unusual results flagged as statistically significant. Once again, these results are split, showing results for disadvantaged children and non-disadvantaged children.

The percentage of children who have reached the national expected standard in the Year 1 phonics screen check and in the EYFS profile is shown, with separate indicators for disadvantaged and non-disadvantaged, girls and boys, SEN with and without statements and without SEN. These measures are all shown for the previous three years.

Finally, the inspection dashboard gives data on absence, persistent absence and fixed-term exclusions, split by different categories, before providing a page of data indicating the school's context. This indicates the school population's self-reported ethnicity, along with indicators of the difference in average prior attainment using KS1 APS for Years 3 to 6, the gender split in each year group from Year 1 to Year 6, the number of children whose first language is not English, the school's stability (a measure showing how many children were in school from Reception to Year 6) and the breakdown by year group of those currently receiving free school meals, and of those with identified SEN.

2.3.1.3.2 Secondary inspection dashboards

These reports begin with an overview indicating a school's strengths and weaknesses, as well as summarising a school's Progress 8 score. Progress 8 is compared to National Floor Standards set by the DfE (and to coasting standards set in 2016), and a school is flagged as either having met, or not having met, Floor Standards. Schools are compared to coasting standards for the previous three years ('coasting' is a DfE measure indicating schools which are deemed to have problematic patterns of attainment).

Children in Year 11 are split into three prior attainment categories, as per the methodology used in RAISEonline. Results are then presented showing whether children recorded 'expected progress' using Progress 8 scores, split into all pupils, 'disadvantaged' children and 'non-disadvantaged', with each measure shown with percentage coverage respectively. Results are also presented for girls and boys, for SEN with and without statements and for those with no SEN. These measures are shown including a confidence interval indicating the spread of possible results any given value is held to represent.

Attainment 8 is presented for 'disadvantaged' children, showing gaps both within school and nationally. Unusual results are flagged using coloured boxes, which indicate how any such result differs from national averages.

The English, mathematics, EBacc and Open elements of Progress 8 and Attainment 8 are shown both for all pupils and for pupils with low, middle and high prior attainment. This is once again split into separate categories. Secondary inspection dashboards include a KS2–KS4 Value Added measure for sciences, languages and humanities, each of which includes a confidence interval. There are separate indictors for disadvantaged and non-disadvantaged, girls and boys, SEN with and without statements and without SEN.

The percentages of Year 11 children attaining the expected standards in English and mathematics (split by prior attainment) are shown over the usual categories. Further indicators of Value Added are shown, including breakdowns by subject, as well as measures based on raw attainment.

Finally, the secondary inspection dashboard gives data on absence, persistent absence and fixed-term exclusions, split by different categories, before providing data indicating the school's context. As with the primary dashboard, this indicates the school population's self-reported ethnicity, along with indicators of the difference in average prior attainment using KS2 APS for Years 7 to 11, the gender split in each year group from Year 7 to Year 11, the number of children whose first language is not English, the school's stability (a measure showing how many children were in school from Year 7 to Year 11), the number of Looked After children and the breakdown by year group of those currently receiving free school meals, and of those with identified SEN. Where the school has a sixth form, a similar breakdown is provided for Years 12 and 13.

2.4 Externally provided data analysis

Schools frequently use information provided by third-party data analysis companies to assist in the interpretation of their data. Companies such as the Fischer Family Trust (FFT), Capita, and Centre for Evaluation and Monitoring (CEM) provide a great many schools with analysis based on both end-of-key-stage tests and proprietary tests provided by the companies themselves.

The Fischer Family Trust (FFT) is a commercial company which began supplying data analysis to schools in the late 1990s. It provides 95% or so of all schools in England with data about their children. The FFT is mainly known for providing 'estimates' of future performance based on prior performance. This is done for Key Stage 2 based on Key Stage 1 results, and for Key Stage 4 based on Key Stage 2 results.

In addition, the FFT provides details for school governors via its governor dashboards arm. RAISEonline/ASP (detailed in section 2.3) is processed and managed by RM plc, which is closely linked to the FFT, having been founded by the same people. RM also manages the Department for Education's school performance tables website, which provides online information about the performance of all schools in England.

Since 2006, RM has managed the national pupil database, the government's vast database which keeps centrally held records on children in English schools.

Capita owns School Information Management Systems (SIMS), which is used in 80% of schools. SIMS provides schools with a wide array of data management and analysis tools, not limited to attendance data collection and tracking, pupil progress analysis, parental payments and communication systems, and management of parents' evenings and engagement.

The Centre for Evaluation and Monitoring (CEM) is best known for systems such as MidYIS (Middle Years Information System) and Yellis (Year 11 Information System), which are IQ-type tests designed to identify students' underlying potential in secondary school. CEM also operates ALIS (A Level Information System) which is used in around 50% of all schools teaching A Levels. CEM provides a variety of testing and reporting packages for primary-aged children, as well as systems to assess nursery- and Reception-aged children.

GL Assessment, an offshoot of the National Foundation for Educational Research (NFER), is best known for the CAT (cognitive abilities test) assessments used by many secondary schools to assess pupils on entry to Year 7. CAT4, the current suite of CAT assessments, measures four areas of reasoning (quantitative, verbal, non-verbal and spatial). The company provides a range of further assessment and administration tools, including progress in English, maths and science packages, a new group reading test and a pupil attitudes to self and school (PASS) survey.

There are many other organisations which provide broader analysis based on educational data, from the Education Endowment Foundation (EEF), a government-funded scheme which evaluates projects which aim to raise pupil attainment, to the OECD's Programme for International Student Assessment (PISA), which aims to evaluate education systems by testing the skills and knowledge of 15-year-old students in countries around the globe.

2.5 Summary

In this chapter, we have looked at the sources of educational data used in schools. We have considered daily attendance data, test data and other non-academic data generated and collated in schools. We have looked at the way in which the government analyses data and provides reporting to schools. We have also looked at externally provided suites of testing and assessments, as well as data analysis provided by third-party organisations.

Much of the analysis detailed in this chapter relies on the use of numbers to summarise children and schools. But numbers, it turns out, are not all the same. And what can be done with different types of numbers is different too. In the next chapter, we will look at what can – and what can't – be done with numerical data, and consider the pitfalls which often arise when we use numerical data in schools.

3

UNDERSTANDING NUMERICAL DATA IN EDUCATION

THE WHAT, HOW AND WHY OF NUMBERS

What you will learn from this chapter:

How to describe information
How to combine numbers and summarise them
How to interpret fractions, decimals and percentages
The four types of numerical data
What can be done with different types of numerical data
The history and development of theories underpinning test data
What this means for databusting schools

Case study 3.1

What do these numbers mean?

Kathryn is a Year 3 teacher, with a new class of 30 children. She has been given a series of test scores from tests the children in her class took the previous summer. In addition, Kathryn has been given the children's test scores from their Year 1 phonics test, as well as some end of Key Stage 1 information from teacher assessments and tests undertaken in Year 2. She also has a table containing the children's ages, as well as responses to a pupil survey the school carries out each July. Finally, she has details indicating which children are girls and which are boys, and information as to whether they have received free school meals in the past. She wants to understand what these numbers can tell her about her class.

She has gathered all this information into a spreadsheet and she is now looking at a great deal of somewhat confusing data and is not sure what it might be telling her. She isn't sure what she should do next or what pitfalls she might fall into. What does she need to know to be able to interpret this mass of information?

Kathryn's colleague, Ben, has just taken on a role within the school's senior leadership team. He is responsible for managing the school's data and he has been given similar information for each of the classes in the school. He has data for the most recent academic year, as well as data for the past five years. He has been asked to summarise the school's current position for a governors' meeting, and he is trying to understand which information is important and how to present it. What should he know and what should he be looking for?

Whilst any teacher will always be aware that the children in their class are individuals, and that the best way to be able to help their children to learn is to develop a personalised understanding of each child, there is an increasing expectation that teachers will be able to interpret and understand numerical data summarising their children. In Ben's case, he needs to understand what the information from multiple classes might be telling him about the whole school.

For many people working in school, what happens when numbers are combined is something of a mystery. It is easy to jump to conclusions which aren't really justified by the data we have, especially when summaries are presented to us in ways which aren't as valid as they may seem. Teachers like Kathryn and school leaders like Ben often find themselves in positions in which they are expected to understand numbers, but may lack some of the knowledge they need to do so.

In this chapter, you will explore the world of numbers and look at different ways of summarising numerical information, at the various types of data you may come across, and discover some of the common errors which are made with numbers. You will also explore the theories of educational testing which have been developed, and you may find that testing children is often not quite as straightforward as many people think it is. You will discover how numbers can deceive as well as enlighten, and learn how to guard against the interpretation and misuse of numbers.

3.1 Describing and summarising numbers

In the first half of this chapter, we will look at the ways that numbers can be described and summarised.

3.1.1 Data sets, data and datum

To many people's surprise, the singular form of 'data' is 'datum'. Whilst you might see this word in many books about numbers, it isn't common in everyday speech. Nevertheless, it is occasionally useful to describe a single piece of numerical information, and datum is the favoured term for a certain type of reader. Most of us will refer to 'data points' or something similar when referring to a particular number within a set of numbers.

It follows therefore that data, whilst often used in the singular, is often written as the plural of datum, which leads to sentences such as, 'The data are useful'. For most of us in school, we'd be surprised by this usage, and we would expect to read, 'The data *is* useful'. This is largely because, in current usage, data is nearly always used to mean 'a collection of information', and therefore its use as a plural seems archaic.

In this book, data is used to mean 'a collection of information'. We will therefore most often discuss 'data' as a singular entity, using the phrase 'data is ...' rather than 'data are ...'. Now that this has been cleared up, we can discuss collections of data, which is what most interests us in this book.

Data which is gathered together is technically a data set. Ben and Kathryn have data sets which consist of different data. A part of this data might look like Table 3.1.

Data is usually presented in a two-dimensional table, with **variables** in columns, and **cases** in rows. Each case – a pupil, for example – has more than one variable, as we have multiple pieces of information about the same child. A variable is something which can be any one of a range of numbers or labels.

Table 3.1 has seven sets of data: a phonics check score, KS1 maths, writing and reading assessments and Y3 maths, writing and reading results.

In summary, a data set is a collection of data which is interrelated in some way, and it is often presented in a spreadsheet with cases in rows and variables in columns. Each variable is a collection of a single type of data, whilst a case contains all the data on each of the variables for a given individual.

Table 3.1 Data on maths, writing and reading for KS1/Y3

	Phonics check score (PCS)	KS1 Maths	KS1 Writing	KS1 Reading	Y3 Maths	Y3 Writing	Y3 Reading
Sophia	32	EXS	EXS	EXS	EXS	GDS	EXS
Faizah	34	GDS	GDS	EXS	GDS	GDS	EXS
James	32	EXS	EXS	WTS	EXS	EXS	WTS
Charlotte	35	GDS	GDS	EXS	GDS	GDS	EXS
Emma	40	GDS	GDS	GDS	GDS	EXS	GDS
Abigail	32	EXS	GDS	EXS	EXS	EXS	EXS
Harper	30	WTS	WTS	WTS	WTS	WTS	WTS
Ava	32	EXS	EXS	EXS	EXS	EXS	EXS
Emily	34	GDS	EXS	EXS	GDS	EXS	EXS
Mason	35	EXS	GDS	EXS	EXS	GDS	EXS
Avery	32	EXS	EXS	EXS	EXS	EXS	EXS
Elijah	39	GDS	GDS	GDS	GDS	GDS	GDS

3.1.2 Summarising data

You will notice that data isn't exclusively numerical. Whilst we often use data as a synonym for number, any information which has been gathered together in a systematic way can be data. Because there are mathematical procedures for summarising numbers, data is often converted into a numerical format in order to summarise it. There are, however, a number of considerations which need to be taken into account when we convert information into numbers. We will come onto these in the second part of this chapter.

For now, we will assume that the data we have is robust enough to be summarised numerically, and we'll begin by looking at ways of combining numbers.

3.1.3 Combining numbers to find means, medians and modes

People are frequently overwhelmed by numbers, especially when there are a lot of them to take in at once. In Chapter 4, we will look at using pictures in the form of graphs and charts to summarise numbers. Pictures need to be generated from underlying numbers, however, and we will begin by looking at the most popular ways which we have to summarise large collections of data.

Ben has data for a Year 9 class. This includes their Key Stage 2 test data, and is presented in Table 3.2.

Table 3.2 Key Stage 2 test data

	FSM	KS2 Maths	KS2 Writing	KS2 Reading	Gender
Amelia	1	27	27	27	F
Samayah	0	29	29	27	F
Faizah	0	31	31	33	F
Mason	0	33	35	35	M
Jacob	1	23	23	23	M
William	1	25	25	27	M
Ethan	0	27	29	27	M
Michael	0	27	27	29	M
Alexander	0	29	27	27	M
James	0	19	19	19	M
Mohamed	0	29	27	29	M
Elijah	0	27	27	27	M

These figures were collected as National Curriculum levels, in which levels were allocated 'points' as per Table 3.3 (see Chapter 2 for more details).

Table 3.3 Allocation of points to levels

Level	Points
2C	13
2B	15
2A	17
3C	19
3B	21
3A	23
4C	25
4B	27
4A	29
5C	31
5B	33
5A	35

We will look at the issues with allocating 'points' in the form of numbers in the second part of this chapter, but, for now, we will assume that these points can be summarised numerically.

The most obvious way to combine these numbers is to calculate an average. This allows us to discuss a 'typical value', or a 'middle value' of a collection of numerical data. The three most common types of average are the mean, the median and the mode.

The **mean** is calculated by simply adding up all the numbers and then dividing the result by the total number of numbers. In Ben's data (see Table 3.2), the mean of the KS2 maths data is 27.16. This would be roughly Level 4B 'and a bit', and is typical of a mean of a set of data: means are often not countable numbers. Whilst the average household might contain 2.3 people, no household comprises of this number of people.

Means are powerful summaries of numbers, but they can be misleading, especially if the largest and smallest numbers in a set of data are not very typical. One millionaire in a staffroom significantly alters the mean wealth of those sharing a cup of tea. Someone with as little as twice the mean wealth of a group of five people will drag the mean upwards by 20%. To get a slightly better picture of a 'typical' number, means are often combined with other measures of 'average' such as medians and modes.

The **median** is the 'middle number' if the data is ranked in order. In Ben's KS2 maths data, the median is 27. The median adds a little more clarity to the summary of the data. In this case, the fact that the mean is higher than the median tells you that there are more children with point scores above 27 than below. In a group of five teachers, a millionaire will not affect the median wealth of the group, since the median is simply the middle value and is not affected by unusual values at the extremes.

The **mode** is simply the most frequent number. In Ben's data, there is one mode – 27. With small groups of data, multiple modes are common. Modes become more useful in larger groups, where a single mode is often similar to the mean and the median.

When combined with the mean and the median of Ben's class, it is now clear that, whilst the children were typically awarded high Level 4B, a large number of the class were awarded Level 4B and below and there are more children with lower point scores than the mean score, so the distribution of scores is skewed towards the lower point scores.

Whilst it is relatively simple to calculate means, modes and medians, they do rely on some basic assumptions about the numbers you are trying to summarise. We will come to these soon, but, first, we need to look at a second way of summarising data: using fractions to split groups into parts.

3.1.4 Summarising numerical data using fractions, decimals and percentages

One of the simplest ways to look at data is to split it using an either/or question, to which there are only two possible answers. Are you male or female? Did you receive free school meals or not? Did you achieve the required standard for the phonics check in Year 1, or not? In the case of Kathryn's class, the answers to these three questions are as follows:

- 13 boys; 17 girls
- 6 children received free school meals; 24 children did not receive free school meals
- 25 children achieved the required standard for the phonics check in Year 1; 5 children did not achieve the required standard for the phonics check in Year 1.

This information is a little wordy, however. The obvious way to summarise each set of data is to present it as a fraction, like this:

- girls: 17/30
- FSM: 6/30
- PCS: 25/30.

Fractions can be simplified, of course, so Kathryn could say 1/5 children get free school meals, or that 5/6 children passed the phonics screening test. Whilst this flexibility in reporting fractions is a very useful property of fractions, it can make it difficult to compare numbers with different denominators.

For this reason, one common way to summarise parts of a whole is to present them as decimal fractions, or proportions. Kathryn's data could be presented like this:

- girls: 0.56666666
- FSM: 0.2
- PCS: 0.833333.

This demonstrates a common issue with decimal fractions: they often have recurring digits. This means that a decision has to be made as to how to show that a number has been truncated. We can use dots to represent recurring digits, or simply show the answer to a given number of significant digits or decimal places.

What's more, since many people don't like dealing with numbers with digits to the right of a decimal point, numbers which include these digits are often converted into percentages. Per cent means 'for every 100', so you simply multiply each number by 100 and add the '%' sign, which should remind the reader to divide by 100 to revert to the decimal fraction.

This turns the difficult decimal fractions into simplified percentages, like this:

- girls: 57%
- FSM: 20%
- PCS: 83%

Naturally, with any summary, you lose detail. As elsewhere in school, summaries can be misleading if they blur the detail too much. This is often the case in primary schools, where data is frequently collected for fewer than 100 cases. Since each case counts for more than 1 per cent of the total, this can make small changes in the underlying numbers look very large when presented as percentages. With just three more girls instead of boys, three more scores above instead of below 32 in the phonics screening test and 3 more children not receiving free school meals instead of being entitled to them, the numbers for Kathryn's class look quite different:

- girls: 47%
- FSM: 10%
- PCS: 93%

It is worth remembering that with just 30 children per class, each child counts for 3⅓%. So, whilst percentages provide a summary of a class, they lose detail and that detail might be important.

For Ben, looking at a range of classes across the school, this loss of detail might be significant. Classes with 12/30, 12/28, 12/25 and 12/24 boys have 50%, 43%, 46% and 40% boys even though each has 12 boys. Looking at percentages without considering the underlying numbers can often be misleading, and this is one area where it is worth having a rule of thumb:

With data presented in percentages, always look at the underlying numbers for a more rounded picture.

So, in summary, fractions are useful when summarising groups, but make it difficult to compare the summaries of groups with different numbers of members. Decimal fractions make comparisons easier, but they can be confusing. As a result, they are often converted into percentages. Percentages can make small differences seem much bigger than they really are, however, so they should always be read alongside the underlying numbers.

Box 3.1 — Don't be misled by percentages

It is surprisingly easy to be misled by percentages, even when they are presented with some of the underlying numbers. This summary of one of Ben's class's test results is not quite what it seems:

> The proportion of children who were assessed as 'working at the expected standard and above' was only 75% this year, whereas last year it was 83%. This represents a worrying drop in the number of children 'working at the expected standard and above', with only 15 compared to 24 children 'working at the expected standard and above'.

When a percentage is reported without all of the underlying numbers, it is vital that you ask yourself what the numbers might be and what you might be missing. In this case, the percentages and numbers have dropped, but does that necessarily mean that the number of children 'working at the expected standard and above' represents a worrying drop? The data on which this is based can be found in Table 3.4.

Table 3.4 Data on children working at/above and below the expected standard

	Working below the expected standard	Working below the expected standard (percentage of total pupils)	Working at the expected standard and above	Working at the expected standard and above (percentage of total pupils)
Last year	5	5/29 = 17%	24	24/29 = 83%
This year	5	5/20 = 25%	15	15/20 = 75%
Year-on-year change	0	25% − 17% = +8%	−9	75% − 83% = −8%

Now that the whole of the underlying data is available, it's easier to see what's actually happening in this class. There was indeed a drop in the number of children 'working at the expected standard and above', but this is entirely explained by the large decrease in the number of children in the class, and the fact that in both years there were five children who were not 'working at the expected standard and above'. So, in contrast to the summary above, the drop in results simply represents the drop in the class size (from 29 to 20 pupils).

Using percentages in this case simply confuses the picture. When you are trying to interpret or present your own data, you need to check that you are not being misled and that you are not potentially misleading others. Percentages allow us to make comparisons, but they also present pitfalls which should be avoided.

3.2 The four types of numerical data

We collect data to provide information about something in which we are interested. The two words – data and information – although clearly related, are often confused, particularly as they have specific meanings in some contexts. In the world of computing, for example, information is often summarised as 'organised or classified data which has some meaningful value for the receiver'. Data, on the other hand, is often used to mean 'factual information'. What you need to know is that, however data or information is described, it isn't all alike. For the simplicity of discussion, the word data will be used here to mean 'what teachers know about their pupils and schools'.

Most teachers will know that information is commonly split into **qualitative** and **quantitative** data. The everyday definitions of these two types of data are broadly as follows:

- qualitative data – descriptive data written in words
- quantitative data – data in the form of numbers.

There is, however, a little more to qualitative and quantitative data than this. Quantitative data are indeed quantities, and these are usually – although not always – represented as numbers. Qualitative data are labels or qualities, usually represented as phrases, words or letters. Data sets are often mixtures of these two broad types of data.

The results of the phonics screening test in Table 3.5 are numbers, whereas the gender data is presented as letters. So which is quantitative and which is qualitative? This might seem straightforward, but the answer might surprise you.

It turns out that some numbers are quantitative and some are qualitative. The difference is decided by what the numbers actually represent. Not all numbers are the same. For example, the numbers used to distinguish areas of a school building

Table 3.5 Phonics screening test results

	Free school meals (FSM)	Phonics check score (PCS)	Gender
Sophia	0	32	F
Faizah	1	34	F
James	1	32	M
Charlotte	0	35	F
Emma	0	40	F
Abigail	0	32	F
Harper	0	30	M
Ava	0	32	F
Emily	0	34	F
Mason	0	35	M
Avery	1	32	M
Elijah	0	39	M

protected by an alarm system have no relationship to each other; Area 6 is not 'higher' than Area 2. In this case, the numbers are qualitative, not quantitative.

One way to differentiate different types of numbers is to consider what they are measuring. Using this criterion, there are four types of numerical data: nominal, ordinal, interval and ratio. As you move through this list, each type of number requires more underlying structure than the last. To determine which type of data a given measurement falls into, the scale of measurement which can be used has to be considered.

Examples of the different types of data might be:

Nominal data: children's names

Ordinal data: 1st, 2nd, 3rd in a list

Interval data: scores in a standardised test

Ratio data: children's ages

Let's look at each of these different types of data in turn, and consider which summary statistics (mode, median, mean, proportion, percentage) can be used for each data type.

3.2.1 Nominal data

Nominal data have labels which clearly identify something real. If you can distinguish between values and collect them together into a data set, the data is nominal at the very least. Nominal data is qualitative and examples might include a child's gender, the colour of their eyes and their responses to simple questions about their likes and dislikes. Any data which has meaningful labels is a nominal measurement at the least, and this is the broadest category into which data is classified.

In school, data which records free school meals (FSM) is nominal, since there is no measurement involved: children are either entitled to FSM or they are not. There is no meaningful measurement which can be made between the two groups. Where nominal data has only two possible values – as it does in the case of FSM – it is also known as 'dichotomous data'.

Summary statistics such as the median or mean cannot be used when analysing nominal data. The mode is the only summary statistic which can be used with nominal data.

3.2.2 Ordinal data

Ordinal data are data with an order which has meaning. If the data has meaningful labels, and some data is clearly 'smaller', 'less' or 'lower' than other data, the data is ordinal. This is still qualitative data, and data which has a rank order is often ordinal data. In school, we regularly use rank order to place children in groups, using scores from a variety of assessments. Where some children are clearly 'better' or 'worse' than others at a given task, they can be ranked in an order.

Scores from tests in which there is a clear difference in the level of knowledge required to answer different questions are often ordinal data. A child who has answered more questions correctly has clearly performed better than a child who has answered fewer questions correctly, but there is no clear indication of how much more knowledge the higher performing child has gained.

In addition, the raw score on the test says little about the difficulty of the test or a child's position relative to those who took the test. Additionally, scores are often converted into percentages, which are only valid if they are of equivalent value, and a score of zero on the test is meaningful – both of which, as you will see below, are problematic.

In this case, the number of questions answered correctly is best used to simply rank the children who have taken the test. The fact that one child has scored, say, 15 out of 20 and another has scored 10 out of 20 is often less meaningful than the fact that the first child is ranked 2nd out of 30 children who took the test and the second child is ranked 20th.

Summaries such as modes and medians can be used with ordinal data. Means of ordinal data are not held to be valid by most statisticians, although some argue that – with care – they can be used in some cases.

3.2.3 Interval data

Interval data has an order and has regular, meaningful differences between values. This data type has all the required properties of ordinal data (it has meaningful labels which can be ordered), and, in addition, there are meaningful distances between values. In a simple spelling test, where each spelling is equally difficult, the difference between 5 marks and 6 marks is the same as the difference between 14 marks and 15 marks – both are a difference of 1 mark. It is important to note here, however, that each mark must be worth *exactly* the same; if this is not the case, the data is ordinal data, not interval data. Creating tests in which this is the case is surprisingly difficult, and we will return to this in Chapter 10.

In a school context, a great deal of data is collected which frequently appears, on first glance, to be interval data, but turns out to be ordinal data. Absence data can appear to be interval data, for example. On close inspection, it often fails the requirements for this category, since there is generally no meaningful distance between values. Some types of absence are clearly more important than other types of absence. A child who has missed eight weeks of schooling in a single block as a result of a medical procedure is somewhat different to a child who has missed six weeks of schooling through irregular attendance, three days a week, for 15 weeks in a row. Only if every day's absence can reasonably be the 'same' can absence data be considered interval data.

Where data is held to be interval data, summaries such as mean, mode and median are all valid. Percentages of interval data need to be treated with care, particularly when they are compared to each other.

3.2.4 Ratio data

Ratio data are interval data with a meaningful zero point. They have all of the properties of interval data (meaningful, ordered values with consistent measurable distances between values) as well as a meaningful zero point. This final requirement makes the identification of ratio data straightforward: if doubling a value results in a value which is 'twice' the initial value, the data can be said to be ratio data.

Test scores are not ratio data, as there is no meaningful zero point. A score of 10 out of 20 does not represent twice the learning that a score of 5 out of 20 represents. A child's age is usually held to be an example of ratio data. A child who is exactly 8 years old is twice as old as a child who is exactly 4 years old. If ages are calculated in years and days rather than years only, a child who is 15 years, 100 days old is twice the age of a child who is 7 years and 282 days old, since zero has an agreed meaning.

This example also demonstrates one of the challenges of ratio data, which is that the precision of the measurement and the method of measurement become important. We often think of 8-year-olds as being twice the age of 4-year-olds, but this rather depends on the actual age of the 8-year-olds and 4-year-olds in question. If we measure the children's ages in days, and we look at the extreme cases, some pairs would be 2¼ times older and some would be just 1⅗ older. What's more, children are alive in utero, and birth dates can often be at quite different stages of development, with some children facing serious challenges due to premature birth.

The accuracy and precision of the measurement is therefore important when considering whether numbers can be treated as ratio data. Where data is ratio data, it lends itself to summary statistics such as means, modes and medians, as well as analyses based on proportions.

3.2.5 Summaries of the four main types of data

Nominal data has meaningful labels which enable grouping.

Ordinal data has a meaningful order of groups.

Interval data has a meaningful order with regular intervals between values.

Ratio data has a meaningful order, regular intervals between values and a meaningful zero point.

3.3 The vexed question of interpreting educational data

Kathryn and Ben have a great deal of information presented as numerical data. But, having considered what they have been given, they know that there are clear differences between the data sets they are analysing.

In Kathryn's case, the information detailing whether children are male or female is clearly nominal data. Each category is separate, but there is no order in the data set. Data of this sort is often used within schools to separate children into groups of boys and girls, and then further analysis is undertaken considering whether there is a difference between the sexes in subsets of other data.

Results of surveys, such as Kathryn's information from pupil surveys taken each year, are somewhat complicated to interpret. Surveys often use what is known as a Likert (or Likert-type) scale, in which children respond with one of five options:

- strongly disagree
- disagree
- neither agree nor disagree
- agree
- strongly agree.

There is considerable debate as to whether Likert scale responses should be considered to be ordinal data or interval data. In most cases, it is much safer to consider survey results as ordinal data, and to be extremely sceptical of any advanced analysis of survey data. Even simple summaries such as means and medians may be misleading, since each respondent may interpret the questions differently, and the interval between questions may be considerably different in value.

Age data is certainly ratio data, although, as noted above, birth can be complicated and some children are born early or late, which can lead to developmental delays which might need to be considered when age data is being analysed. Children are often grouped into autumn, spring and summer categories which can be useful, although this should be treated as ordinal data since any regular interval is lost by this grouping.

Data on whether a child receives free school meals, often used as a proxy for an indication of children who are disadvantaged compared to their peers, is certainly nominal. As with other nominal data, FSM status is often used to create subsets of other data sets for further analysis.

The results of teacher assessments undertaken in Year 2 need to be treated carefully. This kind of data is usually ordinal data, in that there is no consistent interval between data points, and the data simply ranks children in a rough order of current development.

Much of the data which Kathryn and Ben will have access to is test data. This data is perhaps the most complicated to interpret, and there is considerable debate as to whether test score data should be considered ordinal, interval or ratio. Regardless of the academic arguments regarding their status, there is a great deal of evidence that test scores are frequently treated as if they were ratio data – when scores are presented as percentages, for example, they often go on to be treated as if they had a meaningful zero.

Simply using numbers to summarise results in a test encourages many people to treat test scores as if they were interval data, regardless of the validity of this assumption. In many cases, this comes from simple ignorance of the considerations of types of numbers raised in this chapter. In other cases, however, it comes from a lack of understanding of what is known about testing and tests of knowledge.

For teachers such as Kathryn and Ben, as well as for governors such as Andrew and Samaya, some understanding of the history and development of testing and theories of testing is useful to ensure that the limits – and potential uses – of test data are properly understood.

3.4 How testing has developed and what we know about written tests

Written tests of academic ability are a surprisingly recent development in education, not generally appearing until the middle of the 19th century. For most of human history, and certainly for the period in which education has been formalised, tests of ability were undertaken verbally, with questions being asked of candidates in person.

Verbal testing continues at graduate level in the form of the 'viva', in which the person being examined must present themselves and discuss a written thesis with a number of their professors (viva being an abbreviation of 'viva voce', a Latin phrase which translates literally as 'with living voice' and, more informally, as 'by word of mouth').

Written tests were largely pioneered in England by the British civil service, and the Trevelyn-Northcote report of 1854 – heavily influenced by the Chinese system of civil service examination – ushered in the beginnings of widespread written testing in the late 19th century. The first written examinations at Harvard University in the USA were also in the 1850s, and universities in England moved slowly to testing by written examination over the course of the late 19th century and into the modern era.

In 1918, 16-year-olds in England began to be tested via School Certificate Examinations, which led to a 'matriculation exemption' allowing further study in school. At 18, those in school could take a Higher Education certificate, which led to further study, typically at a university.

Early written tests were initially simply written questions which had previously been asked verbally, but which were now expected to be answered at length in the form of an essay. As written testing developed, however, the limitations of this kind of test became clear. Allocating a mark to an essay is essentially arbitrary, particularly when the examiner is asked to award marks which attempt to distinguish between students who are judged to be little more than broadly below, at or above an expected level.

What is more, marks given for essay-type questions are heavily dependent on the subjective view of the person marking the essay. Skilled students can obscure their lack of knowledge in some areas by emphasising others. Where examiners know the students whose papers they are marking, a degree of bias for and against students arises. Even when examiners do not know the students, the difference between adjacent marks is often minimal or non-existent.

As both students and those setting papers sought to improve written tests in the early 20th century, extensive research and development began to codify theories of testing, and to develop frameworks to try to ameliorate the issues identified by academics and practitioners. Much of this continues to be debated, and there are well-known issues with written tests which make scoring and grading written papers a particularly difficult task.

Much of the theory behind testing splits into two broad camps, the second of which – item response theory – was a response to the limitations of the first – classical test theory. We will look at each in turn.

3.4.1 Classical test theory

In classical test theory (CTT), a student's observed or obtained score on a written test is held to be composed of a 'true score' and an 'error score'. This theory builds on ideas developed by 19th century pioneers of statistics, and draws heavily on the mathematical ideas of variance and distributions of observed means of samples from populations, as discussed in Chapter 5.

A 'true score' is defined in CTT as the score which a student would obtain if they were tested over an infinite number of independent administrations of a test. Limitations of time and money mean that a student's true score cannot ever be observed, however. Classical test theory introduces one of the most important ideas in the theory of testing, that of the **reliability** of a test.

In essence, a test is said to be *reliable* if the scores it returns show very little inconsistency from one administration of a test to the next. If this is the case, then the test score contains a relatively low level of measurement error. The reliability of the test does not say whether a test is accurate in any specific sense, since a measurement could be reliable but miscalibrated, for example. As an illustration, a faulty speed camera might record the same speed each time a vehicle passes at the same velocity, but the speed camera may record the speed incorrectly each time.

The **reliability** of a test in CTT is defined as the ratio of the variance of the true score to the variance of the observed score. The variance of the true score – which can't be observed directly – does not change, as the true score is, by definition, fixed. The variance of the observed score, on the other hand, does vary depending on the size of the variance of the error. As the variance of the error decreases, the reliability of the test increases. As it increases, the reliability of the test decreases.

In classical test theory, the reliability of a test is generally measured using Cronbach's alpha (written using the Greek letter α), which provides a measure of a test's internal consistency. Cronbach's α is essentially a measure of correlation (discussed more fully in Chapter 7), in which values are reported in the range from 0 to 1, where 1 is perfectly correlated (i.e. highly reliable) and 0 indicates no correlation (i.e. highly variable).

Cronbach's α attempts to measure the internal consistency of a test by, in essence, producing a numerical correlation between the outcomes students return for each question on the test and the outcomes the students return for all of the other questions on the test. Where all of the students answer all of the questions in similar ways, the value of α increases, and where students give very different answers, the value of α decreases.

There are several known issues with Cronbach's α, not least that it assumes that all of the questions on a test are testing the same concept or construct (which is referred to as unidimensionality). There are also issues with the number of questions on a test, and it is well established that tests with higher numbers of related questions testing the same concepts generally return higher levels of α.

There are various well-known shortcomings with classical test theory in general. An important issue is that under CTT it is not possible to separate the characteristics of the students taking a particular test and the characteristics of the test itself. The argument becomes circular, as the score a student returns depends on the test items (the questions asked and their possible answers), and the test item statistics (the difficulty of items and the powers of discrimination between students) depend on those taking the test. A different set of students would produce a different set of statistics.

In addition, CTT assumes that the error scores are exactly the same for all those taking the test, which assumes that all those taking the test have the same ability, which is rarely the case.

CTT generally suggests that test scores should be treated as if they were ordinal data, not interval data. That said, a great deal of analysis based on test scores often treats numbers as if they were interval data. Generally, where a test uses scores which are held to be normally distributed, and raw scores are converted into standardised scores, test scores are often treated as if they were interval data.

For those working in school, a good rule of thumb is that standardised scores can usually be treated as if they were interval scores. Other test scores are probably best treated as if they were ordinal data.

3.4.2 Item response theory

Item response theory (IRT) addresses some of the shortcomings of CTT. By focusing on each item within a test rather than the test itself, IRT assumes that those taking the test have differing abilities and models the response of students of differing ability to each item in the test. As such, IRT is concerned with measuring latent traits, rather than performance on a test as such. By focusing on items which can be used to discriminate between students with differing levels of ability, the items become the focus, rather than the test, as is the case in CTT.

This allows for a much more sophisticated understanding of students' responses to test items, which in turn allows those using IRT to create tests that are tailored to specific groups of students and to the specific requirements of the test.

Rather than using CTT's concept of reliability, IRT uses a test information function which shows the degree of precision at different values of ability. This allows for the creation of sophisticated banks of test items which can discriminate between those items which provide little information (those which all those taking the test can answer, for example, or those questions which are too difficult for all test takers) and those items which actively discriminate between students (being 'just right' to discriminate between those who have/have not attained a given standard).

Once a bank of test items has been created, tests can then be created using these test items. An advantage of IRT is that, because the test items are 'sample independent' (i.e. they do not depend on those taking the test), different students can answer different questions and the results of their answers can be used to discriminate between students.

This allows for a much larger item bank to be used, which improves the reliability of testing created using IRT. Unfortunately, much of the theory underpinning IRT is immensely complicated and requires high levels of mathematical and statistical knowledge and understanding. In summary, IRT shows that it is possible to create tests which accurately assess a somewhat narrow range of ability for a given underlying concept, but that it is difficult to cater for those performing at the higher or lower levels of ability on a given test.

In school, tests based on item response theory are fairly rare. They do exist and, as computers become more common in classrooms, more tests based on IRT are developed for school. Once again, it is generally held that scores from tests based on IRT should not automatically be treated as interval data, although models within IRT are often used to argue that scores from IRT-based tests can be used as interval data.

3.5 What this means for databusting schools

We are primarily concerned with making sure that Kathryn and Ben do not come to conclusions which are based on misunderstandings of the way in which numbers can be interpreted. Having considered the information in this chapter, our teachers should be aware that they need to be extremely careful when it comes to interpreting numerical data.

Understanding the different types of data, and the common techniques which are used to summarise large and often confusing data sets, is essential for those working in databusting schools. The important differences between ratio data such as children's ages and ordinal data such as teacher assessments mean that we all need to be careful when attempting to bring clarity to complex situations.

Whilst in most cases test scores bring an invaluable relatively unbiased independence to the ongoing assessments we make in school, having an understanding of the theory underpinning testing helps to remind us to take care when we interpret test scores.

For teachers such as Kathryn and Ben, caution should become second nature. Clearly, having robust data is much better than working on intuition alone, but databusting schools are both aware of the potential pitfalls when working with data, and wary of being misled by the numbers they use.

3.6 Summary

We have looked at ways to describe information and at how numbers can be combined and summarised. We have considered how to interpret fractions, decimals and percentages, and looked at the four types of numerical data and what can be done with each of them.

We have also considered the history and development of theories underpinning test data, to help to understand what is known about the reliability and validity of test scores. In the next chapter, we will consider how we visualise complex data, and how visualisations can bring both clarity and confusion to our analyses of data.

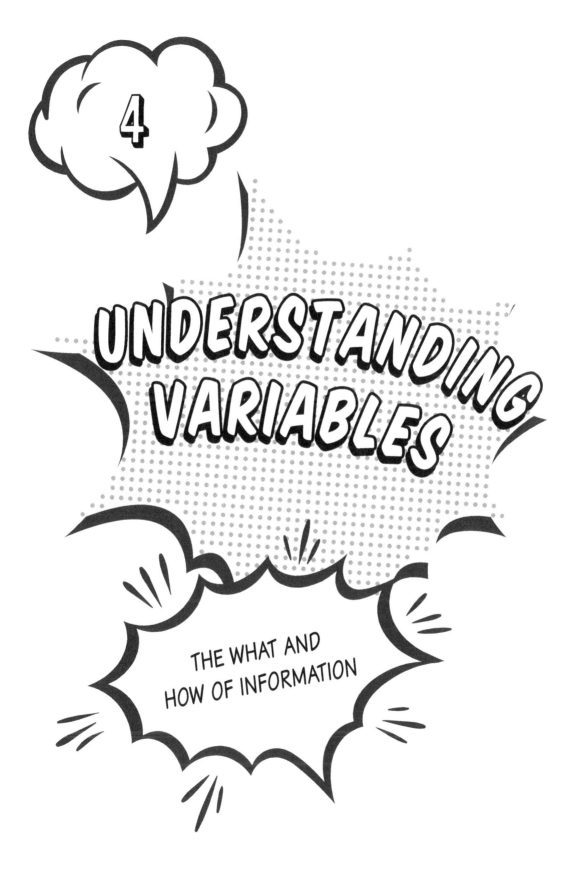

4

UNDERSTANDING VARIABLES

THE WHAT AND HOW OF INFORMATION

Case study 4.1

What do these graphs mean?

Kathryn and Ben are considering creating a series of graphs to summarise the numerical data they were given in Chapter 3. Whilst graphs can seem simple, they clearly contain a great deal of complex information. Both Kathryn and Ben are considering what they can and cannot present visually in the form of a graph.

Whilst both Kathryn and Ben have studied mathematics to a reasonable level, they are somewhat rusty when it comes to the ideas which underpin the graphs they are considering using. Armed with the knowledge about different types of numerical data they gained in Chapter 3, they are keen to use this information to help them understand how graphs work and whether the graphs they use might mislead others.

As this book is aimed at those working in school, more complicated mathematical language has, in general, been kept to a minimum. A majority of readers will follow the ideas presented in later chapters with essentially elementary mathematics. For those who are less certain of the way in which mathematics can be used to summarise complicated real-world situations, the following chapter will review and explain the way in which numbers and pictures can be used.

Readers whose mathematical knowledge is somewhat rusty will find it useful to work through the ideas which follow.

In this chapter, we will explore the way in which numbers can be converted into lines and pictures which help to summarise large amounts of information. You will also learn of many common ways in which graphs can be used to mislead or misdirect the reader, either accidentally or – as happens with surprising regularity – deliberately.

4.1 Describing numbers

In the first half of this chapter, we will focus on numbers, looking at the ways that lines can be described and summarised mathematically. Using lines helps us to depict data visually, which can frequently help us to understand relationships which have a numerical underpinning. We will look at algebra and equations.

4.1.1 Algebra

We have the Arabic world to thank for the term 'algebra'. It translates roughly as 'reunion of broken parts'. If this sounds reminiscent of surgery, this is because the term derives from the Spanish for 'the surgical treatment of fractures'. The mathematical sense, however, comes from a book title, *ilm al-jabr wa'l-muqābala*, which translates as 'the science of restoring what is missing and equating like with like'.

This was written by the 9th century mathematician known as al-Ḵwārizm, from whose name we derive the word 'algorithm' (a set of rules to be followed in a calculation or in mechanical problem-solving, such as that used in column methods of calculation or by a computer). Algebra has been with us for a long time and the deceptively simple idea it describes is to allow a specific case to be generalised. In other words, '6 plus 3 multiplied by 4' gives one specific answer, whereas replacing the numbers with letters which can represent any number – 'a plus b multiplied by c', for example – allows the specific case to be generalised.

In early mathematics, problems were written in words, as above. Luckily for us, algebra has become much easier to understand in the past few hundred years, primarily because of the work of mathematicians Gotfried Leibnitz, Leonard Euler and Carl Friedrich Gauss, amongst many others, which introduced a common set of symbols and rules for interpreting sentences with numbers in them. Hence, we can read and write '6 + 3 x 4' and 'a + b x c'.

Using letters rather than new symbols to represent the counting numbers emerged as scientists began to explore the natural relationships between different measurements. Thanks to different scales of measurement, we often have to convert between metric and imperial lengths, for example. Most people remember that 8 kilometres is roughly the same as 5 miles. So, if you wanted to convert 40 kilometres into miles, you would divide this by 8 – which would give you 5 – and then you would multiply this by 5, giving you an answer of 25 kilometres.

If you wanted to generalise from this specific case, you could simply replace the specific numbers with letters, like this:

$$M = K \div 8 \times 5$$

If you work out that dividing by 8 and multiplying by 5 is the same as multiplying by 0.625, you could write the conversion between kilometres and miles as:

$$M = 0.625 \text{ K}$$

Note that there is no 'x' symbol between the number 0.625 and the letter K.

Mathematicians like brevity and they soon discovered that the 'x' was not needed, so they simply stopped writing it when it was clear what was meant.

Algebra is a hugely powerful way of thinking. It uses simple mathematics to generalise from specific cases, and in doing so, it allows us to visualise complicated relationships using simple graphs. As with many essential ideas in mathematics, it is a threshold concept – once you understand it, it opens up many more ways to understand the world of numbers.

4.1.2 Understanding equations

A relationship between two different numbers, such as M = 0.625 K, is known as a *formula* or an *equation*. Equations allow us to do two different but related things with numbers. The first is to change one of the unknown letters into a known value, and then to calculate the value of other, previously unknown, letters. This requires that we *solve the equation*. The second thing is to draw a picture of the relationship between the unknowns. This *graphic formula*, or pictorial formula, is now known as drawing a *graph*.

4.1.2.1 Solving equations

Using M = 0.625 K, if K = 10, then M = 6.25. So, 10km is roughly 6.25m. This can be solved for any other value of K. (See Figure 4.1.)

4.1.2.2 Graphing equations

The standard format for an equation is to have a single letter on the left-hand side, an equals sign, and various numbers and letters on the right-hand side. Converting from imperial to metric measurements of distance, as we have been doing, is fairly straightforward, since both measurements have the same zero point. Where this isn't the case, there is a numerical adjustment, as in the case for the standard formula for converting between temperatures in Celsius and Farenheit, which is as follows:

$$F = 1.8C + 32$$

Here, the relationship between F (Farenheit) and C (Celsius) is a little more complicated.

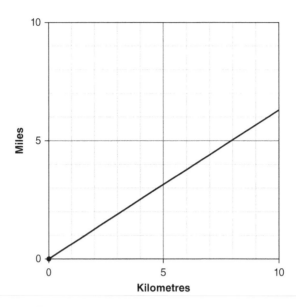

Figure 4.1 Kilometres v miles

So, for example, to convert 20°C into Farenheit, we need to solve the equation, by inserting C = 20 into F = 1.8C + 32, which gives 68°F.

A graph of the conversion can be seen in Figure 4.2.

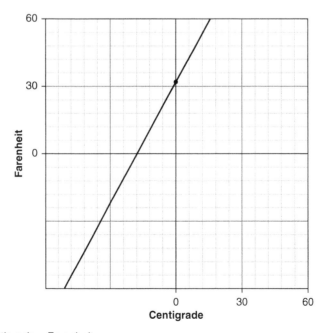

Figure 4.2 Centigrade v Farenheit

Databusting for schools

In Figure 4.2, you can begin to see how algebra becomes a very powerful tool both to find specific values given one unknown, and also to generalise from specific cases. Equations contain *variables* and *constants*. By convention, variables are written as capital letters or lower-case letters from the end of the alphabet (usually x, y or z). Variables are often multiplied by *coefficients*, such as '1.8C' in the temperature conversion equation above. Coefficients dictate the slope (or *gradient*) of the line in a graph. The bigger the coefficient, the steeper the slope of the graph, and vice versa. Figure 4.3 shows a range of coefficients to illustrate the point.

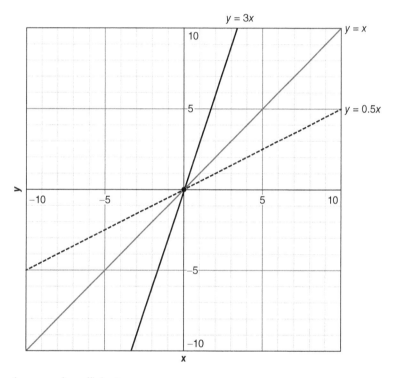

Figure 4.3 A range of coefficients

In Figure 4.3, each of these lines cuts through (0,0) the *origin* of the graph. Equations which include an unchanging number to be added or taken away look like Figure 4.4.

In Figure 4.4, the adjustments move the whole line up or down, depending on whether a number is added or taken away. Because the adjustments aren't changed by variables (+ 7 means you always add 7 regardless of the value of x), the adjustment is referred to as a *constant*.

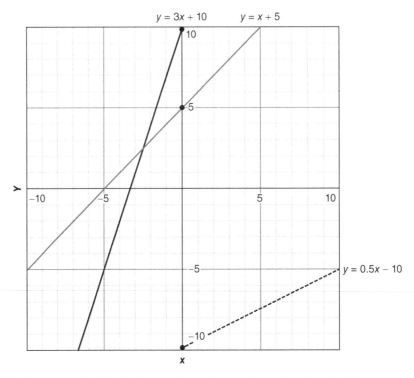

Figure 4.4 Equations which include an unchanging number to be added or taken away

In summary, an equation such as y = ax + b contains *variables* (x and y), a *coefficient* (a) and a *constant* (b). This is the equation for a straight line, which we will use extensively in later chapters.

Straight lines are described using *linear equations*, of the form y = ax + b. Curved lines are described by using more complex variables, using higher powers of variables such as x^2 or x^3 (or, more generally, x^n, where n is any number). Whilst these are also incredibly useful, most education data uses linear equations rather than more complex equations and we will restrict the discussion to linear equations for most of this book.

4.2 Working with equations

Working with algebraic equations requires some understanding of the terminology and definitions which have been developed by mathematicians and statisticians. The following are a number of the common algebraic terms you might encounter.

4.2.1 Common terms and expressions

An **expression**: a number written with variables and constants, such as $3x^2 - 5x + 5xy + 8$.

A **term**: the individual parts of an expression, referred to in the order in which they appear. So, in the expression above, the terms are $3x^2$, $-5x$, $5xy$ and 8. Terms are discussed in terms of their 'term type', which is the name given to each variable. So, the expression above has x^2, x and xy terms, as well as a constant.

Simplifying expressions: the process of gathering all the like terms together and calculating a single term for each term type. If $4x + 3xy$ was added to the expression above, it would become $3x^2 - 5x + 5xy + 8 + 4x + 3xy$. This could be simplified to $3x^2 - x + 8xy + 8$, since $-5x + 4x = -x$ and $5xy + 3xy = 8xy$.

Expanding expressions: this is typically used to describe the expanding or multiplying of brackets. So, $3(2x - 3) + 5(2 - x)$ would become $6x - 9 + 10 - 5x$. This usually allows for further simplification. Here, the two x terms add to make x and the two constants add to make 1, leaving the expression $x + 1$.

Equations: these use the root word 'equal' and are simply expressions which have an equals sign, '=', between them. Each expression is equivalent so, for example, $8 + 2x = 14 - 4x$.

4.3 Reading graphs

Whilst many people have an instinctive feel for numbers, it can be very difficult to work out just what an equation such as $-2x + 8y - 8 = 0$ might tell you. You could put in a variable and work out the answer. So, when $x = 0$, for example, the equation becomes $8y - 8 = 0$. This is only true when $y = 1$, so when $x = 0$, $y = 1$. This begins to indicate the relationship between x and y in this equation.

Solving the equation when $y = 0$ is also fairly straightforward. This gives you $-2x - 8 = 0$. This is only true when $x = -4$, so when $x = -4$, $y = 0$. You could insert any value for x or y and solve the equation for y or x, and in this way you could build up a picture of what happens as x and y vary.

Most brains seem to be much happier to find visual patterns, however, which is why graphs have been developed to turn fairly complicated equations into fairly straightforward lines. The reading of graphs follows a set of simple universal rules:

- **Rule 1:** Where do you start counting from? You need to know where the graph 'begins'. Graphs start at a point known as the 'origin', where both x and $y = 0$.
- **Rule 2:** Points are measured across the page on the x-axis.
- **Rule 3:** Points are measured up (or down) the graph on the y-axis.

Graphs are often shown with variables which only have meaningful positive values, and therefore the origin is usually in the bottom left-hand corner of the picture. The horizontal side of the picture – the x-axis – shows the value of x, and the vertical side – the y axis – shows the value of y. Each axis is labelled with its scale of measurement, so that it is possible to interpret any point on the graph as being x and y away from the origin. The sides are labelled x and y, incidentally, since these are the 24th and 25th letters of the alphabet. Where a graph shows three dimensions, the axes are referred to as x, y and z, where z is, in effect, 'into' and 'out of' the picture.

Each point drawn on the graph is known as a co-ordinate (numbers which 'work together') and in a 2D graph is written in the form (x,y). So (10,36) is the point 10 away from the origin on the x-axis and 36 away from the origin on the y-axis (see Figure 4.5).

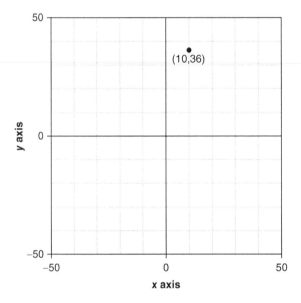

Figure 4.5 Example of a graph

Graphs of straight lines make it clear that there is a relationship between the x and y co-ordinates, which every point on the line clearly shares. In the graph in Figure 4.6, it is clear that the y co-ordinates are simply 5 more than the value of the x co-ordinates. Using the language of algebra, which we looked at earlier in this chapter, this relationship can be summarised as follows:

$$y = x + 5$$

The power of both equations and graphs should be clear. The graph is very easy to read and the equation generates every possible point on the line.

 Databusting for schools

Box 4.1 Plotting co-ordinates on a graph

Try plotting the following co-ordinates on the graph in Figure 4.6:

(0,5), (2,7), (4,9), (6,11), (8,13), (10,15)

What do you notice about the line you have drawn?

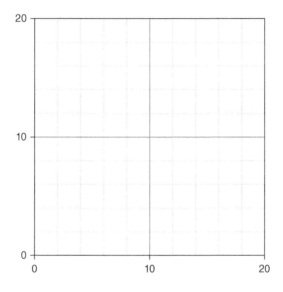

Figure 4.6

Box 4.2 Drawing the graph of an equation

Using the equation $y = 3x - 4$, check which of these points will appear on the line it generates:

(a) (3, 5)

(b) (10, 10)

(c) (4, 9)

(Continued)

(Continued)

Check that you can work out the missing halves of the co-ordinate pairs below:

(a) (2, ?)

(b) (?, 11)

(c) (6, ?)

Plot the points you have found on the graph in Figure 4.7. They should all be on the same straight line.

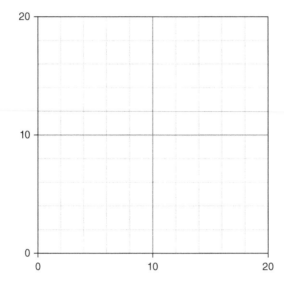

Figure 4.7

The equations we have been working with thus far – with a y term, an x term and a constant – have all resulted in straight lines. These types of equations are referred to as *linear equations* since, when they are plotted as a graph, they produce straight lines.

The constant term in a linear equation is very useful because it has a consistent property, no matter what the coefficients of x or y. If you look back at y = x + 5 and y = 3x –4, you will notice that the line crosses the y-axis at the same value as the constant in the equation. These values (5 in y = x + 5 and –4 in y = 3x – 4) are known as the *Y intercept* – that is, the point at which the y-axis is crossed.

The coefficient of the x term contains valuable information too. It tells you which way the line is sloping – up to the top right if it is positive, down to the bottom right if it is negative – and it tells you something about the slope of the line as well. For y = x + 5, the slope (or 'gradient' to use the mathematical term for the slope) of the line is 1, so that for every step along the x-axis, the line rises 1 step on the y-axis. For y = 3x – 4, the line is steeper, rising 3 steps on the y-axis for every step on the x-axis.

All of this means that, mathematically, a linear equation of the form $y = bx + a$ has a *gradient* of b and an *intercept* of a.

4.4 Summary statistics

Two further concepts that are important here are those used to find *sums* and *means* for sets of numbers. These appear so often that they have been given specific symbols: Σ (read as capital sigma) and $\bar{x}$ (read as x bar).

4.4.1 Σ (capital sigma)

The Greek upper-case letter sigma, Σ, is used to indicate that a set of numbers should be added together (lower-case letter sigma, σ, is used to refer to a different concept, that of a calculation of a measure of spread which we will cover in Chapter 5, and should not be confused with Σ).

ΣX indicates that a set of X values should be added together, and ΣY indicates that the Y values should be added together.

Consider the values for X and Y in Table 4.1.

Table 4.1   Values for X and Y

X	Y
0	−4
1	−1
2	2
3	5
4	8
5	11
6	14
7	17

The sum of the X values, ΣX, is simply the sum of $0 + 1 + 2 + 3 + 4 + 5 + 6 + 7$. In this case, $\Sigma X = 28$. ΣY is $-4 + -1 + 2 + 5 + 8 + 11 + 14 + 17 = 52$.

4.4.2 $\bar{x}$ (x bar)

The symbol $\bar{x}$ is used to refer to the mean of the X values. The mean is one of a number of summary statistics used to provide insight into 'typical' values of a set of data, which we considered in Chapter 3. $\bar{x}$ is calculated by adding together all the values and then dividing the sum by the number of values. This unwieldy sentence can be summarised by the notation below:

$$\bar{x} = \frac{\sum X}{N}$$

So, in the example we have been considering:

$$\bar{x} = \frac{\sum(0+1+2+3+4+5+6+7)}{8} = \frac{\sum 28)}{8} = 3.5$$

Both $\sum$ (capital sigma) and $\bar{x}$ (x bar) are simple but powerful operations and are essential when looking at large sets of data, as are frequently gathered in schools.

Means should only be used for data which fulfils the criteria for at least interval data (see Chapter 3). Where a mean has been calculated for ordinal data – which happens frequently in education data – great care should be taken. The mean of ordinal data *may* provide a useful if inaccurate summary of the raw data, but it may also create misconceptions or mislead the reader.

4.5 Presenting data visually

The past century has seen a bewildering proliferation of images of data, and the rise in computing power has enabled increasingly complex graphs, diagrams and plots of data to be created. Derived from the Greek word meaning writing, a graph has come to mean a picture of a collection of numbers, often drawn using axes which have a known origin. As with all summaries of sets of numbers, it is easy to lose the detail contained within data sets, especially when graphs are drawn which either carelessly or deliberately mislead the reader.

In this section, we will look at the most common graphs: bar charts, pie charts, pictograms, histograms, scatter graphs and time graphs. As a group, these different representations will be referred to as graphs, even when – as often happens – the word graph does not appear in the name of the visualisation.

4.5.1 Bar charts

Bar charts are used extensively to summarise data sets. Figure 4.8 is a typical example of this simple graph.

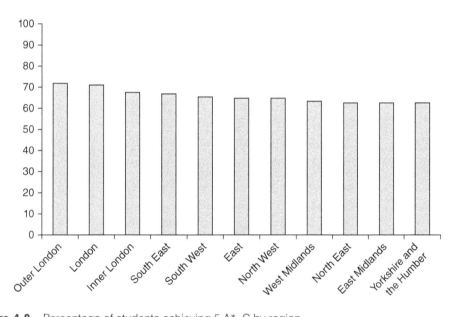

Figure 4.8 Percentage of students achieving 5 A*–C by region

As is clear, bar charts give an immediate indication of the main features of a data set, showing the relative differences between the extremes of the data. It is immediately obvious that more children in Outer London attain 5 A*–C GCSE grades than in any other region, and that the smallest percentage of children with this level of attainment are those in Yorkshire and the Humber.

There are several features of a bar chart which should be understood. First, each of the bars is the same width. This means that a fair comparison can be made between each of the bars. The only dimension which is relevant is the height of the bar.

Bar charts have gaps between bars, as there is no link between each category. Leaving a gap between the south west and the south east, for example, emphasises the fact that these two regions are entirely distinct, with no connection between them. This is different to a histogram, which looks similar to a bar chart, but has adjoining bars for reasons which will be explained below.

Whilst bar charts are usually presented with vertical bars, they can also be presented with horizontal bars. There are no hard and fast rules as to which orientation should be used. Where names of categories are relatively long, horizontal bars can make the chart easier to read and are therefore sometimes preferred. The vertical bars in Figure 4.8 could quite easily be presented horizontally, as in Figure 4.9.

Figure 4.9   Percentage of students achieving 5 A*–C by region

Some bar charts go beyond the simplistic examples we have looked at so far. Where data is grouped in some way, such as data for different years or genders, for example, a bar chart can be drawn which positions data for two or more categories next to each other, such as that shown in Figure 4.10.

These are known as compound or multiple bar charts. They may need additional clarification via a legend box to indicate what each bar colour indicates. A good compound or multiple bar chart can present a great deal of complicated information quickly and succinctly, although it needs to be approached with caution as including too much information in one graph can also confuse the reader.

Bar charts can also be drawn with each bar split into several separate components, such as the chart shown in Figure 4.11. This type of chart is known as a component bar chart and, once again, caution is advised as the reader can easily be overloaded if too much information is crammed into one chart. A limit of five or six separate components is advisable, otherwise the chart simply becomes too difficult to interpret.

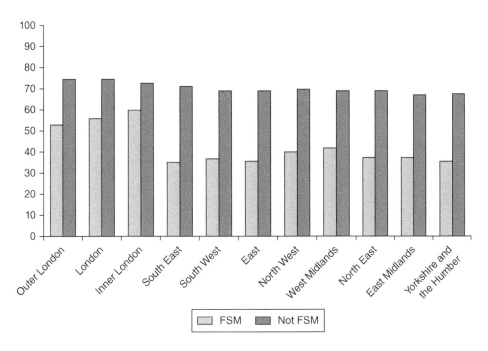

Figure 4.10 Percentage of students achieving 5 A*–C by region and FSM status

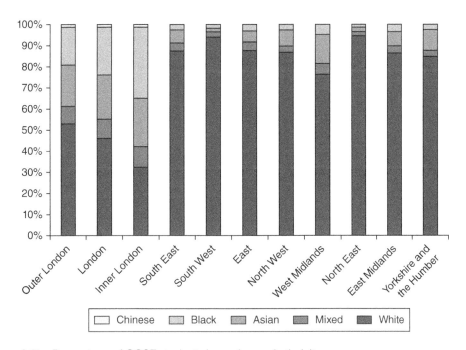

Figure 4.11 Percentage of GCSE students by region and ethnicity

4.5.1.1 How bar charts can mislead readers

The main way in which bar charts are used to mislead readers is in the choice of the scale for the chart. Bars for ratio data – see Chapter 3 – should start at zero wherever possible, as this makes it clear to the reader the relative changes between the different bars. An example of the difference this makes is shown in Figure 4.12, which shows a chart with a vertical scale beginning at 0 and extending to 100%, alongside a misleading chart in which the vertical scale does not begin at zero.

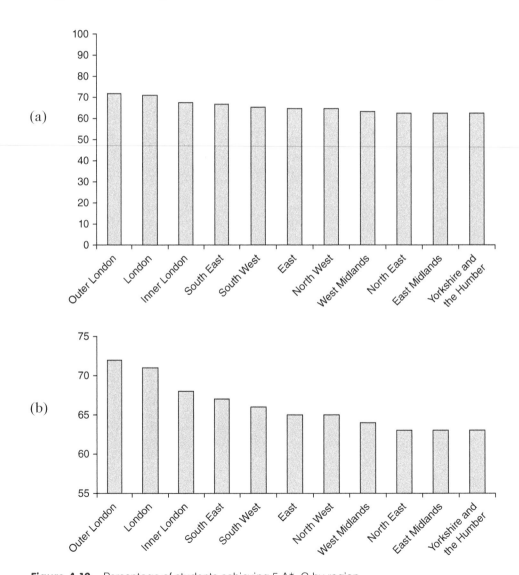

Figure 4.12 Percentage of students achieving 5 A*–C by region

In Figure 4.12b, it appears that the differences between regions are relatively large, indicating that there are substantial differences between them. But, as Figure 4.12a makes clear, the differences are actually quite small – it is simply the misleading impression that a truncated scale makes. Unfortunately, many different spreadsheet programs automatically select scales for charts. Many published charts show that some publications either do not understand, or choose to ignore, the effect a truncated scale has on the reader.

Where you choose to truncate a scale, this should be indicated as shown in Figure 4.13. It is not ideal, but rather than deliberately mislead, it is best to alert the reader to the truncated scale openly rather than to simply truncate without indication.

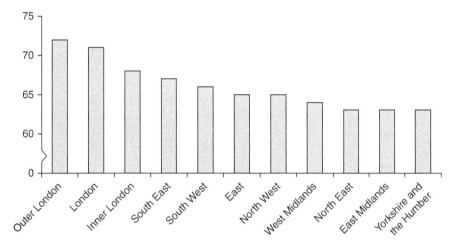

Figure 4.13 Percentage of students achieving 5 A*–C by region

Using bar charts for interval data (see Chapter 3) can sometimes mislead. Temperature in degrees Celsius is often shown in a bar chart, for example. But zero has no real meaning in this case, since it simply reflects the freezing point of water at sea level, not the absence of heat. A graph with data points just above freezing can suggest large fluctuations in temperature when, in reality, these are relatively small changes which may simply reflect measurement error. An example is shown in Figure 4.14. Care needs to be taken in drawing up and reading this kind of chart, so that no misleading impression is given.

In education, many numbers are not ratio data, but scaled scores arranged around a mean and a standard deviation. In these data sets, bar charts are very misleading, as the scale simply has no obvious meaning to the casual reader. PISA scores, for example, have a mean of 500 and a standard deviation of 100. Presenting scores as is done in Figure 4.15 can be misleading, since it is not clear what the relative differences between the countries might be.

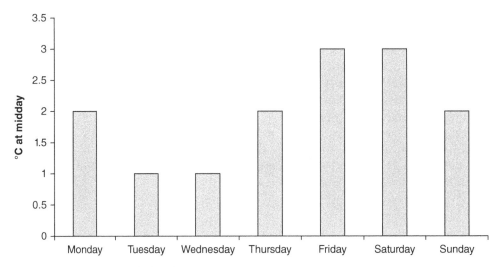

Figure 4.14 Temperature in London

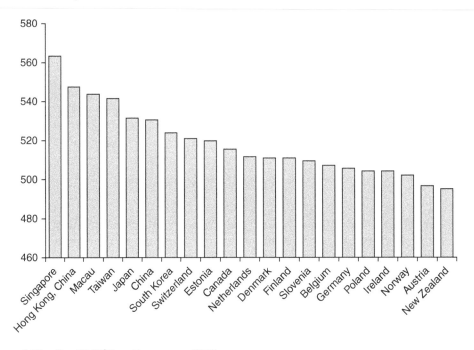

Figure 4.15 Top 20 PISA maths scores, 2016

Where data is presented in percentages, make sure that you consider the numbers used to create the chart. Percentages are an excellent way to allow comparisons between different data, but they can mislead if they are based on data sets with limited numbers of cases. Data for primary school classes and for less popular GCSE subjects, for example, is often compared across year groups; where there are fewer

Databusting for schools

than a hundred students in each cohort, small changes in the underlying data can look much bigger when presented in a bar chart using a percentage scale.

Data which can be presented to suggest differences between subgroups in a data set may also simply reflect either measurement error or sampling error. Student test scores, for example, contain a substantial amount of measurement error: the difference between any relatively narrow range of scores is likely to be negligible, which is why grades are frequently preferred to raw scores. Sampling error occurs when a data set is assumed to be drawn from the same population. One group of 30 students may be randomly different to another group of 30 students, and the difference between the two contains an element of sampling error, which is often ignored when two cohorts are compared in a bar chart. The smaller the sample, the greater the potential for large sampling error (see Chapter 6 for more details on these issues).

In summary:

- Bar charts are best for comparing the differences between groups of data, or to track large changes over time.
- Bar charts should be shown with a scale which includes zero.
- Be aware that data without an easily understood interval can be misleading.
- Beware data which may simply show measurement or sampling error, or which may present misleading percentages based on small sample sizes.

4.5.2 Pie charts

Pie charts are used to show percentage or proportional data, where the reader might want to understand the breakdown of parts of a whole at a glance. Figure 4.16 is a typical example of this simple graph.

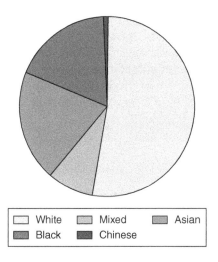

Legend: White, Mixed, Asian, Black, Chinese

Figure 4.16 Outer London GCSE candidates by ethnicity

Pie charts are quite difficult to draw by hand, but, luckily, computers make light work of constructing these charts. To draw them by hand, each data point has to be converted from a fraction of the whole into an interior angle, and these angles are then used to draw the different segments. Figure 4.17 shows the different angles required to draw the pie chart above, and shows that hand-drawn pie charts are difficult to draw accurately.

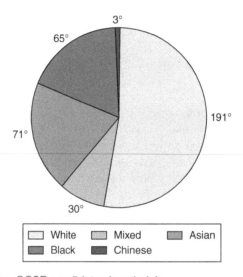

Figure 4.17 Outer London GCSE candidates by ethnicity

Care needs to be taken with pie charts. Ideally, each of the data points which are being illustrated should make up a substantial proportion of the whole. In Figure 4.18, for example, four of the data points are so small when compared to the whole data set that they barely register on the chart. This makes it difficult to label the smaller segments, which can make it difficult to interpret the data.

Pie charts tend to work best when there are between three and six segments. Any more segments and each segment becomes too small; any fewer and the data may as well be shown in a table.

In summary:

- Pie charts are best for showing the proportional differences between parts of a whole.
- Make sure that the chart is well labelled and that it is very clear what each segment represents.
- Don't use pie charts where there are more than six segments – a table or bar chart is better for this kind of data.

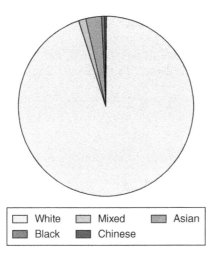

☐ White	▨ Mixed	▨ Asian
▨ Black	▨ Chinese	

Figure 4.18 North East GCSE candidates by ethnicity

4.5.3 Pictograms

Pictograms are often used to summarise data sets for non-specialist readers. They often appear in newspapers and magazines in place of bar charts. Figure 4.19 is a typical example of a pictogram.

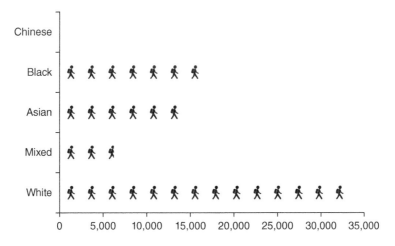

Figure 4.19 Outer London GCSE candidates by ethnicity

As can be seen in Figure 4.19, a single symbol is used to represent a given number of observations. A fraction of a symbol is used to indicate a fraction of the chosen multiple. This makes it easy to determine rough numerical order and proportional differences, but it is often difficult to determine the actual values with any accuracy.

4.5.3.1 How pictograms can mislead readers

Pictograms drawn with unusual perspective can be misleading, as shown in Figure 4.20. Unless the symbols are all the same size, it is easy to mistake a bigger symbol for a bigger number.

Figure 4.20   Outer London GCSE candidates by ethnicity

In summary:

- Pictograms are best for showing data to a non-specialist audience who might not wish – or be able – to read a bar chart.
- Make sure that the symbols are identical in size so the reader is not misled.

4.5.4 Histograms

Histograms show a simple distribution of numerical data. They help to see the spread and shape of a data set. Figure 4.21 is a typical example of a histogram.

Histograms are similar to bar charts, with one crucial difference: the horizontal axis on a histogram represents a **continuous** number scale. Because the adjacent bars are in effect subsections of one variable, they are made to touch. Bar charts, which represent separate categories of variable, are deliberately drawn with bars which do not touch, which emphasises the separation between categories.

The bars on a histogram represent intervals on a number line, and therefore represent quite different types of data to the bars on a bar chart. Histograms clearly show the shape of data which have been measured on a continuous number scale.

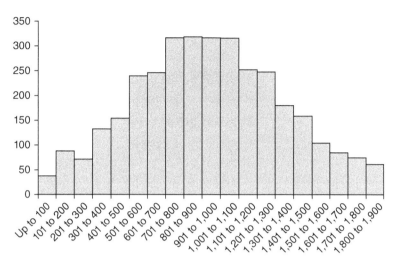

Figure 4.21 Secondary schools by number of pupils

Box 4.3

Box 4.3 Continuous and discrete data

Data can be separated into two broad categories, known as *discrete* and *continuous* data. Discrete data is that which is effectively grouped into separate categories, with no overlap or continuum between categories. A child is either male or female. There is no overlap between these two groups, and the data is therefore said to be discrete. Continuous data could be placed on a number line, as there is a continuum between groups of data. A child's age is continuous data, as '9-year-olds' and '10-year-olds' are related, and it makes sense to say that there is a dividing point at which a child can cross from one group to the next.

Examples of discrete data might include:

Categories	Examples of data
Class size	30 pupils, 25 pupils, 27 pupils, 20 pupils
Sex	Boys, girls
Free school meal status	Currently receives FSM, Ever 6 FSM but not currently
FSM, Never FSM	

In the terminology introduced in Chapter 3, nominal or ordinal data is always discrete data. Interval and ratio data can be discrete or continuous, depending on whether there is a meaningful midpoint between any two values.

(Continued)

(Continued)

Examples of continuous data might include:

Categories	Examples of data
Child's age	3043 days, 4790 days, 4236 days
Annual absence	3 sessions, 10 sessions, 25 sessions
Child's height	132cm, 105cm, 163cm

Unlike discrete data, continuous data is not restricted in the values it can take, only by the precision of the measurement of the variable. So, for example, it would be possible to be more (or less) precise in the measurement of a child's age, or of their attendance in school. It would be theoretically possible to measure these variables in months, days, hours or even seconds, should this be necessary. Of course, there are practical limitations in the degree of precision used, but these numbers are fundamentally different to the measurement of the number of children in a class. A child is either a member of a class or she is not, and therefore this is discrete data. Test scores, which can only have a limited number of values, are discrete data. A child's age, on the other hand, is continuous.

It is useful to have the idea of continuous data being that which can be placed anywhere on a number line depending on the precision of the measure used. With continuous data, it is always possible – if not always practical – to find a third point between any two points. This is fundamentally different to discrete data, which can be thought of as separate boxes into which any new item of data can be placed.

As with bar charts, the heights of the bars in histograms are related to the value each bar represents. When drawing histograms, however, the width of each bar may vary depending on the data which is being represented. Some data may have been collected in unequal class intervals, for example, or two or more adjacent intervals may be amalgamated. So the histogram above could be redrawn to show the small number of schools with over 1,500 children in one interval rather than in four intervals (Figure 4.22 and Figure 4.23).

Histograms will be developed later when we consider distributions of data.

4.5.4.1 How histograms can mislead readers

Histograms are a more specialist representation of data, requiring some knowledge of their construction, and therefore tend to be misused less often. Very occasionally, discrete data will be presented in histogram form (with bars which touch when they shouldn't) which can suggest a distribution, which might be misleading. Because bars can have different widths, histograms are prone to mislabelled axes which imply that all the bars are presented on the same vertical scale, which may not be the case.

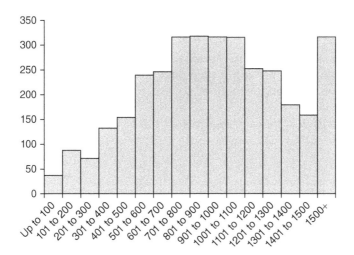

Figure 4.22 Secondary schools by number of pupils

By carefully selecting intervals, it is possible to blur some important differences within a data set, and therefore histograms should be presented where possible alongside the underlying data. Where no original data is available, be careful not to make too many assumptions about any data presented in histogram form.

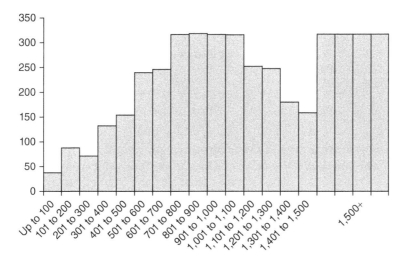

Figure 4.23 Secondary schools by number of pupils

In summary:

- Histograms are best for showing simple distributions within data.
- The height and width of the bars should be taken into consideration.
- Be careful to consider whether the chosen intervals may hide any useful data points.

4.5.5 Scatter graphs

Scatter graphs (also known as XY graphs, scatterplots or scatter diagrams) show simple distributions of paired numerical data, i.e. data sets which have data which is linked in pairs. Pairs might include test scores at two points in time, age and attendance, attendance and test scores, and so on. Scatter graphs help readers to see the patterns within a data set. Figure 4.24 is a typical example of a scatter graph.

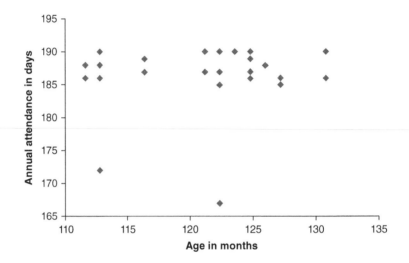

Figure 4.24   Attendance v age

Scatter graphs provide a powerful visual representation of the kind of relationship which *might* exist between the two variables under consideration. A simple scatter graph reveals very quickly whether two variables are related or not, and in what way they might be related. We will look much more closely at the way in which these relationships can be analysed and interpreted when we look at the concepts of *regression* and *correlation* in Chapter 7.

4.5.6 Time graphs

Time graphs show changes in a variable over time. A line drawn from left to right on the graph joins data points over time for each variable.

Figure 4.25 shows the changes in test scores recorded by boys and girls in England over time.

Figure 4.25 Boys v girls O Level/GCSE outcomes

As a slightly more sophisticated graphical representation of data, time graphs can be drawn for data which has been standardised, i.e. the scale has been recalibrated using the mean and standard deviation of the data. This means that data is often presented in a format which varies around a mean score, as shown in Figure 4.26. This can draw out patterns over time, but care must be taken to ensure that the reader is not being misled.

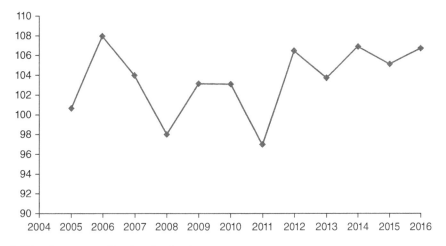

Figure 4.26 Average maths standardised score

4.5.6.1 How time graphs can mislead readers

It is often tempting for readers to read more into the lines on a time graph than they should. Time graphs are useful to give the reader a sense of change over time. Each data point is often independent of the other data points with which it is linked, however. On a scatter graph, it would make no sense to join pairs using a line, as they are not consecutive and are clearly unrelated. A time graph can give the impression that each pair *is* related when they are clearly not.

In the time graph above, for example, each data point represents entirely separate cohorts, and there is therefore clearly no direct link between one point on the line and another, other than that the same (or similar) variable has been measured each year. When the non-time variable represents a mean drawn from a large sample or population, the line can be useful to show the broad trend in the measured variable over time. With small numbers – the mean of a population of 30 children in a class, for example – the line will frequently vary wildly simply because the data underlying the graph is much more susceptible to wide variation.

Figure 4.27 shows the differences between a single class of children and the national picture. The class, representing just 30 children, is clearly much more volatile than the national population, which represents many hundreds of thousands of children.

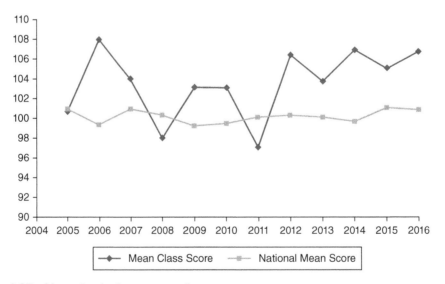

Figure 4.27 Mean standard scores – maths

The usual cautions about a misleading choice of axes apply to time graphs, and readers should consider whether the data being summarised in a time graph is actually continuous data which is at the very least interval data.

In summary:

- Time graphs are best for showing changes in a measurement over time.
- Always remember that each data point is independent of the data points on either side, and variation warrants further investigation rather than inviting assumptions.
- Make sure that the vertical axis is not misleading and includes zero where appropriate.

Box 4.4 — **Selecting graphs to show key data points**

When Kathryn considers how she is going to interpret her data, she might find different types of charts useful for visualising the information she has. Kathryn now knows that bar charts can help when comparing the differences between groups of data, or to track large changes over time, and some of the data she has, such as data grouped by gender or free school meals status, lends itself to these kinds of representations.

She might use a pie chart to consider responses to pupil surveys, as these provide a quick overview of the relative differences in children's different views about school. Where she has data for a number of school years, she might consider a time chart to look at changes over time. In each case, she is using graphs to help her to investigate her data and to draw out areas which might inform various questions she may want to investigate concerning her new class.

In Ben's case, he might try to identify lines of enquiry using similar charts to those Kathryn has created. Once he has drawn his own conclusions from his data, he will need to consider which graphs will best help to summarise his findings when he presents them to his governing body.

4.6 Summary

This chapter has provided an introduction to equations and expressions, and explained how variables and constants are used to describe lines.

It has provided a guide to the following types of graphs:

- bar charts
- pie charts
- pictograms
- histograms
- scatter graphs
- time graphs.

Now that Kathryn and Ben have explored different types of graphs, and have got themselves up to speed on understanding linear equations and basic statistics, they are ready to consider how they might use more advanced statistical techniques to summarise the data that they have. They are also in a position to get the most from more advanced analysis which is available to them in school, either from school data management systems or from outside providers who supply schools with data analysis.

In the next chapter, we will explore measures of central tendency and consider the theory underpinning the use of samples of populations to shed light on wider populations.

5

DESCRIPTIVE STATISTICS

WHERE ARE WE NOW?

Now that we have looked at some of the terminology used to talk about data, we can begin to look at some of the more sophisticated ways in which data can be summarised effectively and efficiently. Picturing data will lead to information on which we can act. After all, we have ever increasing amounts of data in school, and the average computer will give us the computational power to help us summarise all the data we have quickly and easily – provided we know what can be done and how to interpret the results.

Common questions about data are deceptively simple. What does it all mean? How should we interpret the data we have? What does all this data tell us about the current situation we are in?

In this chapter, we will look at ways in which we can get a feel for where we are now. We will look at a seemingly simple question: What does our data tell us about a typical child in our school?

We will look at averages and spreads, and what we can do with these measures. This chapter builds on the ideas in Chapter 3, and you might find it useful to make reference to that chapter for any tricky concepts which crop up here. In summary, Chapter 3 included information about combining and summarising numbers, how and why fractions, decimals and percentages are used, the four types of numerical data and what can be done with each of them. The use of test scores was also discussed, focusing on the tricky question of whether a given set of test score data should be considered interval data or not.

Let's also reconsider what we might want to find out using the data to which we might typically have access.

Kathryn knows how to calculate the mean, median and mode of her test data, and she has entered the scores her children have generated into a spreadsheet program. She now knows that the mean, median and mode of her data are as follows:

Mean: 17.3

Median: 16

Modes: 8, 9, 20

Kathryn is trying to get an idea of the most typical result for her class. With just 30 children, it is highly likely that her class will have a random distribution of test scores which varies considerably depending on the children in the class. There simply are not enough children for any 'smooth' distribution to emerge. Ben, who has much more test score data with which to work, and is therefore more likely to be considering mean scores rather than scores for individuals, will expect to see data which clusters around a typical measure, especially if he works in a large high school with lots of children.

Kathryn is also aware that her data is unlikely to be interval data, as the raw scores are made up of test items which are unlikely to be of the same difficulty. She is wary of reading too much into the summaries she has generated, and is considering other ways to picture her data.

Ben looks at Year 7 CAT scores for each cohort (cognitive abilities tests which were taken in the first few weeks of all the children entering school), which he can be more certain about treating as if it were interval data. He has means, medians and modes for various tests, giving him a lot of data which he would like to interpret.

Both Kathryn and Ben want to know what the data they have can tell them about a child picked at random from their classes, and about what might be expected for particular children. Is a child 'average' or not? And if they are not 'average', how different are they from the typical child in the groups Kathryn and Ben are looking at?

5.1 Considering the spread of values in data

The measures of central tendency which Kathryn has calculated suggest that the children in her class have scored around 17 marks on her spelling test. From this she concludes that 17 marks is a fairly typical result, and most children are indeed near to this score. The mode for her class alerts her to the fact that some children have scored 8 and 9 marks, however – which is much lower than the 17 marks the median and mean suggest is typical.

She is also aware that the data she has may not be interval data and that she might simply have to treat it as ordinal data. At this point, she puts the scores in order and starts to consider the spread of the marks – what is the highest score and what is the lowest score? This range of results is called just that – the **range**. It is calculated by quite simply finding the difference between the smallest and the largest result. The smallest score was 5 and the highest score was 35, making the range 30.

A range of 30 in a data set with 40 possible results suggests that there is a very wide spread of current knowledge in the class. But Kathryn is concerned that there may simply be one child who has scored highly and one who has scored a low mark, with most of the other children clustered around the mean and the median. The second measure of spread Kathryn can use is the *inter-quartile range*.

Quartiles are simply divisions into quarters. The first quartile is the first 25% of the data, the second the next 25%, and so on. The interquartile range is simply the difference between the first and third quartile – the boundaries which contain the middle 50% of values. In this case, the first quartile comes at 8.5 marks (half way between a score of 8 and a score of 9 marks) and the third quartile comes at 24 marks. The inter-quartile range is therefore 15.5 marks.

Quartiles are frequently referred to as being the lower quartile (the lowest 25% of observations) or the upper quartile (the highest 25%).

It is worth noting that, in some data sets, the highest and lowest data points are regarded as 'extreme', or very different to typical data points. This often happens when the range of possible data points is very wide – the speed of cars on a motorway, or salaries of people travelling on an aeroplane, for example.

Test scores are capped, in that the highest score is the total number of marks available and the lowest is zero, and therefore in a well-designed test the data rarely contains extreme values. In some data sets, however, there may be a substantial number of children who were absent and who were therefore awarded no score, and there may be a group of extremely talented children who get everything on the paper correct.

So now Kathryn has a number of summary statistics to consider:

The median, 1st quartile, 3rd quartile, minimum and maximum scores.

These five figures are commonly known as 'five-figure summaries' and they tell you a great deal of information about a data set. It's worth recalling that, following the definitions of data in Chapter 3, the data which is being summarised in this way should be either ordinal, interval or ratio data. In Kathryn's case, these summaries are particularly useful as she cannot be sure that the test score data she has is interval data.

The standard way to put these five figures into a table can be seen in Table 5.1.

Table 5.1 Standard median table

	Median			17	
1st quartile		3rd quartile	8.5		24
Minimum		Maximum	3		35

Whilst this is a relatively simple summary of the data, it is still quite a lot of information to take in in numerical form. Too many numbers often overwhelm us. Fortunately, pictures tend to make comprehension much easier and these five-figure summaries are usually presented as **box plots** (also known as **box and whisker plots**) as a result.

Figure 5.1 is a box plot of the data in the table above.

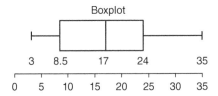

Figure 5.1

As is fairly obvious, the central 'box' section contains the middle 50% of results from the 1st quartile to 3rd quartile. The horizontal lines on each side stretch out to the minimum and maximum observations. The median is marked as a vertical line in the box.

As you get used to looking at these plots, it becomes fairly straightforward to get a quick and useful overall impression of the distribution of the data at which you are looking. Comparing box plots for two sets of data is a very powerful way of looking at multiple statistics at once, and makes it very easy to compare two different distributions of data.

Whilst box plots are particularly useful for picturing ordinal data, they can of course be used for interval and ratio data too. Have a look, for example, at Table 5.2, which shows statistics for the CAT scores of two of the cohorts at which Ben is looking. The box plots for these figures are given in Figure 5.2.

Table 5.2 Statistics for CAT scores for two cohorts

Cohort A		
	97	
78		112
65		140

Cohort B		
	103	
87		120
70		140

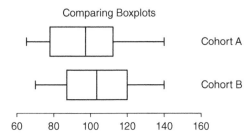

Figure 5.2

For most people, using box plots makes it much easier to spot patterns in data than looking at numbers alone.

5.1.1 Mean deviation

One common measure of spread is based on calculating how far a typical value is from the mean value of a set of data. Values are frequently referred to as 'deviating' from an average value. 'Deviation' is the amount at which a value differs from the average value, and mean deviation is a mean of all of the deviations within a data set. In general, the mean requires data to be at least interval-scale data, which means that Kathryn should be careful when she considers using this statistic for her test data. Ben's test score data, from standardised tests and in standardised form, can be analysed using deviations.

To find deviations, each value is simply subtracted from the mean, as can be seen in Table 5.3.

Table 5.3 Finding deviations using the mean

Name	CAT score	Deviation
Alexander	129	33.1
Amelia	96	0.1
Elizabeth	74	−21.9
Ethan	67	−28.9
Faizah	82	−13.9
Jacob	69	−26.9
Mason	129	33.1
Michael	108	12.1
Samayah	99	3.1
William	106	10.1
Mean	**95.9**	

There is an obvious problem with calculating the sum (and mean) of the deviations. Since the deviations are calculated using a central value, the sum of the deviations – and therefore the mean deviation – is zero. This isn't particularly helpful, since there clearly *is* a spread of values around the mean, which isn't being captured here.

The simple way to cater for this statistical quirk is to treat all differences as positive, since we are actually interested in the absolute difference between values and the mean, not whether the differences are negative or positive. The mathematical notation $|x|$ indicates the absolute value of x, or how much it differs from zero.

So, instead of calculating the sum of $\bar{x} - x$, we calculate $\bar{x} - |x|$, as shown in Table 5.4.

 Databusting for schools

Table 5.4 Calculating absolute deviation

Name	CAT score	Absolute deviation
Alexander	129	33.1
Amelia	96	0.1
Elizabeth	74	21.9
Ethan	67	28.9
Faizah	82	13.9
Jacob	69	26.9
Mason	129	33.1
Michael	108	12.1
Samayah	99	3.1
William	106	10.1

This is much more useful, as we now have a measure of spread around the mean, the *mean deviation*.

The alternative to treating all deviations as positive is to square each deviation before finding the sum of all the squared deviations and then the mean of the squared deviations, since the squares of both negative and positive numbers are treated as positive in calculations (by convention, $-2 \times -2 = 4$, for example, and for any x, $(-x)^2 = x^2$).

The mean of squared deviations is itself squared. This has come to be known as the 'variance'. Taking the square root of the variance gives a number known as the 'standard deviation'.

The variance is abbreviated using the lower-case Greek letter sigma squared (remember that upper-case sigma, Σ, is used for 'the sum of'). The standard deviation, being the square root of the variance, is written as σ.

These two statistics are written in formula form as follows:

$$\text{Variance} : \sigma^2 = \frac{\Sigma d^2}{n}$$

$$\text{Standard deviation} : \sigma = \sqrt{\frac{\Sigma d^2}{n}}$$

In summary, the **variance** is a measure of spread. It gives an indication of how much the values in a data set vary from the mean. Because of the need to square differences from the mean, the variance is a slightly inflated measure of spread.

The **standard deviation** is simply the square root of the variance, and also gives a slightly better indication as to how much the values in a data set vary from the mean.

Standard deviations are powerful statistics, as they contain a great deal of information in a simple numerical format. Understanding how standard deviations can – and cannot – be used is one of the keys to becoming a databusting educator.

Whilst these statistics seem a little unwieldy, they do lead on to some very useful ways of summarising large amounts of data. The standard deviation is one of the most commonly used measures of spread and it is worth considering what different values for σ might look like.

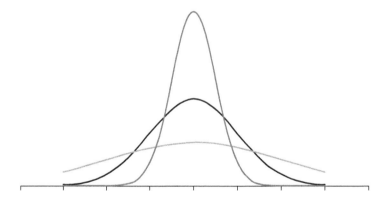

Figure 5.3

As you can see in Figure 5.3, the size of σ dramatically changes the distribution of a data set (or vice versa, if you prefer). You also need to consider the mean when looking at σ, since the spread around a mean close to zero might suggest something quite different to a similar spread around a mean which is some distance from zero.

As an aside, it should be noted that there is more than one way of calculating the standard deviation. The appropriate method depends on the way in which the data has been organised and the nature of the data under consideration. Whilst this is beyond the scope of this book, one important distinction which should be made is that statisticians use the σ symbol to indicate a standard deviation which is calculated for a *population*, and an *s* for a standard deviation which is calculated from a *sample* of a population.

5.2 Populations and samples

Kathryn has a child in her class who enjoys doing online maths games. The child, Janice, says that in a game against other children online, she completed 25 mental calculations in a minute and that another child managed to complete 45 calculations in the same time. The game is specifically restricted to those who are currently in Year 3. Janice thinks that this score was not that of another Year 3 child and she suspects that something unusual is going on.

Kathryn knows that her class is quite good at this online maths game and that Janice is a typical member of the class. So, just how likely is it that someone similar to Janice could post a score of 45? On the basis of Janice's own score, this seems unlikely. But perhaps Janice is slower than a typical child playing the game. A sample of one does not seem particularly robust and it would not be particularly sensible to conclude that someone was cheating based on Janice's score alone.

Taking the population as a whole, how likely is it that a primary-aged child could answer 45 questions in a minute? Whilst it might be possible to have every Year 3 child in the country play the game, this is clearly far too much to ask.

To try to find out what a typical score might be, Kathryn took a sample of children in her class. She looked at scores posted in the previous week and found that 15 children had played the game. The scores she found ranged from a minimum of 14 questions to a maximum of 38.

To check that her class was typical of a class playing the game, Kathryn asked various colleagues teaching Year 3 in other schools around the country to gather their scores. She was sent scores for 26 children, which ranged from a minimum of 12 questions to a maximum of 39.

On the basis of this set of data, Kathryn was able to say that she had reasonable grounds to suggest that Janice's suspicions were correct and that the score of 45 was unusual. She was able to use a sample of the population to make predictions about the population as a whole, without having data for every member of the population.

This example introduces some of the key ideas which need to be explored to enable us to understand what we know about our current position, based on facts which we have at hand. It introduces the idea of a population, and of a sample of that population.

As a broad simplification, a sample is selected so that a property of a wider population can be explored. It might be that we want to gather information about a particular aspect of a population's behaviour, or that we want to compare two different populations to see if they are measurably different. Whilst there are many caveats around sampling, and a great deal of caution has to be applied to any conclusions based on sampling (see Chapter 10 for more on this point), it does give us potentially valuable information with which to get a sense of where we are now.

5.2.1 Definitions

5.2.1.1 A 'population'

In the field of mathematics, which focuses on extracting information from data, a 'population' is defined as any large group of things which we are trying to measure. Ideally, to make inferences about a large group, we would collect data for every member of the population.

The modern era – often referred to as the era of Big Data – has made it much easier to collect and process population data. Companies can now track, for example, every transaction which contributes to a company's turnover. In education, we frequently have access to population data, in that we have all of the test results or ages of a particular cohort of children. Where we have all the data for the entire population in which we are interested, technically we have 'census' data.

For a great deal of the information which we want about children, however, we are interested in comparing a small group of children with the wider population of similar children. The population has to be tightly defined, so we know that what we are trying to estimate via a smaller sample of the population will enable us to make the inferences which we often want to make.

A population could therefore be 'all children in our region in similar schools', 'all children with similar starting points nationally' or 'all children in Year 4 or 9'.

5.2.1.2 A 'sample'

Where we do not have access to data for the whole population which we wish to examine, we need to generate or gather data for a subset of the population. This subset is referred to as a 'sample', and selecting (and gathering data from) a 'sample' subset is called 'sampling'.

It is perfectly acceptable to take more than one sample and this is often done to check the validity of the procedure used to select the sample. The size of a sample – the number of observations which are used as a sample – is referred to as n.

Samples are not typically drawn from every possible member of a population, as data for some sections of the population is usually easier to obtain than data for others. Where this is the case, the section for which we do have information is referred to as the 'sampling frame', and a representative sample is generally drawn from this subset of the population.

The case of Kathryn's data above illustrates some important features of sampling. First, a sample needs to have enough information to be useful. That is, it needs to be big enough to provide a representative cross-section of the population. If it does not, it might give a biased, incorrect impression of the wider picture. Second, whilst a large sample is much more likely to be an accurate representation of the wider population, collecting, collating and analysing the data is frequently simply too costly and time-consuming to undertake.

Databusting for schools

Box 5.2

How a sample is biased

In the previous year's class, Kathryn had a particularly high-achieving group of children. The class had very few children working at a low level for their age, and a significant number of children with high-achieving older siblings. Would it be fair to compare this year's cohort to last year's?

It may seem, on the surface, that given this year's class is the entire population of Year 3 children in the school, this is a population in itself. It may also seem that this year's class is a sample of the national cohort of Year 3 children.

In fact, neither argument is valid. A sample has to be representative of a wide population, and in both cases described above this is not the case. The class is at best an extremely small sampling frame with just 30 members, which would make it impossible to draw a representative sample of the population from the class.

5.2.2 Selecting a representative sample

Whilst there are several well-known techniques for selecting a representative sample of a population, the best known is *random sampling*. This is defined as follows:

A random sample is one in which every item in the population has the same probability of being selected.

For a random sample, there has to be some way to ensure that each item is chosen at random. This means that each item has the same probability of being chosen, and that there is no hidden bias which means that any item is more likely to be chosen than another. Kathryn's samples were clearly not random samples of the population, as she simply took data from those children who had chosen to play a particular online maths game.

Creating a representative sample which can be used to make predictions about a wide population can be extremely useful to help us understand where we are now. For example, if Ben's school has 1,400 students (a sampling frame of size 1,400), he might want to select a sample of size $n = 30$ (that is, 30 students from a potential 1,400 students) to find out how often children read at home. To get a representative sample, Ben needs to find a way to ensure that each child has an equal chance of being selected.

The classic approach would be to allocate a sequential number to every member of the group and then find a method to generate n numbers from within this range of numbers.

The items which correspond to the randomly generated numbers then become the 30 items in the sample.

Samples are generated either 'with replacement' or 'without replacement'. With replacement simply means that any item selected is placed back into the sampling frame. This ensures that subsequent selections have the same probability as the original selection. If a sample is generated 'without replacement', the next item selected has a slightly higher probability of being selected. In Ben's case, a sample generated without replacement would see the final item added to the sample selected with a probability of 1/1371 and not the 1/1400 with which the first item was selected. Whilst this is a difference of just 0.000015, it might make a difference with some levels of analysis. In most cases, the difference is so small that samples are generated without replacement. Furthermore, as in Ben's example, in many cases each 'item' is actually a child, and it would seem odd (even if it is perfectly valid) to use the same child's responses twice.

Generating random numbers has been a subject of much debate. In the past, statisticians have used random number tables which allowed a somewhat laborious manual selection of random numbers. These days, all computers provide some way of generating random numbers, although even these can be shown not to be truly random. For most purposes, however, computers can generate numbers which are as good as random, and can be used to generate lists for selecting a random sample.

Let us assume that Ben decides to generate a list of 30 children whom he will survey. He has access to the school database containing information on all of the children in the school. He puts the children into a non-random list, in this case using the children's names to order every pupil alphabetically. Using a random number generator, he creates a sample of 30 children.

5.2.2.1 Sampling variation

Ben looks at some summary statistics for his sample. He finds that 17 of the 30, i.e. 57% of the children selected, are girls. As he suspects that gender might be an important factor in reading habits, he wants to know if his sample is typical of the gender split in the school. As he has access to this data, he can see that the school population is 55% female. This is quite close to the 57% in the sample, but given that the sample size of 30 is quite small, it would be reasonable to expect a fairly wide variation if we were to choose several samples. In fact, it is possible to measure sampling variation and to use this to give some insight into the degree of confidence with which estimates about populations can be made from sampled data.

As well as looking at the gender split, Ben also looked at the split across age groups. Since he has a sample of 30, and children in the sample come from across seven year groups in his school, the variation by year group is quite wide, with two children in Year 8 and seven in Year 13, as in Table 5.5.

It is clear that different samples will produce slightly different distributions of ages, but because we have information about the whole of the school population, we can see whether any particular sample is broadly representative of the school.

Table 5.5 Ben's sample by year group

Year	Frequency
7	4
8	2
9	3
10	5
11	6
12	3
13	7

In this case, whilst the sample is slightly biased towards Years 13 and 11, it is still a representative sample of the school.

There are several alternatives to random sampling, of which the most commonly used are *systematic sampling, stratified sampling* and *cluster sampling*.

Systematic sampling is a way of selecting a sample from an ordered sampling frame. For example, Ben could list all of the children in the school by year group and then by age, and then select every fortieth child, starting at a number randomly selected between 1 and 40. This has the benefit of ensuring that the distribution of year groups is more even, without skewing the sample too much in any particular direction.

Stratified sampling is used where there are significant subgroups within the main population. Ben's school has a significant group of children who qualify for free school meals (FSM), which is frequently used as a proxy for systematic educational disadvantage. In order to ensure that the FSM group is equally represented in his sample, Ben could partition his sampling frame into two separate sampling frames. This would ensure that each group – FSM and non-FSM – is more likely to reflect the population of the school.

Ben could also separate his children into their term of birth, with those born between September and December grouped as Autumn Born, those with birthdays between January and April categorised as Spring Born and the youngest children in each year group – born between May and August – identified as Summer Born.

Cluster sampling is a way of reducing complexity by accepting that it is frequently easier to gather data from those in natural groups – in a tutor group, for example, or in a subject which uses setting rather than mixed-ability groupings – than it is to draw from the wider population. School populations are naturally split into classes, and schools themselves are clusters within the national population of school pupils, and therefore lend themselves to cluster sampling.

Since people naturally group themselves by physical location, and there are distinct differences between different parts of the country, there are many groups of children who can be said to be gathered into clusters. Different regions, counties and administrative areas lend themselves to cluster sampling.

5.2.3 Dealing with error in samples

Whilst it makes a great deal of sense – in terms of cost, time and effort – to select a small subgroup from a population from which to extrapolate results, there are clear and obvious risks with this strategy. One of the best studied phenomena is that of the 'observer effect', as typified by the experience of researchers exploring productivity at the Hawthorne Works, in Illinois, in the early part of the 20th century.

The Hawthorne Works had commissioned a study to examine the effects on productivity of various changes within their factory. Part of the enormous Western Electric organisation, the Hawthorne Works produced a variety of products primarily for use in domestic settings such as telephones, refrigerators and electric fans. With 45,000 employees at its peak, any improvements which would lead to greater productivity were clearly hugely beneficial.

Experimenters tested the effects of changes such as altering light levels, relocating work stations, and so on. In nearly every case, the changes which the experimenters made resulted in improved productivity during the experimental period. When the longer-term effects of the alterations were examined, however, it was found that productivity generally reduced following the experimental period, and generally reverted back to the levels prior to the experiments.

Whilst there are many interpretations of the experience at the Hawthorne Works, the studies have been dubbed the 'Hawthorne effect', which is generally understood to be the tendency of some people to work harder and perform better when they are participants in an experiment. In sample surveys, the Hawthorne effect includes the likelihood that those being surveyed will give the answers which they think are expected, rather than answer accurately.

The observer effect more generally is the tendency for those who are participating in a process to be affected by the process itself, which can change behaviour or responses to the process.

Broadly, there are three main types of error in sampling theory. The first type of error is measurement error. Any method of data collection which attempts to measure something is subject to measurement error. Even those tools which we have for physical measurements have a finite degree of accuracy – a ruler can only measure to the nearest centimetre or millimetre, for example. Measuring knowledge is subject to a much greater degree of inaccuracy. There is no 'unit of reading' which Ben could use, for example, and however he decides to measure reading, his measurements will necessarily be imprecise and subject to error.

The second type of error is introduced by human error, such as a badly designed sampling procedure which results in a sample which is in some way biased, either by design, through a lack of rigour or due to the limited knowledge of the principles of sampling. The classic example of this kind of error is that which is seen in many polls reported in news media, particularly those snap polls on topical issues often conducted by media outlets, who encourage members of the public to choose between one of two fairly polarised options. A typical example is a poll which asks who the next prime minister should be. The outcome of the poll is inevitably biased by the self-selecting nature of the sample of the population who choose to answer the poll.

The third type of error is sampling error. All sampling is prone to error, and because of their very nature all samples will vary to some degree. Whilst sampling error can't be eliminated, statisticians have developed ways in which it is possible to quantify how much variation can be expected under certain conditions. This allows us to use statistics based on sampling error to report results with a 'degree of confidence' about the predictions which can be extrapolated to the wider population.

In Ben's case, he could use a measure of sampling error to suggest, for example, that he is '95% confident that between 150 and 210 of the school population do not read for pleasure'. This kind of statement is referred to as an interval estimate. Interval estimates can be useful when considering what a sample might indicate about the wider population.

There is of course a pay-off between sample size and strength of interpretation. The larger the sample, the more confidence you can have that the sample results are an accurate reflection of the population. A larger sample therefore leads to a smaller confidence interval. This might seem a little counter intuitive – why does something get smaller when the sample increases in size? An example might help to clarify this idea. Consider how much you would trust a sampling exercise which suggested that most people read between one and six books a month, having surveyed five people. Now consider how much you would trust a sampling exercise which surveyed 50 people, and suggested that most people read between two and four books a month.

Of course, in either survey, one person may read a great deal or not at all, but a typical person selected at random from the population would be unlikely to be at the extremes of the distribution, and much more likely to lie within the confidence interval which we can calculate based on the sample results.

5.3 Distributions of data

Both Ben and Kathryn's investigations are affected by the underlying distributions of the data which they are analysing. A distribution is simply the pattern in any data set, and there is a huge amount of thought which has gone into the way in which data are distributed.

Understanding how common distributions can be modelled can help us to understand what our data might show us, as we can compare what we see to what we might expect to see if our data was distributed in a standard form.

Certain distributions are likely to reoccur frequently, and it is possible to summarise other likely distributions quickly and easily with a few key statistics. We will look at two common distributions which underpin a great deal of data analysis.

5.3.1 The uniform distribution

Having looked at his results, Ben decides to test whether his method of selecting a sample of children was truly random. Looking at the number of children selected from each year group within his sample of 60 children, he can examine for bias by investigating what would happen if he had selected 60 separate samples from the school population. Remember that he has 200 children per year group, making a total of 1,400 children in his school.

Let's imagine that his 60 samples return the results in Table 5.6.

Table 5.6 Ben's sample results

Year group	7	8	9	10	11	12	13
Frequency	11,000	11,500	12,300	11,300	11,700	12,200	12,000

This set of numbers doesn't reveal a great deal, other than that there were more Year 9s selected in the 60 samples, and fewer Year 7s. What Ben needs is something against which to compare his results. Now, the obvious expectation with an unbiased random sample selection procedure is that the numbers for each year would be exactly as expected – 1/7 of 1,400 children, on 60 different occasions, i.e. 1/7 x 1400 x 60, which is 12,000 children (Table 5.7).

Table 5.7 Uniform distribution

Year group	7	8	9	10	11	12	13
Frequency	12,000	12,000	12,000	12,000	12,000	12,000	12,000

If this is graphed, as it is in Figure 5.4, it is clearly a 'uniform distribution' and it is named as such. Every outcome is equally likely.

There are several important points to make about a frequency distribution like this. First, this is what is *likely* to happen, not what *will* happen. The difference is crucial. A pair of unbiased dice is likely to total seven on one out of six throws, but this is not what will happen once in every six throws. This is simply the most likely outcome.

 Databusting for schools

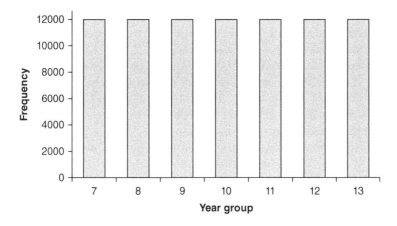

Figure 5.4

It is also worth noting that this is a graph showing the frequency distribution. As such, this is a bar chart, as introduced in Chapter 4. The bars do not touch, since each bar is independent of the bars alongside.

Figure 5.5 shows the probability distribution of the expected outcomes for the repeated samples.

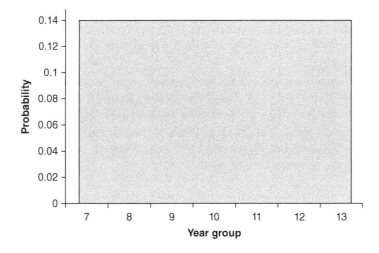

Figure 5.5

This graph is fundamentally different to the previous graph. It is a histogram, and the vertical scale now shows the probability of being from Year 6, which is 1/7 or 0.14 (to two decimal places). This means that the area of the rectangle – the 'area under the curve' is equal to 7 x 1/7, i.e. 1. This is an important aspect of data analysis of probability distributions. This makes it fairly straightforward to find out the probability of a range of outcomes.

If Ben wanted to find out the likelihood that a child in his data set was in Years 8 or 9, all he would need to do would be to find the area under the graph which corresponded to those two years, i.e. 2/7 or 0.285714.

Now we can return to Ben's initial question. Is his method of selecting samples truly random? It should be clear that simply noting that the actual distribution of year groups is different to the likely distribution suggested by the uniform distribution graph is naïve. Suggesting that the selection method is biased because the match is not exact is clearly unreasonable.

The shape of the uniform distribution is a rectangle because this is what is *likely*, not what *will* happen. In reality, we would be surprised to get an exact match – although it *could* happen, it probably will not. The reason for this is simply natural variation. We are only selecting 60 samples, which is quite a small number relative to the population as a whole. If we were to increase the number of samples, the results would likely be more like the uniform distribution.

But, as discussed, this would be expensive and time-consuming – and time is money, after all. We could actually expect to have anything between 8,000 and 16,000 children from any one year group. But given that we never know in advance what the actual distribution will be, the best we can do is to use the model which we can create by making assumptions about the likely distribution of children.

So, in summary, we need to consider two key issues:

1. What do we compare our distribution to? Ben needs to decide what the *expected values* of his distribution are likely to be. In the case of equally distributed variables, the expected values are clearly an equal split across the different categories.

2. What is the natural variation? Even if the selection process was truly random, it would be unreasonable to expect the actual distribution to match the modelled distribution. The key question is therefore, 'Given the results from the sample I have, how reasonable is it that this might represent the population?' This will be the focus of the next chapter, where we look at making inferences based on samples.

The uniform distribution is used in cases where each outcome is equally likely, but many variables are not distributed in this way. Some distributions tend to cluster around a particular value. We will look at an important one of these distributions next.

5.3.2 The normal distribution

The uniform distribution is a useful introduction to the concept of probability distributions, but it is not that useful when looking at the kinds of distributions of data in which the likely outcomes are not all exactly the same. When looking at the number of children who play a particular sport, or who enjoy maths, or feel confident in their writing ability, and so on, it is clear that the potential responses are not uniformly distributed.

In many typical situations, a different shape of distribution is much more likely to appear. Somewhat confusingly, this is called the normal distribution and it looks like Figure 5.6.

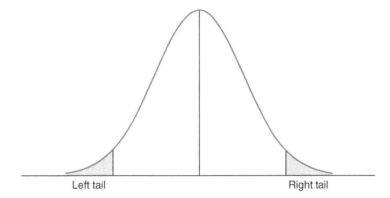

Figure 5.6

This 'bell curve', with which many people are familiar in outline at least, suggests that some things are distributed around a central point, with 'tails' to either side. If actual values are plotted on a histogram, the result is considerably more 'blocky'. This is because the data has to be grouped into intervals, which means that no matter how small these intervals are made, the data will always be somewhat jagged.

The distributions of the heights of 1,000 children might look something like Figure 5.7, for example.

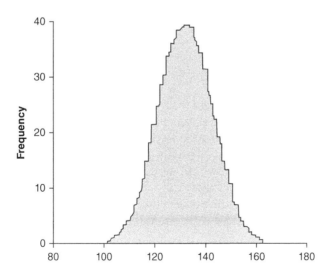

Figure 5.7

If the sample was made infinitely large, with infinitesimally small intervals, the curve would look like the normal distribution. Given that this would never happen in practice, however, it is clear that the normal distribution curve is a model rather than a representation of actual data.

The normal distribution model can be created using just the mean and the standard deviation of a data set. The standard normal distribution is a perfectly normal distribution with a mean of zero and a standard deviation of one. This is also known as the z-distribution and it looks like the distribution in Figure 5.8.

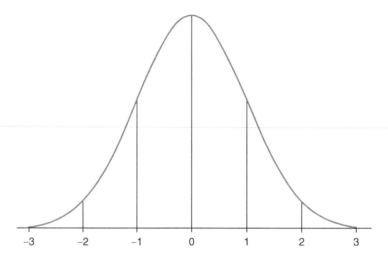

Figure 5.8

The z-distribution is extremely useful because it is defined in terms of standard deviations. On the x-axis above, +2 is 2 standard deviations above the mean, +1 is 1 standard deviation above the mean, 0 is the mean, −1 is 1 standard deviation below the mean and −2 is 2 standard deviations below the mean. These numbers are also called *z-scores*.

Because they can be *standardised* from raw data such as test scores from standardised tests, z-scores can be extremely useful in analysing education data. Remember that standardisation is the name given to the process by which raw scores are compared to the mean and standard deviation of a sample or a population. This has many advantages over using raw data alone, as it allows for comparisons between different data which would not be entirely fair if raw scores alone were compared.

The formula for converting raw scores to z-scores uses either the sample or the population mean and standard deviation, and looks like this:

$$z = \frac{x - \bar{x}}{\sigma}$$

Databusting for schools

In simple terms, the mean value is subtracted from the actual value, and the result is divided by the standard deviation. Standardised scores, as introduced in Chapter 2, are created in the same way.

Remember that z-scores are reported in standard deviation units. This is why, in each formula, above, the mean is subtracted from the value of a given raw score. This gives a result which represents the distance between the raw score and the mean. This difference is of the same order as the variance, and is therefore measured in the same units as the variance, i.e. in SD^2.

This is then divided by the standard deviation, which converts the difference into standard deviation units.

At this point, it is necessary to consider the precision of the calculations which we are able to perform to calculate z-scores. Since the calculations involved in calculating z-scores are likely to stretch to many decimal points, the final z-score is likely to have to be rounded in some way. After all, a z-score of 0.26378164… is simply too unwieldy for most purposes. Typically, z-scores are reported to two decimal places, so this would be rounded to 0.26.

5.4 Using standard normal distributions as a comparison tool

Where data can be assumed to come from a distribution which is roughly normal, the standard normal distribution can be used to shed light on that data. In Kathryn and Ben's cases, where they have standardised scores which have come from standardised tests, this can prove to be extremely useful.

Remember from Chapter 2 and the discussion above that standardised scores are created by subtracting a raw score from the mean and dividing the result by the standard deviation. Provided we are certain that the data which we have can be treated in this way, we can use the standard normal distribution to estimate the distribution of scores on standardised tests. Whilst we do not have a population mean and standard deviation, the creators of the standardised tests the school uses have estimated the population mean and standard deviation using a representative sample of the population, and these are used when calculating standardised scores for individual test takers at Kathryn and Ben's schools.

In general, test scores are standardised so that they have a mean of 100 and a standard deviation of 15. These numbers are usually referred to as 'points', i.e. 105 points. When plotted on a graph, they look like Figure 5.9.

The mathematics of the standard normal distribution suggests that roughly two thirds of the scores will be in the range 85 to 115, and about 96% of scores will be between 70 and 130. Using the standard normal distribution in this way means that we can refer to scores being either within the average range – generally taken to be those within 15 points of the mean of 100 – or outside this, either above or below the average.

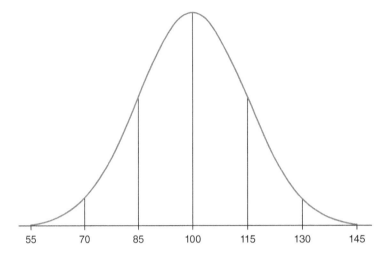

Figure 5.9

Standardised scores are often 'age standardised' as well, in that children within a particular age range within a cohort – often an age of a given number of years and months, rather than simply a number of years – are compared to each other using standardised scores. This means that a child who is, say, 8 years and 1 month old is not unfairly compared to a child in the same cohort who is 8 years and 11 months old. Whilst both can be allocated age standardised scores for a test, the calculations for each score will use different data.

Standardised scores from most educational tests use the same distribution of scores, normally distributed with a mean of 100 and a standard deviation of 15 points. This means that scores from different tests can be meaningfully compared or added together in a way which would not be valid for raw test scores.

Standardised scores are frequently recorded with an associated percentile rank. Percentile ranks are calculated using the standard normal distribution to work out the percentage of those who recorded a score at the same level or below that of a given test taker's score. This allows us to refer to a student as being at the '40th percentile', for example. This means that 40% of students recorded a score which was the same or lower than the student in question.

Standardised scores and percentile ranks convert as in Table 5.8. It is worth noting that percentile ranks are ordinal data, as the intervals between ranks are not equal. Percentile ranks closer to the mean have associated scores which are bunched together, whereas those further from the centre of the score range change considerably with small changes in standardised scores. Combining percentile ranks from different tests is not valid, and neither is comparing percentile ranks on different tests or at different times.

Databusting for schools

Table 5.8 Standardised scores and percentile ranks

SS*	PR*	SS	PR	SS	PR
139+	99+	109	72	89	24
133–138	99	108	70	88	22
130–132	98	107	68	87	20
128–129	97	106	66	86	18
126–127	96	105	63	85	16
125	95	104	60	84	14
123–124	94	103	58	83	13
122	93	102	55	82	12
121	92	101	52	81	11
120	91	100	50	80	9
119	90	99	48	79	8
118	89	98	45	78	7
117	87	97	42	76–77	6
116	86	96	40	75	5
115	84	95	37	73–74	4
114	82	94	34	71–72	3
113	80	93	32	70	2
112	78	92	30	70–	1
111	77	91	28		
110	74	90	26		

Note: * SS = standardised score; PR = percentile rank

Partly because of the bunching effect of percentile ranks, which can clearly be seen when they are shown on a number line below the standard normal distribution, as in Figure 5.10, scores are frequently presented in 'stanines' which introduce a regular interval using standard deviations. Stanines – standard nines – divide the normal distribution into nine intervals, each with a width of 0.5 standard deviations, other than the 1st and 9th stanine, which include all of the values in the tails of the distribution.

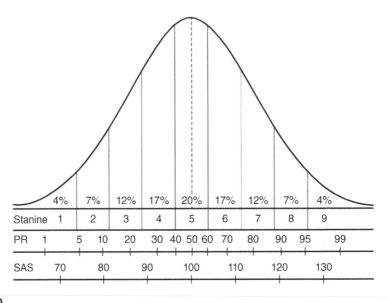

	4%	7%	12%	17%	20%	17%	12%	7%	4%
Stanine	1	2	3	4	5	6	7	8	9

PR	1		5	10	20	30 40 50 60	70	80	90 95		99

SAS		70		80		90		100		110		120		130	

Figure 5.10

As ever, caution is required when analysing standardised test scores. Databusting educators should always consider the effects of measurement error, and how data may be affected by both human error and sampling error. In Chapter 6, we will consider how confidence intervals have been introduced into education data analysis in an attempt to take sampling error into consideration, and we will look at criticisms of this in Chapter 10.

In attempting to aide understanding, those who create standardised tests may, on occasion, however inadvertently, create confusion for those interpreting the results of testing. Using standardised scores requires some understanding of the underlying mathematics and assumptions on which the scores are based, as you have seen in the discussions in this chapter.

An example of the difficulty in interpreting scores often arises when, for example, 'reading ages' are used to summarise the standardised results of some tests of reading ability. In summary, standardised tests which report a reading age use the standard normal distribution to compare children's reading scores to the typical scores for children of a particular age group. This results in scores being reported as, for example, a 'reading age of 9.2 for an 8-year-old child'.

This kind of standardised result simply means that the child scored above the average of those in a representative sample of 8-year-olds who took the test. It says nothing whatsoever about the development of reading skills at a particular age, nor does it imply that the child who took the test reads at the level of children with a chronological age of 9 years 2 months.

Additionally, it is worth noting that not all reading ages which are reported are derived from standardised testing, and there are other ways in which reading

Databusting for schools

ages are calculated. In attempting to make sense of a standardised score of 76 for a child aged 9.06 years, say, reporting this as a reading age of 8.03 years may simply cause more confusion than simply reporting this as a standardised score of 76.

That said, using standard normal distributions as a comparison tool can provide useful insight into what test scores might actually be telling us. Most scores bunch together, as per the standard normal distribution, and extreme scores are more unlikely and therefore often of more interest. Small differences in scores in the centre of the distribution do not indicate that students with similar but different scores vary a great deal, and there is little difference between a score of 95, say, and 105. Scores at the extremes are more variable, and small differences in raw scores in these areas of the score distribution can lead to clear changes in percentile rank or stanine for a given score.

5.5 Summary

This chapter has provided an introduction to using box plots to summarise data sets, and explained that samples are used to shed light on populations. We have also considered how to identify and manage error, and how the uniform distribution and normal distribution can help to model likely outcomes. We have also looked at how the standard normal distribution can help to shed light on standardised test scores.

By using means and standard deviations derived from a representative sample of the population, Ben and Kathryn can use scores their own students record on tests to place those students on a population-level scale. If they were to plot the scores their own students record on the tests, however, they would be highly unlikely to see a pattern which resembles the standard normal distribution.

It would be much more likely that their data would be skewed in some way, or have some unusual, non-uniform pattern. Data is said to be skewed if it tails off more quickly on one side, either to the left or to the right. Samples from normally distributed populations often do this, particularly when the tails of the distribution are open-ended. Ben and Kathryn may have data which has more than one mode, unlike the normal distribution.

In reality, samples of populations can often look very different to the population from which they are taken. Means of samples, however, come from a normal distribution of sample means. This fact is exploited in more complicated analysis – such as the creation of confidence intervals and margins of error – in which education data is treated as if it were a representative sample of the wider population, which we will explore in Chapter 6.

6.1 Introduction

Up to this point, we have considered how we can summarise the large amounts of data which we collect about children. We have used both numbers and images to try to make complex data manageable. Using the ideas explored in Chapter 5, for example, you should be able to interpret information which is presented as in Box 6.1.

Box 6.1   Five-figure summary of verbal reasoning CAT scores

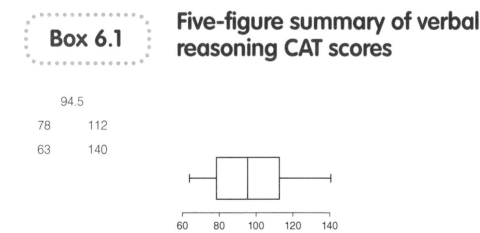

Figure 6.1   Five-figure summary

Ben has been considering a cognitive assessment test report for one of his cohorts, which includes information presented in this format. He can see that the data which is summarised by the box plot and its associated five-figure summary has a wide range, which is slightly skewed to the left. He can see that 50% of the children summarised are clustered around a mean score of 94.5. Ben wants to know how accurate this summary is, and whether it tells him something useful about the cohort.

Ben is now aware of measurement error, human error and sampling error. He has to rely on those who create tests to take steps to reduce measurement error when they design and test their tests. Nevertheless, some measurement error will inevitably creep into the testing process. Ben will aim to reduce human error as much as possible, simply by being aware of the issues which may affect the performance and recording of scores on tests.

When it comes to sampling error, Ben once again has to rely on the creators of the tests he is using. There are serious concerns with the use of statistics in this way, which we will consider in Chapter 10. Nevertheless, databusting educators need to understand the process by which sampling error is used to interpret the results of standardised tests. We will look at this in the first part of this chapter.

6.2 Point estimates and interval estimates

In Chapter 5, we saw that sample means vary randomly from the population mean. If we were to take two different samples, we would have two different sample means which, even if we were taking samples from the same population, would differ simply because of sample error. Most samples would have sample means which would be close to the population mean, but some would have sample means which differ considerably from the mean.

It can be shown that sample error should, in theory, be normally distributed across the samples. So some sample means will be low, some high, and on average – and average alone – the sample error will be zero. That means that it is possible to estimate *population standard error* and approximate the *sample standard error* using the estimate of *population standard error*.

Statisticians have labelled sample statistics such as the sample mean and sample standard deviation as *point estimates*. A point estimate is the best sample estimate which we have for a *parameter* and it is called a point estimate because it is a single value, or point. All of the statistics we have discussed so far have been point estimates. A sample mean is a point estimate of the population mean, for example.

Point estimates can be somewhat misleading, however. They can lead to a false sense of certainty. Means of samples can easily be misinterpreted as accurate representations of means of the underlying population. This, however, is often not the case. The accuracy of point estimates is entirely driven by the standard error of the mean. And different sampling distributions can have the same sample mean, but quite different sampling distributions. Consider the data summarised in Figure 6.2.

Both of the sampling distributions in Figure 6.2 have identical means, which is equal to 1 in both cases. But their standard errors (the standard deviations) are not the same at all. When we take a sample from the left-hand distribution, the sample mean is more likely to be further away from the mean than when we sample the right-hand distribution.

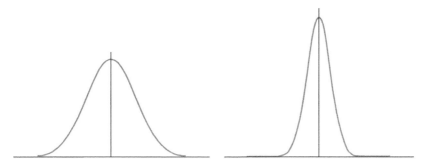

Figure 6.2 Sampling distributions

If Ben were to have cohorts drawn from the sampling distribution on the left, any summary based on the means for each cohort would not reveal the underlying variation which should be expected from year group to year group. If he was to report only point estimates such as the means for each cohort, those he presents may begin to see trends which simply do not exist in the underlying data.

The obvious solution to reporting misleading point estimates is to calculate *interval estimates* which contain information about both the sample mean and the sampling distribution from which the sampling mean was drawn. Interval estimates provide a range of realistic values for a particular parameter, using the sample which was used to estimate that parameter, which provides much more information about the parameter than a point estimate is able to do.

There are different ways to calculate interval estimates. Each depends on the information which is available for the sample and the population. We will focus here on two different ways to compute *confidence intervals*, which are the most common type of interval estimates for means.

Whilst teachers like Ben and Kathryn are unlikely to calculate confidence intervals for their data themselves, they are likely to have access to data which does use this common statistical analysis. Much of what follows in this chapter is necessarily technical and involves a great deal of higher level mathematics. Understanding how confidence intervals are calculated, and therefore having an insight into the potential problems with their use, is part of becoming a databusting teacher.

6.3 Confidence intervals

A confidence interval is simply a range of values where, given a particular sample size, a particular parameter and a particular *level of confidence*, we would expect sample statistics to fall. The most typical levels of confidence which are used are 95% and 99%, and these can be summarised as follows:

A 95% confidence interval: the means of 95% of samples of the same size drawn from a population with the given mean will fall between these two values.

A 99% confidence interval: the means of 99% of samples of the same size drawn from a population with the given mean will fall between these two values.

A 95% confidence interval includes 95% of the possible samples we could take from a population, whereas a 99% confidence interval includes 99% of the possible samples we could take. Clearly, a 99% confidence interval will be wider than a 95% confidence interval, since it includes an additional 4% of the potential samples from the population.

The reason why 95% and 99% confidence intervals have the status they currently hold is largely due to precedence. Whilst it is possible to calculate a confidence interval of any size, it is almost unheard of to see anything other than a 95% confidence interval (which includes 19 out of 20 means of samples) or a 99% confidence interval (which includes 99 out of 100 means of samples).

Confidence intervals can seem to be a simple idea, but in practice they are often misunderstood and misinterpreted. This is partly because the concept is built on underlying concepts which may not be appreciated by the casual observer, primarily that sample means are drawn from a normal distribution of means. Because this is not readily understood, it is common to see and hear incorrect interpretations of confidence intervals.

So, how should Ben explain what a confidence interval actually means?

A 95% confidence interval suggests that the means of 95% of samples of the same size drawn from the same population with the given mean will fall within a range of values.

Unfortunately, confidence intervals are often interpreted incorrectly as the *probability* that the mean of a given sample lies between the two values of the interval. After all, a 95% confidence interval can easily be assumed to mean that we are 95% confident that the mean is actually within the interval we describe, but this is not the case: '95%' refers to the statistical calculation that, given what we know about the distribution of sample means, we can say that 1 in 20 sample means will lie outside of the interval we have calculated.

Since we don't actually know what the population mean is, it may be that it is outside of the confidence interval which we have constructed. What is certain is that it does exist, regardless of any method we use to try to measure it. To suggest that there is a '95% chance' that the population mean lies within our confidence interval makes no sense, no matter how appealing that idea might be.

Given the frequent misinterpretation of confidence intervals, and their regular use within education data and analysis, it is important to take the time to understand what confidence intervals can imply about the summary statistics we have to hand. Confidence intervals are calculated and presented as upper and lower bounds. Whilst the central point between the upper and lower bound is usually the mean of a sample, this isn't reported as part of the confidence interval for a sample.

If, for example, we have a 95% confidence interval with a lower bound of 8.3 and an upper bound of 9.7, calculated from a sample of 50 observations, we know that the mean is 9.0 (half way between 8.3 and 9.7). What does this imply about the interval we have calculated? The following two statements are quite different:

- 95% of sample means (drawn from samples with 50 observations) drawn from a population with a mean of 9.0 will be within an interval from 8.3 to 9.7
- There is a 95% chance that the population mean is between 8.3 and 9.7

The only valid conclusion is that the first sentence is correct. Whatever Ben's sample findings, the population mean is either between the upper and lower bounds – in this case, between 8.3 and 9.7 – or it is not within this range of values. Ben's calculations do not affect this, so it isn't correct to say that the population mean is subject to chance.

Confidence intervals, whilst somewhat limited in the information they provide, are an improvement on a point estimate of a parameter. Ben can, for example, find confidence intervals for the data he has for both verbal reasoning and quantitative reasoning CAT scores, and he can present it like this:

Verbal reasoning CAT scores CI = (89, 100)

Quantitative reasoning CAT scores CI = (91, 98)

So the point estimate of 94.5 (the mean) is broadened out into a confidence interval which stretches from 89 to 100 in the case of verbal reasoning, and from 91 to 98 in the case of quantitative reasoning. This tells Ben something about the precision of the point estimates. Whilst both point estimates are the same, the estimate for quantitative reasoning is more precise than the estimate for verbal reasoning. If Ben was to suggest that the population means for his school were both 94.5, he would expect 95% of samples of the same size measuring verbal reasoning to fall between 89 and 100, whereas 95% of samples of quantitative reasoning scores would be expected to fall in the narrower interval between 91 and 98.

6.3.1 Calculating confidence intervals

Calculating confidence intervals is fairly straightforward and it is useful to understand the decisions which have to be made in order to produce confidence intervals. There are two main types of confidence interval, which depend on the data you have to work with. As Ben is now familiar with the difference between sample and population data, he understands that he can use sample data to find a sample mean and a sample standard deviation. He also knows that, if he were to have data for the entire population, he could find a population mean and population standard deviation.

If Ben knows the population standard deviation, he can calculate the confidence interval of the mean with a *known* population standard deviation. If he does not know the population standard deviation, he can calculate the confidence interval of the mean with an *unknown* population standard deviation. These two confidences are different in subtle ways.

6.3.1.1 Confidence intervals with a known population standard deviation

Where the population standard deviation – σ – is known, the limits of the confidence interval are a function of the mean, the standard error of the mean and a z-score. The confidence interval is symmetrical about the mean, so it is simply a case of finding out how far either side of the mean the confidence interval stretches. This is calculated using the following simple formula:

$$CI = \bar{x} +/- z d\sigma_{\bar{x}}$$

Confidence intervals are usually written as $CI = \bar{x} - z d\sigma_{\bar{x}}$, $CI = \bar{x} + z d\sigma_{\bar{x}}$.

It is worth looking a little closer at this to see what is going on when we construct a confidence interval. The sample mean, $\bar{x}$, is the midpoint of the interval. It is, in effect, our best guess at the population parameter. But since it is a little fuzzy – we wouldn't expect it to be absolutely accurate, simply the best guess – we use it to generate a range of sample means which we would interpret as being reasonably likely to be means drawn from the same population.

The spread of the interval which we generate is simply a product of the z-score and the standard error of the mean. If you aren't too sure what a z-score represents, now would be a good time to revisit Chapter 5. In summary, remember that z-scores are measured in standard deviations, and represent how far a given value is from the sample or population mean. For a 95% confidence interval, the z-score is 1.96, which can be interpreted as follows: '95% of the distribution of sample means lies within 1.96 standard deviations from the mean'. Figure 6.3 shows what this looks like.

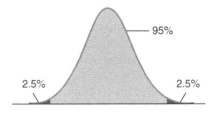

Figure 6.3 95% Confidence interval

All we need now is the standard error, which is calculated as follows:

$$\sigma_{\bar{x}} = \frac{\sigma}{\sqrt{n}}$$

In Ben's case, he has been told that the population standard deviation for verbal reasoning CAT scores is 20, and he has scores for 50 children. So:

$$\sigma_{\bar{x}} = \frac{\sigma}{\sqrt{n}} = \frac{20}{\sqrt{50}} = 2.82842712\ldots$$

His mean is 94.5, so his CI = 94.5 +/− 1.96 x 2.82842712…

= 94.5 +/− 5.5437171645…

= [88.95, 100.04] to two decimal places

= [89,100] to the nearest whole numbers

So Ben can interpret this as suggesting that, if 94.5 is the population mean, then 95% of the samples drawn from that population will be within 89 and 100.

6.3.1.2 Confidence intervals with an unknown population standard deviation

It is very unusual to have a known population standard deviation and standard error. Even when a large amount of data is available, errors and missing data mean that we simply have a biased sample which might give us values which are close to the population statistics we want, but are not entirely accurate. Remember, we are trying not to be wrong, so we need to be very careful about the assumptions which we are making.

A further consideration is that sample sizes can bias distributions and the smaller the sample, the more likely the bias. This is particularly relevant for Kathryn, who has very few data points to use in her analysis.

The problem of small samples was one which exercised William Gosset, who worked for the Guinness Brewery in the early 20th century. He noticed that the distributions of means of small samples tended not to look like those described by the z-distribution. This is because any given value in a large sample is likely to be closer to the population mean than any given value in a small sample.

Remember that the z-distribution is a picture of the distribution of the *means* of samples. In samples where n is smaller than N, the sample means tend to be more extreme than in bigger samples. This problem is particularly acute when n is very small, and you can see the problem if you look at the distributions in Figure 6.4.

Gosset worked out what the distributions for small samples looked like and he published these under his pen name of *Student*. Rather than z-distribution, Gosset's

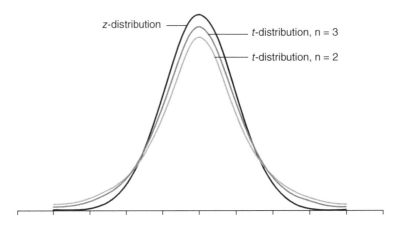

Figure 6.4 Distributions

values have come to be known as 'student's t-distribution', a name which has confused many people ever since. The t-distribution has a shape which is dependent on the sample size, as you can see above.

The differences between the z-distribution and the t-distribution (which is really a whole set of distributions depending on n) are not that great once n is bigger than 30. But with samples smaller than 30, and especially with those under 10, the tails are much bigger than those in the z-distribution.

At around the same time that William Gosset was publishing his t-distribution findings, statisticians noticed that using $\sqrt{n}$ to estimate standard error gives values which are too big. This is because of the observation that when samples are small, more extreme scores become important in the calculations of variance. This can be demonstrated by looking at two different samples with the same mean:

Sample 1: 5, 10, 14

Sample 2: 5, 9, 10, 11, 14

The means of both samples are 10 and both have relatively extreme scores (lowest of 5, highest of 14). The larger sample has more scores which fall closer to the mean, and this is much less unusual with larger samples, where more scores have the opportunity to be closer to the mean. The standard deviation for the first sample is much larger than that for the second. The simple method for managing this is to divide by $\sqrt{n-1}$ rather than $\sqrt{n}$.

Putting these two things together – t-distributions and dividing by $\sqrt{n-1}$ – the formula for calculating confidence intervals when σ is unknown is as follows:

$$\text{CI} = \bar{x} +/- ts_{\bar{x}}$$

This formula requires the computation of the sample standard error, $s_{\bar{x}}$, and uses scores from the t-distribution rather than the z-distribution.

If Ben had not been given a population standard deviation, he would have to use the formula above. He would have to estimate using the sample standard deviation. In his case, this is 22. He would now need to identify the appropriate t-score, using the values which William Gosset published. Because t-scores vary depending on the size of the sample, he needs to use this to find the t-score he requires. This will have 1 subtracted from it (so he finds a t-score for $n - 1$). This number is known as the *degrees of freedom* for the confidence interval surrounding the mean.

Degrees of freedom is a very confusing concept for many people. In essence, it refers to the number of independent variables from which an estimate can be derived. Distributions require a calculation based on the mean, which is dependent on the values in the sample. So, the degrees of freedom is the number of cases in the sample, n, minus the one dependent variable used to calculate the distribution of the sample, i.e. $n - 1$.

Ben has a sample of 50, so his d.f. = 50 – 1 = 49. In a t-table, the 95% confidence interval for 49 d.f. is 2.009575 (to 6 d.p.).

The final statistic Ben requires is the standard error, which he can estimate as follows:

$$s_{\bar{x}} = s_{(\bar{x})} = \frac{s}{\sqrt{n}} = 22 \div 7.071067 \left(\text{to 6 d.p.} \right) = 3.050855$$

So, using $CI = \bar{x} +/- z d\sigma_{\bar{x}}$ his confidence interval is:

$$= 94.5 +/- 2.009575 \text{ x } 3.050855$$
$$= [88.37, 100.63]$$
$$= [88, 101] \text{ (to the nearest whole number)}$$

This means that Ben can interpret this as suggesting that, if 94.5 is the population mean, then 95% of the samples drawn from that population will be within 88 and 101.

If we look at the two different values which Ben has calculated, we can see that:

$$CI_{z95} = [88.95, 100.04]$$
$$CI_{t95} = [88.37, 100.63]$$

When the population standard deviation is not known, the confidence interval estimate is less precise. This means that the interval is wider and we are less confident about our estimate.

6.4 Understanding margins of error

News reports often refer to margins of error, particularly when reporting polling results. Opinion polls are frequently reported as being 'accurate within a 2% margin of error' or '20%, plus or minus 3%'.

Margin of error usually refers to half of a confidence interval, which is then converted into a percentage of the value being estimated. So, for example:

An estimated mean of 10

A 95% confidence interval of [7,13]

From this, the margin of error is 3 points, because both 7 and 13 are 3 points away from 10. Because 3 points is 30% of 10 points, the margin of error is 30%.

In Ben's case, let's look at his data. The confidence interval we calculated with the t-distribution was as follows:

$$CI = 94.5 +/- 2.009575 * 3.050855 = 6.130922 \text{ (to 6 d.p.)}$$

To calculate the margin of error, we need to take the value we calculated (6.130922) and convert this into a percentage of the mean:

$$
\begin{aligned}
MoE &= 6.130922/94.5 \\
&= 0.064877 \\
&= 6\%
\end{aligned}
$$

So, we can conclude that the margin of error for Ben's estimate is 6%.

6.5 Understanding the null hypothesis

Now that we have introduced confidence intervals and shown you how they are calculated, we can begin to look at using data to make inferences about the wider picture. In order to understand the remainder of this chapter and the ideas it contains, you need to have a solid grasp of the mathematical ideas in Chapter 5 and the first half of Chapter 6. I suggest that you re-read them until you are certain that you understand the full implications of sampling theory.

Up until now, we have looked at ways of summarising data and of using data to tell us something about the information which we have already collected. Now we are going to look at using what we know to try to make inferences about the samples and populations in which we are interested.

But, first, we need to recap on some basics. Using advanced statistics is tricky. The assumptions which we make are crucial, and data has to be treated extremely carefully. Mostly, we are trying not to be wrong. The danger of over-interpreting data is ever present. And worst of all, we have to face the often unpalatable truth that statistics can't ever 'prove' anything.

One of the ideas which will help to illustrate this is the Law of Truly Large Numbers. Attributed to Persi Diaconis and Frederick Mosteller, this simply states 'with a sample size large enough, any outrageous thing is likely to happen'. As you will have read in Chapter 5, distributions are simply probabilities. In every sample, *something* has to happen. Given enough opportunities, virtually anything is possible. Even something as simple as a series of coin flips will, if repeated often enough, eventually result in something which is highly unusual. This was demonstrated effectively by UK illusionist Derren Brown in his 2009 TV Series *The Events*, in which he spent nine hours filming coin flips until, by chance alone, he finally flipped 10 heads in a row.[1]

Of course, flipping an unbiased coin results in a 50% chance that the result will be heads. In the language of statistics, to test whether a coin was fair or not we would need to *test a hypothesis*. A hypothesis is simply what you think, based on your experience, *should* happen. This doesn't involve any mathematics; it relies on a series of very fallible, very human qualities: intuition, experience, bias, and so on.

Your hypothesis can then be *tested*. In essence, you decide what you think will happen and then formulate a statement which you then try to disprove. In the case of an unbiased coin, you should expect that any sample of flips will be drawn from a population of flips of a fair coin. A fair coin should show heads 50% of the time, so:

$$H_0: \mu = 50\%$$

H_0 is the **null hypothesis**. It is a simple statement of what we assume about a population parameter, which we will then try to disprove. The null hypothesis is what you assume to be true. In this case, contrary to the evidence which Derren Brown shows in his film, we assume that a fair coin will show heads 50% of the time. We therefore assume that the population mean (μ, pronounced 'mu') will be 50%.

With this hypothesis, we would not expect a series of 10 coin flips to show exactly 5 heads, however. It's much more likely that you will flip close to 5 – 3, 4, 6 or 7, for example – and that flipping 0 or 10 would be highly unlikely (although as the Law of Truly Large Numbers implies, sometimes you will see 10 heads in a row, of course).

To test our '$\mu = 50\%$' null hypothesis, we would construct a confidence interval around our population mean and see if the sample mean which we generate falls within the interval. If I set a 95% confidence interval, with ten flips, a population mean of 50% and a population standard deviation of 5, the confidence interval I draw would be:

$$CI_{Z95} = \bar{x} +/- z\sigma_{\bar{x}} = 5 +/- 1.96 \times 5/\sqrt{10} = 5 +/- 3.099032 = \left[1.9, 8.1\right]$$

The confidence interval ranges between 19% and 81%.

My two coins show 1 and 7 heads respectively. The sample mean for the first coin (0.1) falls outside of the confidence interval I have constructed. As a result, I would reject the null hypothesis and suggest that it is unlikely that this coin comes from a population of fair coins.

The coin which showed 7 heads (0.7), however, has a sample mean which is between the limits of the confidence interval I have drawn. So the null hypothesis is not rejected, as there is not enough evidence that this coin didn't come from the population of fair coins.

These two statements are quite different:

- As a result, I would reject the null hypothesis and suggest that it is unlikely that this coin comes from a population of fair coins.
- So the null hypothesis is not rejected, as there is not enough evidence that this coin didn't come from the population of fair coins.

When the null hypothesis is rejected, we make the positive assertion that the sample is not from the population which we have described in the null hypothesis. When the null hypothesis is retained, we have to conclude that we don't have enough information to reject the null hypothesis. It is worth considering the clear difference here and to reflect on its implications.

Put simply, we can never conclude that, statistically, the null hypothesis is true. We can simply say that we have assumed it to be true and that we have found no evidence to reject this assumption.

Rejecting the null hypothesis is also referred to by using one of the most misused of all statistical terms: that a result is **statistically significant**. In this case, the difference between the first coin and the fair coin is statistically significant; the difference between the second and the fair coin is not. The use of the word 'significance' (or 'significant') is *not* the same as the everyday use of the word and great care must be taken when using the term.

As the example of Derren Brown's 10 coin flips shows, a statistically significant result may be due to factors which are not readily apparent. Where a null hypothesis is rejected, and a result is statistically significant, the best interpretation is that further investigation is required. There are several further considerations to take into account when trying to examine the bigger picture using hypothesis testing, which we will consider now.

6.6 Testing hypotheses

Now that you have a good understanding of the null hypothesis, you should have a grounding in hypothesis testing, the process by which we seek to assess whether or not a sample statistic is likely to have occurred, assuming a given null hypothesis. Whilst teachers such as Kathryn and Ben are highly unlikely to use hypothesis testing in their current roles, an introduction to the theory and practice underpinning this form of statistical analysis is useful to understand the issues with using this kind of methodology when investigating questions in education.

The following steps should be followed every time a hypothesis test is constructed:

1. State the research question.
2. State the null and alternative hypotheses.
3. Set the desired significance level and decision rule.
4. Construct a sample to test the null hypothesis.
5. Conduct a statistical test.
6. State the results of the test.
7. Conduct additional analyses as appropriate.
8. State the conclusions.

Box 6.2   Kathryn's research project

Kathryn has been asked to take part in a research project with a group of local primary schools. The group want to test whether different types of memory recall projects improve children's recall of times table facts. Kathryn is keen to participate and would like to use hypothesis testing to assess the effectiveness of the programme.

Her experience tells her that children tend to get better at times table recall over the course of Year 3. After all, children are subject to many different influences, and times table recall is a key part of the curriculum and of wider life experience for children who are in Key Stage 2.

Kathryn is particularly interested in the way in which memory and recall might be developed through repeated practice.

The best way to introduce hypothesis testing is to take you through a worked example. The following example, typical of all hypothesis testing, will involve the calculation of a **p-value**. Whilst there is some controversy about this kind of test, which we look at in Chapter 10, it is useful to understand the process by which hypotheses are tested using p-values.

6.6.1 State the research question and determine variables

Kathryn knows that a research question must state whatever problem it is that she wants to address using statistics. She knows that the key elements to a good research question are:

1. The research question must be testable.
2. She can't conclude that there is 'no difference'.
3. She should state the research question as specifically as possible.

Research questions must assess differences and must be specific. Kathryn could not simply ask, 'Do children benefit from a particular kind of memory development project?' or 'Do boys and girls react the same way to a particular memory development project?' In this example, 'benefit' is simply too non-specific and we don't know which boys and girls this question refers to. How would children benefit? Do we want to know about boys and girls in the whole country, in our region or in our school?

Testable questions come once we have considered what question we actually want to answer. For example, we might ask 'Do children in our project group outperform their classmates in times table recall?' or 'Do girls in our project group have better times table recall than boys in our project group?'

In Kathryn's case, she decides that she wants to know whether the research project benefits participating children more than children who do not participate in the project. She sets up her research question as follows:

RQ: Do children in the project improve their times table performance more than those children who do not participate?

Kathryn thinks that a specific focus on developing recall of patterns and sequences will help children to recall times tables. She decides to collect data from written assessments at the beginning and end of the project, which she will use to answer her research question.

6.6.2 State the null and alternative hypotheses

To create a null hypothesis, several questions must be answered. We will come to them in turn:

1. What is the parameter to be tested?

So far, we have mostly considered just one parameter, μ, the population mean. Means are useful, of course, but they are not the only parameter we may wish to consider. Standard deviation, for example, might be a parameter we are interested in if we are aiming to ensure that all children make similar amounts of progress (or, at least, to reduce the long tail at the lower end of a distribution which we often see).

For Kathryn, the parameter she is testing is the improvement in the mean attainment of the groups of children in the project she is running. She wants to see if this is better than that which would be expected by chance alone. She wants to compare the mean attainment of her group prior to the project $\bar{x}_a$ with the mean attainment of the group at the conclusion of the project period $\bar{x}_b$, $\bar{x}_b - \bar{x}_a$. The parameter she is testing is therefore $\mu_b - \mu_a$.

2. What do we wish to test against that parameter?

The null hypothesis is derived from our assumptions about the population which we are studying. In this case, the population is Year 3 children similar to those in Kathryn's class. Kathryn has a set of times table tests which the school has administered over the past few years at the end of Year 2 and at the end of Year 3. She has data for the whole of her current Year 3 class, which includes their end of Year 2 times table test results.

3. What is the theoretical relationship between the parameter and the test value?

Kathryn now needs to decide how the parameter she has described $(\mu_b - \mu_a)$ is related to the test value she has identified $(\bar{x}_b - \bar{x}_a)$. She is interested in determining whether the memory recall project affects the project group, such that they can be said to represent a different population to the population from which the rest of the class is drawn.

If she is simply interested in determining whether the two populations are different, Kathryn needs to use a **two-tailed test**. In this type of test, the null hypothesis is rejected if the sample statistic falls in either tail (outside the confidence interval we can calculate). The limits of the confidence interval are known as the **critical values** for the two-tailed test.

Kathryn is interested in finding out whether the children in her project do better than the general population, however, and not whether they are simply drawn from a different population. In this case, Kathryn wants to know if her test population is actually the same or worse than the general population of Year 3 children.

Take a moment to consider this. Kathryn cannot test to see if her test group is 'better', but she can test to see if it is *not* the 'same or worse'. The two might seem similar, but they are not, and this is at the heart of hypothesis testing.

6.6.2.1 State the null hypothesis and alternative hypothesis

Now that we have answered these questions, we can state the null hypothesis for Kathryn's test:

$$H_0 : (\mu_b - \mu_a) <= \bar{x}_b - \bar{x}_a$$

We have decided that the parameter to test is $(\mu_b - \mu_a)$, the test value will be $\bar{x}_b - \bar{x}_a$ and the appropriate relationship is less than or equal to. This is what Kathryn thinks will be true unless she can prove otherwise. She thinks that there will be no difference between the project group and the general population unless she finds evidence to suggest that this is not true.

For many, this will seem somewhat odd. Why undertake the project if you don't think it will make any difference? Experience has shown, however, that we are easily fooled by our intuition, biases and general desire to prove ourselves right. Without setting rigorous, measurable criteria against which we can test our assumptions, we can easily be fooled into seeing what we want to see.

With hypothesis testing, we are generally happy to be proved wrong, since this opens up more areas for us to explore. But if we are right, and the null hypothesis holds, we have to accept that our test shows that two populations are likely to be the same.

If the null hypothesis does not hold, an alternative hypothesis must hold instead. The alternative hypothesis (denoted H_1) must contain all of the possible values rejected by the null hypothesis. In Kathryn's case, this is:

$$H_1 : (\mu_b - \mu_a) > \bar{x}_b - \bar{x}_a$$

6.6.3 Set the desired significance level and decision rule(s)

As previously noted, the wording of a 'significance level' is somewhat confusing and the concept is widely misunderstood. In essence, however, the term simply describes at what point a null hypothesis would be rejected. We know that samples are drawn from a sampling distribution, with most samples having means which are close to the centre of the distribution.

If a sample mean falls within the tails of the sampling distribution, we would reject it. The significance level simply describes the size of the tails which we have chosen to reject. If we are comparing a sample to a 95% confidence interval, a significance level of 5% indicates that we would reject the null hypothesis if 5% of samples would be likely to fall into the tails of the sampling distribution. Significance levels are labelled with the Greek letter α, so a 5% significance level would be written as $\alpha = 0.05$.

The default significance level used in the majority of published significance testing is 5%. It is not unusual to see significance levels of 1% and 10% in different fields of research. We will consider commonly identified issues with significance levels in Chapter 10.

6.6.4 Construct a sample to test the null hypothesis

Once Kathryn has set her decision rule, she can then set about collecting data. We looked at the issues with attainment data in Chapter 3 and we explored samples in Chapter 5. Given that Kathryn has specified her experimental design before completing the project, and therefore before collecting her data, she should be able to stick to the objective standards she has set herself.

Box 6.3   Type I and Type II errors

As should now be clear, a sample is drawn from a wide distribution of samples. There is therefore the clear possibility that any given sample may be in or near the tails of the sampling distribution. Consider the theoretical sample means A, B, C and D in Figure 6.5.

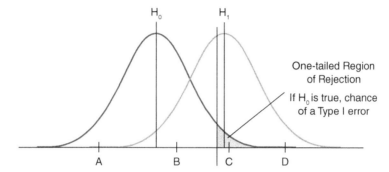

Figure 6.5   Theoretical sample means

Samples A and B are not in the tail and therefore the null hypothesis is not rejected. If H_0 is true, this is the correct decision. In the case of C and D, however, the null hypothesis is rejected. H_0 is true, this is not the correct decision and an error has been made. This type of error – where H_0 is rejected even though it is true – is known as a **Type I error**. This is often referred to as a 'false positive'.

The probability that we will incorrectly reject the null hypothesis is the same as the significance level, so if $\alpha = 0.05$ the null hypothesis will be incorrectly rejected in 5% of cases.

There is also the possibility that the null hypothesis will be retained when it should have been rejected. This is known as a **Type II error** and is often referred to as a 'false negative'.

In this case, the theoretical samples A, B, C and D are actually from a separate population with a different distribution, as shown in Figure 6.6.

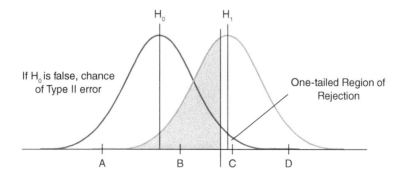

Figure 6.6   Theoretical samples

(Continued)

(Continued)

Here, A and B are in the tail of the H_1 distribution and have been incorrectly identified as being from the H_0 distribution.

Good research design tries to minimise both Type I and Type II errors. Setting a low α minimises Type I error. A large sample minimises Type II error (which is known as β). As with many things in hypothesis testing, judgement is required when assessing the possibility of Type I and II errors and, as ever, there is always the possibility that our results might be wrong at any point.

There is a whole field of research design on which Kathryn can draw and which we will consider further in Chapter 8.

6.6.5 Conduct a statistical test

Once Kathryn has completed her project, and has collected the data she needs, she can conduct a statistical test. This will involve testing or identifying a p-value. In this case, this represents the probability that Kathryn's sample statistic (her $\bar{x}_b - \bar{x}_a$) came from the population represented by the null hypothesis.

If Kathryn's sample group is different to the general population of Year 3 children, she will find that her p-value will be quite small. Whatever p-value Kathryn finds will be compared to the α she set in the research design. Assuming that she set an α of 0.05, any p-value less than this will indicate a statistically significant result, and the null hypothesis will be rejected; anything higher than 0.05 will not indicate statistical significance.

6.6.6 State the results of the test

The formulation for stating the results of a hypothesis test is as follows:

(test statistic) = (your result), p = (p-value) [if you know the p-value]

(test statistic) = (your result), p (>,<) 0.05 [if you don't know the p-value]

Calculating p-values is covered later in this chapter.

6.6.7 Conduct additional analyses as appropriate

Kathryn might compute a confidence interval, for example, or wish to conduct further analysis at this point.

6.6.8 State conclusions

At this point, Kathryn needs to interpret her results. She needs to turn all of the data she has into everyday terms which carry meaning for a general audience, whilst retaining enough formality to ensure that her conclusions are clear to those who understand hypothesis testing.

Her conclusion should start with a formal statement, which is then explained for a general audience.

The formulation for this is as follows:

1. A formal statement about the null hypothesis.
2. A formal statement about statistical significance.
3. A sentence interpreting the results with reference to the research question.
4. An interpretation of any additional analysis.

In Kathryn's case, her project results were presented as follows:

Research question: Do children in the project improve their times table performance more than those children who do not participate?

$$H_0 : (\mu_b - \mu_a) <= \bar{x}_b - \bar{x}_a$$

$$H_1 : (\mu_b - \mu_a) > \bar{x}_b - \bar{x}_a$$

$$\alpha = 0.05$$

$$\text{Critical value} = +1.645$$

$$z = 1.98, p < 0.05$$

$$CI_{95} = [0.50, 0.78]$$

Conclusion: Reject the null. The difference is statistically significant. The research project performance is better than the non-intervention group. If we assume that the research project sample will replicate in future, we would expect 95% of sample means to fall between 0.50 and 0.78.

6.7 Typical tests used to generate p-values

To generate a p-value, you need a null hypothesis, a **test statistic** and data. A test statistic is a single number, such as a mean, which summarises the data. In most cases, the test statistic is assumed to follow a normal distribution and the most common tests which are used to generate p-values are z-tests and one-sample t-tests. Whilst there are other tests, we will look at these two tests for now.

In order to test whether a sample is drawn from a population which is different to our hypothetical population, hypothesis testing requires that we have a given population mean. This can be problematic, but for now we will assume that we have a value for a population mean.

When we conduct these tests, we are going to compare sample means with population means, and we will state the results in terms of standard errors.

6.7.1 Computing critical values in z-tests

Where we also know the standard deviation (the σ) for the population to which we are comparing our sample, we can use a t-test. It can be useful to draw the sampling distribution for the mean and standard deviation of the population to clarify what we are testing. In Kathryn's case, the population mean is 35 and the standard deviation is 7, which looks like Figure 6.7.

There are three main variants of the t-test: two-tailed, left-tailed and right-tailed. Two-tailed tests are used where we simply want to know if the sample is significantly different to the population and we are not particularly interested in whether this difference is at a given end of the sampling distribution. One-tailed tests, either left-tailed or right-tailed tests, position the critical value closer to the mean either on the left- or right-hand tails of the distribution.

It's worth looking at the critical values for each test to see where the areas of rejection are (Figure 6.8).

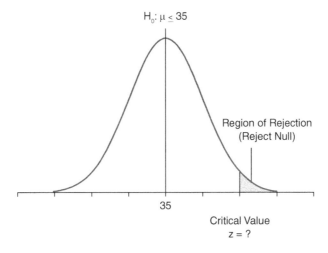

Figure 6.7   Theoretical samples

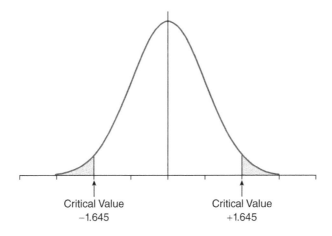

Figure 6.8   Locating the critical values

For tests with $\alpha = 0.05$, the most common significance level, the critical values are as in Table 6.1.

Table 6.1   Critical values

	$\alpha = 0.05$	$\alpha = 0.01$
Two-tailed t-test	±1.96	±2.58
Left-tailed t-test	−1.645	−2.33
Right-tailed t-test	+1.645	+2.33

6.7.2 Calculating z-test values

Remember that a z-score is calculated as follows (we covered this in Chapter 5):

$$z = \frac{x - \bar{x}}{\sigma}$$

To calculate a z-score, we compare a raw score with a *sample* mean. In the z-test, which compares the sample to the population, we compare the raw score to the *population* mean. For z-scores, the differences we find are reported in standard deviation units. For z-tests, because we are comparing each score to the population mean, the differences are reported in *standard error* units. The standard error of the sample mean is defined as a measure of how precisely the population mean is measured by the sample mean.

The formula to calculate the z-test is therefore calculated using the sample mean ($\bar{x}$), the population mean (μ) and the population standard error ($\sigma_{\bar{x}}$), as follows:

$$z = \frac{\bar{x} - \mu}{\sigma_{\bar{x}}}$$

The population standard error is estimated using the population standard deviation (σ) using the following formula:

$$\sigma_{\bar{x}} = \frac{\sigma}{\sqrt{n}}$$

In our case, we know $\mu = 5$ and $n = 15$. We can calculate $\bar{x}$, which is 6.2.

The standard error is calculated first:

$$\sigma_{\bar{x}} = \frac{7}{\sqrt{15}} = 1.807392$$

We can therefore calculate z as follows:

$$z = \frac{6.2 - 5}{1.807392}$$

$$z = 0.663940$$

$$z = 0.66$$

This z-test value is the value which we use to compare to the critical value which we have identified. In this case, the results are within the area of the sampling distribution outside the tails, and therefore the null hypothesis would not be rejected.

6.8 Computing critical values in one-sample t-tests

Finding a critical value for a one-sample t-test is similar to the method used for a z-test. The main difference is that the t-distribution is actually a whole range of distributions depending on the size of the sample, and therefore to the degrees of freedom with which we have to work (see above for a reminder of the tricky concept of degrees of freedom).

The degrees of freedom are $n-1$, so in Kathryn's case, the degrees of freedom are $15 - 1 = 14$. Using this information, she can find the t-test statistic she needs, which is ±2.51 for a two-tailed test with $\alpha = 0.05$. This is written as follows:

$$t_{crit} = \pm2.51$$

6.8.1 Calculating t-test values

The formula for a t-statistic is similar to the formula for a z-statistic. The main difference is that a t-test is used when the population standard deviation is not known. If it is known, a z-test is preferred. Because the population standard deviation is not known, we can't find the population standard error. The solution to this problem is to use the sample standard error to approximate it.

The formula to calculate the t-test with a particular number of degrees of freedom is therefore calculated using the sample mean $(\bar{x})$ the population mean (μ) and the sample standard error $(s_{\bar{x}})$, as follows:

$$t(df) = \frac{\bar{x} - \mu}{s_{\bar{x}}}$$

In Kathryn's case, the values she has are as follows:

$$\bar{x} = 6.21$$

$$\mu = 5$$

$$S = 8.342523$$

$$n = 15$$

The standard error is calculated first:

$$s_{\bar{x}} = \frac{s}{\sqrt{n}} = \frac{8.342523}{\sqrt{15}} = 2.154030$$

This then gives us:

$$t(14) = \frac{6.21 - 5}{2.154030} = 0.561738 = 0.56$$

This one-sample t-test value is the value which we use to compare to the critical value which we have identified. In this case, the results are within the area of the sampling distribution outside the tails, and therefore the null hypothesis would not be rejected.

6.9 Summary

In this chapter, we have considered that we can point estimates to create confidence intervals, and how confidence intervals can be used to make inferences about data. We have looked at margins of error and how these are calculated using the summary statistics which can be generated. We have also looked at null hypothesis testing and the way in which it can be used to shed light on research questions. Much of this kind of analysis is clearly based on advanced statistics, and it is not without its critics. We will look more closely at the controversies surrounding the use of these techniques in education in Chapter 10. Databusting schools need to be aware of both the methods which are commonly used to create statistics to summarise schools, and of the criticisms which are made of these methods.

In Chapter 7, we will look at the use of correlational statistics, as we consider how variables are related and what this might tell us about our students and our schools.

Note

1. See www.youtube.com/watch?v=n1SJ-Tn3bcQ

7.1 Introduction

Whereas many hypothesis tests look at differences, there are times when we might want to look at relationships between variables. For example, we might want to find out what the relationship between a child's height and their weight might be, and how this might be described using the data which we can collect. Clearly, we would expect a relationship between the two variables, since children get heavier as they get taller.

Before we can really understand whether one thing leads to the other, or whether the variables are interrelated, we want to understand what we could use to describe and picture the relationships we find.

Box 7.1   Ben's correlated variables

Ben has data sets which include several variables on each child in each year group. He has been asked to look into correlations between age and CAT scores so that his teaching team can look for any children who appear to have unusual CAT scores for their age. He is interested in finding out whether any children have higher or lower scores than might be expected. To do this, he needs to start by exploring whether there is a relationship between age and CAT scores.

7.2 Introducing correlation coefficients

Where we have continuous data, such as that described as interval- or ratio-level data, it is possible to compute a **correlation coefficient**. Whilst there are many types of correlation, all are descriptive statistics which summarise the relationship between two variables using a single number. This does require a high degree of precision, as demanded by ratio and interval data, so we need to be careful when choosing to subject data to correlational analysis. Where the data is robust, how-ever, reducing the relationship between data to a number can provide useful insight into the relationship which exists (or does not exist) between the data sets.

The most common correlation coefficient was developed by mathematician Karl Pearson. It is known by the somewhat complicated name of the **product-moment correlation coefficient**, abbreviated to **Pearson's r** or **PMCC**. Pearson was a pioneer in statistics and was heavily influenced by the field of physics, which is where he borrowed the idea of a 'moment' from. In physics, 'moments' refer to expressions which, for example, recognise that the way in which a force is applied changes dependent on the distance from which the force is applied.

Pearson pioneered the use of moments in statistics. Moments are given numbers to denote their order, with the first moment of a probability distribution being the mean, the second being the variance. The product-moment of Pearson's r refers to the mean of the product of the mean-adjusted random variables. If this sounds com-plicated, it serves as a reminder that this is extremely theoretical statistics, which isn't quite as simple as is often presented. Luckily for the general reader, Pearson's r can be represented very effectively in a visual way, and the key idea – whether two items are dependent or not – is easy to grasp.

The PMCC is frequently referred to simply as the 'correlation' between values, and we will do that here. As with several other everyday terms used in specific con-texts in statistics, correlation is often misinterpreted. The phrase 'correlation does not imply causation' is often used to remind us that a correlation in statistical terms does not imply that one thing causes another. There are many famous examples of data sets which are clearly correlated but equally clearly unrelated in the everyday sense of both words.

> **Box 7.2**

Correlation does not imply causation

For endless examples of the surprising correlation between unrelated data sets, take a look at the remarkable examples published by Tyler Vigen on his spurious correlations website (www.tylervigen.com/spurious-correlations). Many variables have extremely high correlations, even though they clearly have no causal relationship whatsoever. A classic example is the correlation between ice cream sales and murder rates in the United States of America. As ice cream sales increase over the course of the year, so does the murder rate.

Of course, the consumption and sale of ice cream don't *cause* the murder rate to ebb and flow, but there is a clear correlation. The underlying factor seems to be warmer weather, which encourages people to want ice cream and, at the same time, brings peo-ple outside and into contact with other people. In cities like New York, that results in higher homicide rates.[1]

The phrase 'correlation does not imply causation' should underpin the whole of this chapter. We might be able to accurately describe correlations between variables, but we must remember that all that this simply tells us is whether there is a relationship between variables or not.

What the PMCC does is to describe the extent to which two variables are linearly related, i.e. the extent to which we can say that a line can be drawn showing a direct relationship between two variables. We covered linear relationships in Chapter 4, and you will remember that a 'linear relationship' is that described by a straight line. Examples of different linear relationships are shown in Figure 7.1.

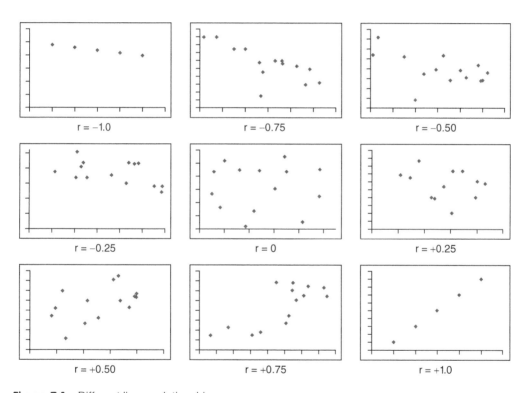

Figure 7.1   Different linear relationships

As you can see, whilst it is difficult to see correlations with values from −0.25 to +0.25 with the naked eye, those with values of −0.5 to −1.0 and +0.5 to +1.0 are much easier to pick out. Even so, the only one-to-one, straight-line 'perfect' relationships are those with values of −1.0 and +1.0, and all the other correlations are much fuzzier, particularly those around +/− 0.25.

It is important to bear this in mind as we explore correlations. With data, as with life, most relationships we find are less than perfect. Whilst we can describe lines very well, we must always bear in mind the fact that our lines are generally somewhat fuzzy.

The PMCC is an index, and as an index it has no meaningful unit of measurement. On its own, it doesn't tell you too much, but *comparing* different PMCCs can be very useful. Two things about correlations are worth noting: first, the magnitude of the relationship. As noted above, −1.0 and +1.0 are 'perfect relationships, and the closer the correlation is to either value, the stronger the linear relationship. So r = −0.8 is said to be a stronger relationship than r = 0.4, although 0.4 is clearly greater than −0.8. The closer to zero, the weaker the relationship, and zero indicates that there is no relationship between the variables at all.

The second is the direction of the correlation. In positive relationships, both variables move in the same direction at the same time. In Ben's data for age and CAT scores, he finds that as age goes up, CAT scores go up too, and as CAT scores decrease, age decreases too. In negative relationships, one variable decreases as the other increases. For example, the fewer the number of days a child is absent from school, the higher their grades at school tend to be, and the relationship is said to be negative.

7.3 Calculating correlations

In calculating simple correlations, we are looking at data sets which have two variables for the same case. You might want to refresh these terms so that you can follow the thinking behind the calculations which are involved. We start by finding the *covariance* for the variables we are analysing. This requires that we find the difference between each variable and the mean for that variable for each case, multiply them together and then find the sum of all these products. Once we have calculated this sum, we divide it by the degrees of freedom, which is $n - 1$ in this case.

All of these calculations are neatly summarised by the expression below:

$$cov = \frac{\sum(x - \bar{x})(y - \bar{y})}{n - 1}$$

Whilst these calculations might seem odd, they are quite similar to the method which is used to calculate the variance which we looked at in Chapter 5. Remember that the difference between each variable and its mean can be positive or negative, and to find the variance we square the difference to give a positive difference from the mean (and then we take its square root to find the standard deviation). In the case of the covariance, we simply find the distance from the mean for each variable for every case and multiply them together, add the results and then divide the sum of difference products by the degrees of freedom.

With variance, large values result from data sets with lots of scores which are far away from the mean, and smaller values result when the scores are close to the mean. Because we are multiplying by two different variables to find the covariance, the values will be small if *either* distance from their respective means is small. If *both* distances are small, the value is close to zero and adds little to covariance. The opposite is also true, and larger covariances occur when both distances from their respective means are large. When we divide the sum of difference products by n − 1, we end up with the *average* distance each pair is from describing a straight line.

All this means that the larger the covariance, the closer the relationship is to a straight line. The smaller the covariance, the more likely it is that the relationship is weak or non-existent. Figure 7.2 shows the effects of each pair of variable differences.

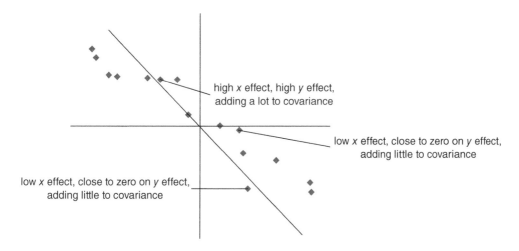

Figure 7.2   Effects of pairs of variable differences

You may have spotted one of the big problems with covariance as we have gone through the calculation in Figure 7.2. When we calculate variance, we simply square the differences between a single variable and its mean. When calculating covariance, we use the difference between each variable and its mean. Where the scales of the two variables are substantially different, the calculations run into difficulties.

Consider, for example, one data set which has values which vary between 1 and 20 and a second data set with values from 30,000 to 40,000. The second data set will have a much greater covariance simply because the scale is so much bigger. For this reason, a covariance without context is largely meaningless.

This is managed by removing the original scale of the data, and setting the range from −1 to 1. This process simply involves dividing by each variable's standard deviation, *s*. This then converts a *covariance* into a *correlation*, which is a standardised covariance. Correlation then becomes an index, as it does not have a natural scale, and it has outer limits of −1 and +1.

$$r = \frac{\sum(x - x^c)(y - \bar{y})}{(n-1)s_x s_y}$$

Because z-scores are simply score minus mean divided by standard deviation, r can be expressed using z-scores as follows:

$$r = \frac{\sum z_x z_y}{n-1}$$

Correlation is now a standard function on most spreadsheet programs and it is very simple to find the r for two variables. The key, as ever, is to be able to interpret correlations which you compute. Understanding what typical correlations in 0.25 point increases look like (as per Figure 7.1) is useful. It is also possible to test hypotheses using r as the parameter.

7.4 Using correlations in hypothesis tests

Using the steps discussed in Chapter 6, the process for testing a hypothesis regarding correlations would be as follows:

1. State the research question.
2. State the null and alternative hypotheses.
3. Set the desired significance level and decision rule.
4. Construct a sample to test the null hypothesis.
5. Conduct a statistical test.
6. State the results of the test.
7. Conduct additional analyses as appropriate.
8. State conclusions.

7.4.1 State the research question

In Ben's case, he wants to know whether age is related to CAT scores.
    RQ: Is there a linear relationship between age and CAT scores?

7.4.2 State the null and alternative hypotheses

We need to compare our sample to a hypothetical population. The symbol used for a population correlation is ρ, the Greek character rho. The null hypothesis is that there is a correlation of 0 (no relationship), and the hypotheses are therefore:

$$H_0: \rho = 0$$
$$H_1: \rho \neq 0$$

7.4.3 Set the desired significance level and decision rule

We set the significance level to $\alpha = 0.05$. Because we have two variables (x and y) and we have two degrees of freedom, we will conduct a one-sample t-test with n-2 degrees of freedom. Ben has 15 cases, so we will use the critical value for 13 d.f. which is:

$$t_{crit} = \pm 2.160$$

7.4.4 Construct a sample to test the null hypothesis

Ben has the data for this Year 7 group and he has taken a representative sample of the year group using the guidelines for random samples described in Chapter 5.

He creates a sample of 15 children, and finds a correlation between age and CAT score of r = 0.536542. This looks like Figure 7.3.

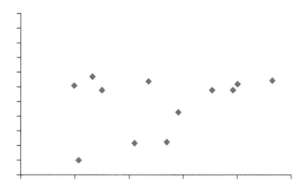

Figure 7.3   Correlation between age and CAT score

As you can see in Figure 7.3, it is quite difficult to see the relationship between the variables using the naked eye, and this is typical of an r near 0.50.

7.4.5 Conduct a statistical test

In this case, Ben has to convert his correlation (which was r = 0.536542) into a t-statistic. This is done using the following:

$$t(n-2) = \frac{r\sqrt{n-2}}{\sqrt{1-r^2}}$$

This then results in the following:

$$t(13) = \frac{r\sqrt{13}}{\sqrt{1-r^2}}$$

$$t(13) = \frac{0.536542 * 3.605551}{0.680777}$$

$$t(13) = +2.841649$$

7.4.6 State the results of the test

The critical value was $t_{crit} = \pm 2.160$ and $t(13) = +2.841649$, so the observed t-statistic is in the tails and therefore the null is rejected.

$$r(13) = 0.54, p<0.05$$

7.4.7 Conduct additional analyses as appropriate

As with previous hypothesis tests, if we find statistical significance, we have additional steps to undertake. For correlations, we can compute a **coefficient of determination**, or r^2. Second, we can also conduct a **regression analysis**.

7.4.7.1 Coefficient of determination

The coefficient of determination is a number which indicates how much of the variance in one variable is predicted by the variance in the other variable. It is found by simply squaring the value of r, so in Ben's case it is $0.536542^2 = 0.287877$.

This can be said to mean that age predicts 29% of the variance in CAT scores, and that CAT scores predict 29% of the age of the child. As ever, it is worth repeating that correlation does not imply causation. This can be seen quite clearly here, since a CAT score is clearly unable to *cause* a child to be a particular age. There is a relationship, clearly, but there is no indication as to the cause of that relationship.

7.4.7.2 Simple linear regression

There are many different analyses which fall into the category of **regression**, which is the term used to describe the process of trying to find a 'line of best fit' between two variables. Finding a line can be very useful, since we can begin to predict how one variable will behave if we know another variable. We have a lot of data on children's height and weight, for example, and we can therefore use one to predict the other. This is particularly useful if it causes us to ask questions when we find examples of pairs of data which do not follow the pattern we have identified.

Simple linear regression is the prediction of one variable using another variable. It should be noted that, in order for the analysis to be valid, both variables must be interval- or ratio-level variables, so you need to be confident that your data is robust enough to stand up to scrutiny. Ben is using age data, which is ratio data (with certain caveats, since date of birth varies somewhat depending on birth circumstances – nothing in data should be taken for granted!) and CAT score data. Are CAT scores interval or ratio data? It's a very moot point.

All regression analysis aims to summarise data using a line of best fit or **regression line**. Mathematically, this is the line which describes the data better than any other line can. We saw examples of regression lines above, along with the data from which they can be drawn.

Simple linear regression uses a technique known as **ordinary least squares**. This requires that we compute the line which looks at every possible difference between each data point and the line, and finds the smallest sum of the squares of the differences (squares are used once again to ensure that all the values used are positive). The differences are known as '**residuals**' and a regression line has the smallest possible residuals for all of the data points in the data set.

From Chapter 4, you will recall that the formula for a straight line is of the form:

$$y = ax + b$$

where a is the gradient (or slope) of the line and b is the y-intercept (where the line crosses the y-axis), and x and y are the variables we are looking at.

In Ben's case, he wants to use age (which should be predictable) to predict CAT scores (which appear to be more unpredictable). In this case, he wants age to be his x variable (or predictor) and CAT scores to be his y variable (or criterion). The predictor is referred to as an independent variable (because it can vary independently) and the criterion is the dependent variable (because it depends on the predictor).

7.4.7.3 Calculating the regression line

Once you have calculated the correlation (r), calculating the slope of the regression line is straightforward:

$$b = r\frac{S_C}{S_p}$$

where b is the slope of the regression line, r is Pearson's PMCC and the standard deviation of the criterion is divided by the standard deviation of the predictor. In Ben's case, $S_c = 72.564738$ and $S_p = 10.435262$, so:

$$b = 0.536542\frac{72.564738}{10.435262}$$

$$b = 3.731006 = 3.73 \text{ to } 2 \text{ d.p.}$$

To calculate the y intercept (a), we use the formula below:

$$a = \bar{x}_c - b\bar{x}_p$$

where $\bar{x}_c$ is the mean of the criterion variable, $\bar{x}_p$ is the mean of the predictor variable and b is the regression slope. So, in Ben's case, we have $\bar{x}_c$ and $\bar{x}_p$, and therefore

$$a = 85.75 - 3.73100643 * 138.56$$

$$a = -431.218251$$

So, our regression line is:

$$y = 3.73x - 431.22$$

7.4.7.4 Predicting values from the regression line

Once you have a regression line, you can predict a specific range of values of the criterion given a specific range of the value of x. Simply solve the equation for the regression line for the x in which you are interested. Bear in mind that the model which you have created will only hold for values of x in the range of the original data set. Beyond these limits, the regression line may alter in ways in which our model cannot predict.

Whilst the regression line can be written using rounded values, it is important to use the full values which you have calculated when predicting values, since rounding will skew the results. In Ben's case, for example, he wants to see what CAT score his model predicts a child who is 140 months old will attain. Using the full values, it suggests a CAT score of 91.12. Using rounded values, the predicted score is 90.98.

7.4.8 State conclusions

RQ: Is there a linear relationship between age and CAT scores?

$$H_0: r = 0$$
$$H_1: r \neq 0$$
$$\alpha = 0.05$$
$$t_{crit} = \pm 2.160$$
$$r(13) = 0.54, p < 0.05$$
$$r^2 = 0.287877$$
$$y = 3.73x - 431.22$$

Conclusion: Reject the null hypothesis and accept the alternative. The correlation is statistically significant. There is a linear relationship between a child's age and their CAT score; 28% of the variance in CAT score was explained by the child's age in months.
   A simple linear regression was justified because:

(a)   The correlation was statistically significant.

(b)   There was good reason to assign age as the predictor and CAT score as the criterion.

(c)   We wanted to predict the criterion from the predictor.

It is hugely important to remember that correlation is not causation and that the regression analysis here does not change this: we cannot conclude that age causes CAT scores, simply that in this case study the variables were related statistically.

7.5 Multiple regressions and beyond

Regressions are tremendously powerful tools. We have looked at simple linear regressions and it is beyond the scope of this book to go very much further. It is worth mentioning a few other regressions however, as they may crop up in research which you might read. One more powerful and very common regression which is often used in educational research is **multiple regression**. This uses, as it implies, multiple predictors to produce a line of best fit rather than just two particular variables.

Beyond multiple regression models lies a further field of modelling known as **multilevel modelling**. As the name implies, this kind of modelling works with data at different levels. For example, data sets with student performance data at both student, classroom and school level lend themselves to this type of modelling. Multilevel modelling is quite some way beyond this book, but you may come across it in research you read. It's a relatively new field and is rapidly evolving as statisticians explore different ways to analyse complicated data sets.

7.6 Rank correlation

As noted above, calculating a PMCC requires data which is interval or ratio data. Much of the data which we have in school isn't that robust, however. Frequently, we simply have ordinal data. Fortunately, there is a technique for calculating correlations for this kind of data. Developed by Charles Spearman, another big beast in statistics, the **Spearman's coefficient of rank correlation** (denoted by r) provides a method of analysing data which is ordinal.

When we test a class's knowledge in simple tests, the marks we have aren't necessarily of the same value. What we can do, however, is to rank the children from 1 to n, where n is the total number of children in the class. So, for example, let us imagine that Kathryn's Year 3 pupils have been ranked in their spelling tests at the beginning and the end of a half term, as can be seen in Figure 7.4.

	Test 1	Test 2
Sophia	1	2
Faizah	2	5
James	3	3
Charlotte	4	1
Emma	5	4
Abigail	6	6
Harper	7	8
Ava	8	12
Emily	9	10

	Test 1	Test 2
Mason	10	9
Avery	11	15
Elijah	12	20
Jacob	13	7
Benjamin	14	11
Mohamed	15	17
Madison	16	16
Amelia	17	19
Samayah	19	13
Isabella	19	
Mia	20	21
Aiden	21	14
Sofia	22	18
Ethan	23	22
Alexander	24	26
Olivia	25	23
Michael	26	28
William	27	
Jayden	28	27
Logan	29	24
Elizabeth		25

Figure 7.4   Ranking of pupils over two tests

What do the results in Figure 7.4 suggest about the children's positions within the class? Do children who rank highly stay in similar positions, or is the opposite true? We could plot the rank positions in the first test against those in the second test. One problem which immediately springs to mind is what to do with those children who did not take the test for some reason. A simple solution is to award them the lowest rank available, so Elizabeth (who did not get a rank in test 1) would be given a rank of 30. An additional problem is that, in some cases, more than one child will not have been given a rank. These children simply take the mean of the lowest available ranks, so Isabella and William share ranks 29 and 30 for the second test and are each allocated 29.5 as their rank.

Figure 7.5 is the scatterplot of the ranks for the whole class.

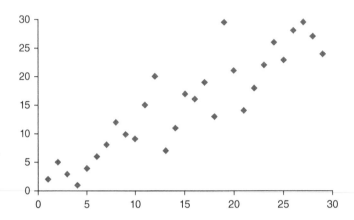

Figure 7.5 Scatterplot of ranks for the whole class

There seems to be a clear pattern in the scatterplot in Figure 7.5, which suggests a positive relationship between the two tests. Spearman's enables us to quantify this difference. To use r we need the difference, d, in the ranks and the following formula:

$$r' = 1 - \frac{6\sum d^2}{n(n^2 - 1)}$$

Using the rank data from Kathryn's class gives the following:

$$r' = 1 - \frac{6 * 443.5}{30\left(30^2 - 1\right)} = 0.901335$$

As with the PMCC, the coefficient of rank correlation is designed to give a value between –1 and 1, and the values can be interpreted largely in the same way in which the values of r are interpreted. Thus, 0.901335 is a strong positive correlation and shows a high degree of correlation between the two test ranks.

If we were simply to look at the children in the top ten for test 1, we would see the following:

$$r' = 1 - \frac{6 * 39}{10\left(10^2 - 1\right)} = 0.763636$$

Databusting for schools

And if we were to look at the children who were in the top ten in test 2, we would find the following:

$$r^{'} = 1 - \frac{6*56}{10\left(10^2 - 1\right)} = 0.642424$$

Both of these results are quite different to our strong positive rank correlation for the whole class, and this indicates yet another statistical pitfall into which it is very easy to fall. When we just look at the top ten ranks, we have different children in the calculations each time, with some dropping out and some coming in. This points to an important general idea in statistics, which is that we cannot generalise beyond the remit of the data which we have.

The analysis for a subset of the children in a class over two tests is different to the analysis of all the children in the class. Conclusions which are drawn for each grouping are separate and can't be extrapolated beyond the scope of each data set.

7.7 Summary

In this chapter, we have considered how to interpret links between variables, and how to use and interpret correlation coefficients. We have also looked at ways to picture correlations using scatter graphs.

Much of the latter part of this chapter considered dependent and independent variables, and explored the use of lines of best fit to create regressions of relationships between variables. In the next chapter, we will explore how to critically appraise presentations of data, looking at common ways in which data can mislead those analysing it.

Note

1. See www.nytimes.com/2009/06/19/nyregion/19murder.html?pagewanted=all&_r=1

8

CRITICALLY APPRAISING STATISTICS

USING WHAT YOU HAVE LEARNED

8.1 Critically appraising presentations of data

In 2013, Ben Goldacre, best-selling author of *Bad Science* (2009) and an influential advocate of evidence-based practice in medicine, wrote a report for the UK government which advocated further advances in the development of evidence-based practice in education. In his report, Goldacre encouraged those involved in education to establish a culture where 'evidence is used as a matter of routine':

> Learning the basics of how research works is important, not because every teacher should be a researcher, but because it allows teachers to be critical consumers of the new research findings that will come out during the many decades of their career. It also means that some of the barriers to research, that arise from myths and misunderstandings, can be overcome. (Goldacre, 2013: 16–17)

In the preceding chapters, we looked at how numbers work, how relationships in data sets are summarised and visualised, and how we use statistics to describe both where we currently are and how we might make inferences about the bigger picture. A goal of this book is to encourage all of those using data in education to critically appraise data as a matter of routine. To paraphrase Goldacre, teachers should ensure that they know enough about data to be able to use it in ways which is justifiable. Understanding the limitations of the data we generate ourselves, and being able to appraise data provided by others, has become essential for those of us working in education.

In order to critically appraise statistics and data analysis, we need to be aware of the many ways in which we might be misled, and to develop a framework for appraising studies which use educational data.

Most humans find complex data difficult to read and interpret. As we have seen, there are any number of ways of summarising data using measures of average, limits, sectional data, and so on, and most of these are difficult to summarise quickly and easily. As a result, we frequently present data visually to exploit our ability to absorb large amounts of data via a wide variety of graphs, diagrams and charts.

Unfortunately, a number of misleading representations – both intentional and accidental – are often found when we critically appraise presentations of data. There are many ways in which an argument can be distorted by playing fast and loose with averages, selecting a particular representation of a proportion, or tweaking a graph or two.

In the first part of this chapter, we will look at three areas of data presentation which can potentially mislead: graphs, proportions and averages.

8.2 Critically appraising graphs

Graphs are simply visual representations of complex data. As such, a key observation which should be made when considering any graph is that it is simply one of many different ways of presenting one particular aspect of a data set which is of interest. There is no one graph for a particular data set which is 'correct' in any meaningful sense. Graphs are used to illustrate points which can be made about a given set of data, and there are frequently different ways in which the point can be visualised. That said, whilst there is no one correct graph, there are usually a number of graphs which are clearly 'incorrect' for the type of data which are being represented, and we will consider how to spot some of these misrepresentations here.

8.2.1 Graphing discrete data

Table 8.1 Discrete and continuous data

Child	Age in months
Joe	86
Sam	96
Sameena	84
Isobelle	93
Iqbal	91
Shannon	91

Child	Age in months
Trevor	92
Gloria	88
Martha	94
Matthew	95

The first column in Table 8.1 is a set of children's names, which is a set of *discrete* nominal data. There is no connection between any one child's name and another. Age, on the other hand, is *continuous*. There is a linear relationship between the values, and, as discussed in Chapter 4, there is a clear connection between any two values. The graph which you choose to represent this data will depend on whether you wish to focus on the names or on the ages of the children. Discrete data such as children's names are usually graphed using a bar chart or a pie chart, whereas continuous data are usually shown using a histogram.

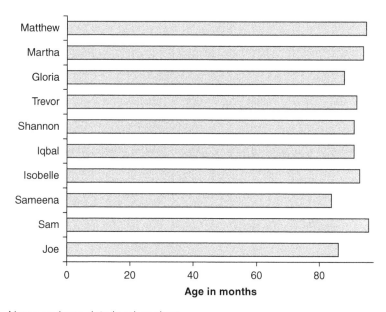

Figure 8.1 Name and age data in a bar chart

Figures 8.1 and 8.2 show the name and age data in bar charts. In this case, Figure 8.2 is slightly easier to read and it is immediately obvious that Sam is the oldest and Sameena is the youngest child. Bar charts can be drawn either vertically or horizontally; horizontal charts are sometimes easier to read, particularly if the category names are lengthy or unfamiliar, and if there are a large number of bars. With a bar chart, it is usually difficult to see the distribution of the data.

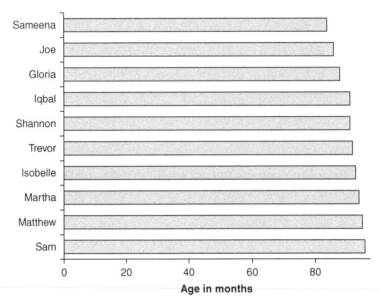

Figure 8.2 Name and age data in a bar chart

Pie charts are frequently used to show discrete data, and on many occasions they can provide a useful overview of the way the categories are distributed. Modern computer software has made the creation of pie charts effortless, and they often provide useful visualisations of data. In this case, however, a pie chart would simply consist of 10 equally sized sections of a circle and would not provide any useful information.

Since age data is continuous, we could represent this data using a histogram. This does not use the names of the children – the second variable which is used is the frequency of any given range of values, as shown in Figure 8.3.

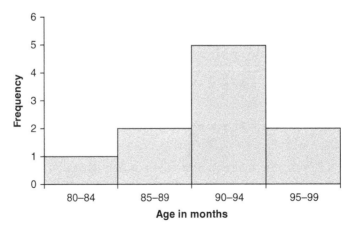

Figure 8.3 Distribution of ages

Databusting for schools

Figure 8.3 shows the distribution of ages, which allows us to see that most children's ages are in the range of 90 to 94 months. There are different ways to draw histograms, however, and it would be perfectly legitimate to draw histograms with groups of ranges of, for example, 4 or 6 months. Both of these histograms would show a slightly different distribution.

Of these graphs, Figures 8.2 and 8.3 are the most sensible visual representations of the data. They are quite different, however, and each has its benefits and drawbacks. The bar chart keeps all of the raw data and makes it easy to see the children's relative ages at a glance. The histogram shows the distribution of the age data and makes it clear roughly how old the class are. The choice of which graph you might use depends entirely on which aspect of the data you wish to highlight.

Table 8.2   Discrete transport use data

Mode of transport	Frequency
Car	8
Walk	7
Bicycle	5
Public transport	5
Other	5

The data in Table 8.2 is once again discrete and shows the methods of transport used by a class of children travelling to school. It would probably make sense to start by creating a bar chart of this data, as shown in Figure 8.4. Since there are

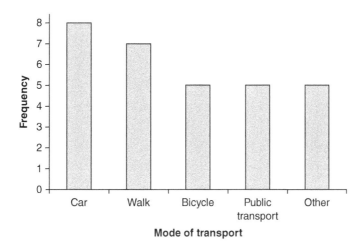

Figure 8.4   Bar chart: travelling to school

relatively few bars, with easy to comprehend categories, this probably makes more sense as a vertical chart rather than a horizontal one.

In the previous data set, there was no logical order to the headings. In this case, however, it might be argued that the headings imply a distance travelled: those travelling on foot or by bicycle might be assumed to live closer to the school. If this is felt to matter, the data could be redrawn as in Figure 8.5.

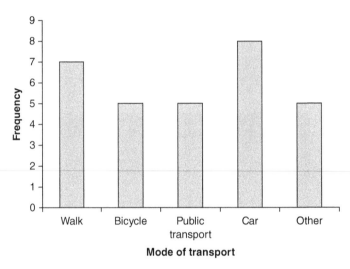

Figure 8.5 Bar chart: travelling to school

It would be possible to create a line graph using this data, as in Figure 8.6.

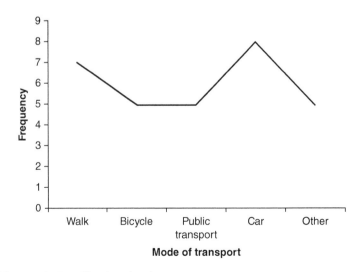

Figure 8.6 Line graph: travelling to school

Line graphs indicate a direct connection between different points and should therefore only be used for continuous data. To draw a graph such as Figure 8.6 implies that each point on the line means something, which is clearly not the case. If the line connects two measurements of a child's height, for example, then at some point in time, the child will have actually been the height indicated at every point on the line. This isn't the case with discrete data, where there is no such correlation, and this makes a line graph inappropriate in this case.

In education data, line graphs are often used to show trends over time. These types of time graphs need to be treated with care, however. Where examination results are shown over a number of years, the results are for entirely different cohorts of children. In many cases, the cohorts are quite different in make-up, and this can lead to time graphs which show considerable variation over time simply because the children who have generated the data each year are different. Time graphs should only be used when the underlying data is robust enough to be used in this way.

Box 8.1 Creating different impressions with the same data

The choice of the scales which you use for both the x-axis and the y-axis makes a huge difference to the impression you make with a graph. This is very clear when you look at the graphs below, which all represent the same data set. Using a 'stretched' or 'compressed' scale on one axis gives a completely different impression, and it is possible to exaggerate small differences or to compress large ones.

Modern computer software allows you to create an image of a graph very easily, and it is possible to exaggerate the height or width of the graph by simply changing the ratio of the axes. Be very careful, therefore, when you are reading graphs, as you may find that the impression you are given has been chosen to potentially mislead you.

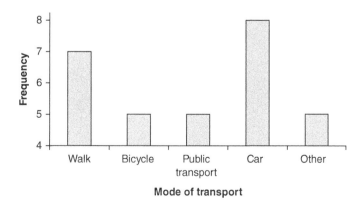

Figure 8.7 Bar chart: travelling to school

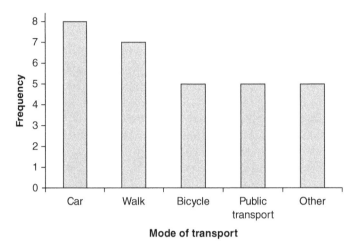

Figure 8.8   Bar chart: travelling to school

The two bar charts in Figures 8.7 and 8.8 show the importance of using the correct starting point for the y-axis. Figure 8.7, which starts at four rather than zero, leaves you with the impression that the relative differences between the values of the categories are considerably larger than they actually are. Figure 8.8 shows the bars starting from zero; the relative differences now look much smaller than they do in Figure 8.7. Modern computer software makes this kind of misleading y-axis surprisingly common, as many graphs are generated with truncated y-axes rather than starting from zero.

Where it is deemed necessary to show a truncated y-axis – usually to highlight marginal changes in large values – the usual practice is to 'break' the y-axis to ensure that the reader is fully aware that the y-axis may be misleading. Figure 8.9 shows how this might look. But be very wary of graphs with truncated y-axes as they often imply much greater differences than are the case.

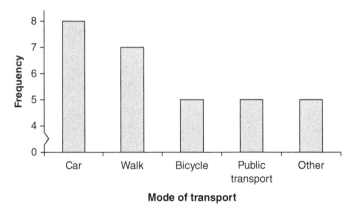

Figure 8.9   Bar chart: travelling to school

Databusting for schools

Discrete data is often shown in a pie chart, which highlights the proportions of a data set in each category. Each section of a pie chart should be meaningful, and the relative proportions between the categories should be clear at a glance. As you can see in Figure 8.10, the proportions in this data set lend themselves to being represented via a pie chart.

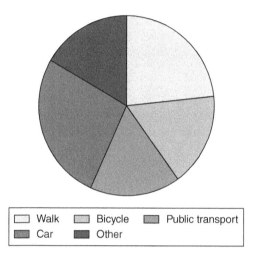

Figure 8.10 Pie chart of a data set: travelling to school

Figures 8.8 and 8.10 are the most sensible visual representations of the data here. Figure 8.8 keeps the original data and shows the relative differences between the modes of transport. Figure 8.10 shows the differences between the proportions of children using each mode of transport. Once again, the choice of which graph is used to illustrate the data set depends on what you wish to highlight.

8.3 Working with proportions

As was noted in Chapter 4, percentages are often used to help to make sense of the relative differences between numbers. Most of us find it difficult to imagine parts of a whole, and numbers which use tenths, hundreds, and so on, are difficult to visualise. Percentages – created by simply multiplying a number by 100 and using '%' to remind you to divide the percentage by 100 to get the decimal number – make comparing proportions much easier. Many people find it a great deal easier to think of 35% of a total than to think of the decimal number 0.35 multiplied by the total. Shoppers, for example, clearly find it easier to comprehend '20% off' than they would '0.2 reduction' (and the percentage has the advantage – for retailers – of appearing to be a much bigger discount).

Fractions are often easier to visualise than either percentages or decimals, but are much harder to compare when their denominators are different. As a result, we often find that converting numbers to percentages, and then creating visual displays of those percentages, makes it much easier to understand the underlying patterns in data.

But percentages can be both confusing and misleading, and they need to be treated with care. Table 8.3 shows the kind of data set which lends itself to being summarised using percentages. We will look at using percentages before discussing the various pitfalls which working with percentages introduces.

Table 8.3 Absence data

Number of sessions absent	Year 1	Year 2
0–9	100	110
10–19	120	121
20–29	115	116
30–39	45	46
40+	20	22

The changes in Table 8.3 are difficult to draw out from the numbers involved, especially since the figures vary so widely – in this case, from 20 up to 121 children. Most children miss around 10–19 sessions each year, but what is the underlying picture year on year? Is the picture of overall absence improving or not?

Percentages lend themselves to this type of problem and help to show the changes which have happened year on year. The annual changes for each category are as follows:

0–9 sessions = (110 – 100) ÷ 100 = 10 ÷ 100 = 0.1 = 10%

10–19 sessions = (121 – 120) ÷ 120 = 1 ÷ 120 = 0.008333 = 0.83%

20–29 sessions = (116 – 115) ÷ 115 = 1 ÷ 115 = 0.008696 = 0.87%

30–39 sessions = (46 – 45) ÷ 45 = 1 ÷ 45 = 0.02222 = 2.22%

40+ sessions = (22 – 20) ÷ 20 = 2 ÷ 20 = 0.1 = 10%

Using the percentage changes, the numbers of children absent in each category's year-on-year figures look somewhat different. The number of children missing 40 or more sessions has increased by one tenth as much again, whereas the number of those missing 10–29 sessions has increased by under 1%. And whilst the differences in numbers which were very small to begin with look more dramatic when presented this way, the eagle-eyed will also have noticed that all of the figures have increased, however. This indicates that the number of children in each category in the second year is greater than it was in Year 1 (there is an overall increase, from 400 children in Year 1 and 415 children in Year 2), which has an immediate distorting effect.

The change in pupil numbers represents a 3.75% increase across the board. Whilst it is possible to account for this change in the overall figure, the very wide difference between the smaller and the higher figures involved makes this somewhat complicated. As ever, with a broader focus, some detail is lost.

In this case, we could go back to looking at the annual figures and calculate the percentage in each category relative to the number of children as a whole. This would look like Table 8.4.

Table 8.4   Percentage in each category relative to number of children as a whole

Number of sessions absent	Year 1	Year 2
0–9	25.00%	26.51%
10–19	30.00%	29.16%
20–29	28.75%	27.95%
30–39	11.25%	11.08%
40+	5.00%	5.30%

Looking at the figures in Table 8.4, we can see that the percentage in each category has changed by relatively small amounts. These changes could, in turn, be summarised as per Table 8.5, which shows quite a different picture.

Table 8.5   Annual changes shown by percentage increase/decrease

Sessions absent	Annual change
0–9	(26.51% – 25.00%) ÷ 25.00% = 6%
10–19	(29.16% – 30.00%) ÷ 30.00% = –3%
20–29	(27.95% – 28.75%) ÷ 28.75% = –3%
30–39	(11.08% – 11.25%) ÷ 11.25% = –1%
More	(5.30% – 5.00%) ÷ 5.00% = 6%

The way these figures are presented depends on your scruples and the point which you want to make. Very small changes in raw data can seem very large when considered as percentage changes. Larger changes in underlying data can appear smaller when presented as changes in overall percentages. Looking at data in a particular way can obscure lines of inquiry which might be being ignored – in this case, the question as to why the increase in pupil numbers has resulted in more children who miss 40+ sessions compared to the picture painted by the Year 1 data.

A further complication can arise when the effects are exaggerated, either deliberately or accidentally. If we were to look at the actual numbers of sessions missed by the children in our example, they might look like Table 8.6.

Table 8.6   Actual numbers of sessions missed

Number of sessions absent	Year 1	Year 2	Change
0–9	500	770	54%
10–19	1800	1694	–5.89%
20–29	2875	2668	–7.20%
30–39	1575	1564	–0.70%
40+	900	968	7.56%

So, those who missed 0 to 9 sessions over the year missed a total of 500 sessions in Year 1 and 770 sessions in Year 2, which represents 270 more sessions missed by this group. This group missed an additional 54% of sessions compared to Year 1, whereas the 68 sessions missed by all those in the 'More than 40' category represented a 7.56% increase; 270 more sessions is almost four times more than the 68 sessions, but 54% is more than seven times bigger than the 7.56% increase. Which is more interesting – the overall change in underlying data or the percentage change in each category?

A further issue with using percentages to show proportions is that there are usually a number of choices of figures which could be used. Two figures are required to find a proportion – a numerator and a denominator – and there is a lot of leeway in the choice which can be made, particularly when we are looking at complicated real-world problems. In the last example, we began by considering the proportion represented by the number of missed sessions in each category compared to the total number of sessions which were missed. We could choose another denominator, however. For example, we could compare the proportion of sessions missed to the total number of sessions over a school year.

In this case, there are 400 children who attend two sessions a day, five days a week for 38 weeks. This is 190 sessions per child, or 152,000 sessions a year. Using this figure as a denominator, the number of sessions missed can be seen in Table 8.7.

Table 8.7   Proportion missed of the total number of sessions over a school year

Number of sessions absent	Year 1	Year 2	Change
0–9	0.33%	0.49%	48.43%
10–19	1.18%	1.07%	−9.29%
20–29	1.89%	1.69%	−10.55%
30–39	1.04%	0.99%	−4.29%
40+	0.59%	0.61%	3.67%

These kinds of difficulties appear regularly when looking at information presented using percentages. This is one reason why summary statistics are best presented along with raw data so that anyone reading the information presented can explore the analysis themselves. It is also why summaries, particularly those written for newspapers or magazines, should generally be treated with scepticism in the first instance. It is simply too easy to mislead, either willfully or accidentally, using percentages and proportions.

One particular point to notice with percentages is the difference between a percentage change and a change in percentage points. A change from 80% to 90% represents a 12.5% increase. It can also be presented as a 10 percentage point increase. In addition, a change from 90% to 80% represents an 11.1% *decrease*. And it is not possible to reverse a percentage by using the same percentage to change a figure back – 10% more than 100 cannot be reversed by reducing the answer by 10% (10% less than 110 is not 100!). All of this means that it pays to be careful both when presenting figures using percentages and when interpreting data presented using them.

8.4 Mobility and missing data

One perennial problem in education data is that schools and their populations are fairly fluid. Children move in and out of schools all the time, and groups, on whom data is based, keep changing. This causes immense problems when comparing numbers over time. What's more, the differences are not random, as those who move between schools outside of the usual entry and exit points tend to be dissimilar to those who do not.

Movement of children is referred to as 'mobility' and this is measured in various different ways. One way is to add the number of children leaving a school to those who join, and to divide this by the number of children in the school (as with the discussion about proportions in section 8.2 above, the point at which any or all of these numbers are measured changes the calculation, of course). RAISEonline/ASP, on the other hand, provides statistics for pupil mobility at Key Stage 2 based on the number of children on roll for all of Years 5 and 6.

Research into pupil mobility suggests that just under 5% of children move school between any given school years, and that those who move school are different to the school population as a whole:

> Pupils from lower social background are more likely to switch schools than other pupils, and this is true for pupils at all stages of schooling; pupils who change schools are more likely to have a low previous academic attainment record than pupils who do not change schools; pupils placed in schools with high Key Stage performance levels move less than pupils from lower performance schools; pupils who move school and home simultaneously are typically more socially disadvantaged than otherwise. (Machin et al., 2006: 3)

In addition to these problems, the data held for children in school is often of variable quality – some is incorrectly recorded or simply missing, particularly for those who move into school outside the usual starting points. Children who have entered school from other parts of the UK, from outside of the country or from the independent sector frequently join with no comparable attainment data. These children are not drawn from the same population as those already in the school, and therefore their missing data means that any analysis based on the remaining children for whom data is available has to be treated with caution.

8.5 Selective use of measures of central tendency

We looked at measures of central tendency in Chapters 5 and 8. The simplest measures are the mean, the mode and the median, and care needs to be taken with these measures, as they can easily obscure the underlying data. Take the following statement:

> This year, our increased KS2 average scores show that children are making greater gains in mathematics.

The common error here is to believe that the average provides information about the spread of values on which the average is based. But this is not the case. There simply is no information about the spread contained within the average, as the following example – in which the average score rises but the majority of children actually have lower scores – shows.

A small group of students took a spelling test. In the first week, all of the children scored 10 out of 20. In the second week, one child scored 20 out of 20, but the other students scored 9 marks.

Week 1: $(10 + 10 + 10 + 10 + 10 + 10) \div 6 = 10$

Week 2: $(20 + 9 + 9 + 9 + 9 + 9) \div 6 = 10.8$

The average mark has increased to 10.8, but five out of the six students actually scored less than they did in the first week.

The opposite situation is equally problematic, and unusual distributions of results can obscure successes. Take, for example, a calculation of average progress for a cohort with a student who does not sit their GCSE English examination due to illness. If this child is recorded as having made zero progress, but remains within the calculations of overall progress, their zero score will lower the overall average score. Whilst this case is unlikely – and this child's progress score would be removed from progress calculations – a substantial minority of children often make less progress than expected for a number of reasons beyond the control of the school. Where this is the case, overall good progress can be obscured by the unusually low progress of a small number of students.

8.6 Problems with 'significance'

We looked closely at using statistical significance in Chapter 6. Tests of significance are a valuable tool for many scientists, and hypothesis testing is used in a wide variety of fields. The appeal of tests of significance is simple. We often want to know whether a given sample is similar or different to the population from which it is drawn. Measuring entire populations is frequently expensive and time-consuming. Developing a hypothesis and testing whether it is true is extremely useful. Tests of significance seem therefore to offer many advantages when attempting to make sense of complex real-world situations.

Unfortunately, the use of significance testing – more properly referred to as using sampling theory – is not without controversy. There is a great deal of confusion about significance testing, as we touched on in Chapter 2. Following are a number of problems which have been identified.

Significance testing requires randomly distributed samples from a population.

It is a fundamental requirement of the use of statistical significance that a randomly distributed sample is tested against a hypothesis. Statisticians use the phrase 'independently and identically distributed' (i.i.d.) when referring to randomly distributed variables. Each random variable must have the same probability distribution as any other random variable, and all of the variables must be independent of each other. In layman's terms, this means that there is an equal likelihood that any given random variable appears within a sample, and that the fact that any one case appears in a sample does not affect the probability of any other case appearing in the sample.

Where one is testing a bowl of soup, for example, a spoonful of the soup contains particles which are equally likely to have been scooped up, and each particle has no effect on any other. If one then did something to this spoonful of soup, and compared the results to a second random sample of the soup, one could use significance testing.

In education, students are very rarely i.i.d., particularly when they are grouped in classes within schools. This means that it makes no sense whatsoever to use tests of significance to suggest that any difference between classes means anything other than that the children in different classes are simply different. It isn't possible to say, as RAISEonline/ASP does, that one group of children is 'significantly above' or 'significantly below' any other group. They might have higher or lower results than the national student population, but we know nothing other than that they have higher or lower results than the national student population: tests of statistical significance are not justified in this situation.

We want to know whether two samples are different, but we can only make assumptions about populations based on samples.

Sampling theory is often used to make inferences about a population based on a small sample of that population. These inferences are then used to test whether any difference with a second sample would also be found in the population from which the samples are taken. So, for example, if we draw three yellow and seven blue balls from a bag of 1,000 balls, we might use this information to make inferences about the number of yellow and blue balls there are in the bag. This is what sampling theory relies on: being able to use samples to make inferences about populations. Having made an inference, we then test to see whether that sample is similar to the assumed population.

The problem with this is that we simply don't know what the population actually looks like, and we can't work this out from the sample. In our soup example above, any large enough sample of the soup is, to all intents and purposes, identical to the soup population. But with the relatively small number of balls in the bag, or of children in schools, this simply isn't the case. The bag may also contain red, white and blue balls for all we know.

It would be *much* simpler to calculate the likelihood of drawing three yellow and seven blue balls from a bag we *know* to contain 600 yellow and 400 blue balls, and in fact this is a simple exercise in probability. What's more, this is what most hypothesis testing boils down to: using assumptions about the population made using one sample, we find the likelihood that a difference at least as large as the one found in the first sample will be found in the second sample.

This isn't very useful, however. What we really want to know is whether there is a difference between the two samples, whereas what we have found is the probability of getting the second sample, given the assumptions made about the population using the first sample.

If this feels confusing, then you are in good company, as many people misunderstand sample theory and make simple errors as a result. Tests of significance rely on using a sample to make predictions about a population, and then using this prediction to test whether a second sample is different to the first.

8.6.1 Misunderstanding p-values

There is a large body of literature to show that most researchers who use p-values don't understand them, and those who find them difficult to understand are in good company. The precise meaning of a p-value is often misunderstood because it is the product of a complicated set of assumptions, underlying theory and multifaceted calculations. Any definition is therefore extremely complex to summarise.

Essentially, however, a p-value is a 'statistical summary of the compatibility between the observed data and what we would predict or expect to see if we knew the entire statistical model (*all* the assumptions used to compute the *P* value) were correct' (Greenland et al., 2016: 339). A p-value, therefore, is, to a large extent, a summary of probability. It is, however, extremely hard to summarise the implications of what p-values represent.

It is much easier to show the mistaken beliefs which many writers and researchers have about p-values, and what many people *think* p-values represent. One of the most common interpretations is that a p-value represents the probability that an observed result in a sample will be erroneously labelled as being different because of sampling and measurement error.

The OECD's PISA programme, for example, suggests that when it tests samples:

Each separate test follows the convention that, if in fact there is no real difference between two populations, there is no more than a 5 per cent probability that an observed difference between the two samples will erroneously suggest that the populations are different as the result of sampling and measurement error. (OECD, 2004: 58)

But this isn't quite correct, however. All that a p-value below 5% indicates is that there is a small chance of obtaining a result at least as extreme as the one observed (all other assumptions being valid). Flagging results as 'significant' and suggesting that tests of significance based on p-value might indicate that 'populations are different' because p is less than 0.05 all too often lead to confusion and misinterpretation.

8.6.2 Misunderstanding statistical significance

The use of p-values to calculate the probability that a null hypothesis might be false is, far too often, reduced to an idea of results being 'statistically significant'. The concept of 'statistical significance' is extraordinarily difficult to define and to summarise. It is also extremely easy to misinterpret. This is in part because in everyday use, as we noted in Chapter 2, 'significant' means 'important' or 'momentous', whereas 'statistically significant' results merely indicate success or failure in a (complicated and robust) mechanical test, and carry no inherent value judgement; at best, they mean that a result is of interest and worthy of further exploration.

The OECD's attempts to define 'statistically significant' provide a good example of the difficultly involved:

> In the tables and charts used in this report, differences are labelled as statistically significant when a difference of that size, or larger, would be observed less than 5 per cent of the time, if there was actually no difference in corresponding population values. (OECD, 2004: 329)

Correctly interpreted, this simply means that a statistically significant result is unusual, although there is a small but entirely reasonable chance that it might represent a result which is drawn from the population under consideration. 'Statistically significant' results do not imply any difference, as many assume. Rolling a one followed by a six on a die has a considerably lower than 5% chance of occurring, for example, but this does not provide any evidence that the die is biased in any way.

What is more, the somewhat arbitrary cut-off of 'significance at the 5% level' follows the suggestion made by pioneering statistician Ronald Fischer (Fischer, 1935: 13), who suggested that this was a convenient level at which to reject the null hypothesis (that there is no discernible difference between a sample and a population). Even Fischer recommended that the significance level be set according to the circumstances of a particular research design.

Since Fischer and others popularised the idea of significance testing, there has been an ongoing debate about the appropriate significance level, with many suggesting that tests of significance should use, for example, a 1% cut-off. The widespread use of a 5% cut-off in the recent past has worried many of those who are able to take a wider perspective on the effect of the simplistic use of tests of significance.

Concerns about many researchers' 'convenient, yet ill-founded strategy of claiming conclusive research findings solely on the basis of a single study assessed by formal statistical significance, typically for a p-value less than 0.05', has been raised by Ioannidis and others. As Ioannidis says in his landmark study which focuses on medical research, 'Why most published research findings are false' (2005), 'Research is not most appropriately represented and summarized by p-values, but, unfortunately, there is a widespread notion that medical research articles should be interpreted based only on p-values'.

Academic journals, which entrenched the use of p-values for a long period, requiring research to report p-values, and in most cases reported only those studies which identified results which passed a test of significance, have begun to change the way they view p-values. Academic journal *Basic and Applied Social Psychology* has gone the furthest so far, announcing in early 2015 that it would no longer publish papers containing p-values. In 2016, the influential American Statistical Association released a statement on statistical significance and p-values, in which it issued principles to guide the use of p-values, advising that they cannot determine whether a hypothesis is true or whether results are important.

ASA president Jessica Utts made the Association's position clear:

Over time it appears the p-value has become a gatekeeper for whether work is publishable, at least in some fields. This apparent editorial bias leads to the 'file-drawer effect,' in which research with statistically significant outcomes are much more likely to get published, while other work that might well be just as important scientifically is never seen in print. It also leads to practices called by such names as 'p-hacking' and 'data dredging' that emphasize the search for small p-values over other statistical and scientific reasoning. (2016: 1)

At school level, the most egregious use of 'statistical significance' is often in data sets such as RAISEonline/ASP (see Chapter 2), in which statistically illiterate 'tests of significance' are used (which test samples which are not identically and independently distributed against population statistics which contain no sampling error) and then claim that 'Green shading indicates that the school value is significantly above the national value. Blue shading indicates that the school value is significantly below the national value' (DfE, 2016: 33). At best, figures shaded in this way simply indicate that a result is relatively high or relatively low, but offer no possible interpretation whatsoever as to the reason why this might be.

8.6.3 Misunderstanding confidence intervals

When using tests of statistical significance to identify results worthy of further investigation, a confidence interval is often calculated to allow for easy identification of results which seem unusual, or to suggest that a particular outcome is 'significant'. Confidence intervals are mechanical calculations (see Chapter 6) based on derived statistics which simply indicate the range of results which would, given the distribution of potential results which is postulated via earlier calculations, be expected in 95% of cases. Results outside of any confidence interval are once more 'worthy of investigation' rather than 'significant' as a lay person would understand the term.

Data sets such as RAISEonline/ASP, once again, as with their incorrect use of the statistical concept of 'significance', incorrectly imply that a data point outside a confidence interval is definitively 'better' or 'worse' than would normally be expected.

8.6.4 Being extremely wary of significance testing

In conclusion, there are a great many reasons why we should be extremely wary of any claims of statistical significance. The statistics involved are complex and rely on conditions which are frequently not in place. Too often, results which are unusual are treated as if they were 'educationally significant' when there is no support for such a conclusion.

With modern education data, we often have information for the entire population, and statistics which are based on dealing with inherent error in random sampling are simply irrelevant. Whilst some have postulated theoretical super-populations to manage this problem, they lead off into equally irrelevant suppositions about the educational performance of small cohorts in particular schools.

One of the most trenchant critics of null hypothesis significance testing (NHST) is Professor Stephen Gorard, who has waged an active campaign to educate those who use NHST for problems with 'significance'. As Gorard says, 'Statistical testing is often inappropriate, and is always insufficient to help to decide whether one set of measures is markedly greater than another' (2013: 181). Gorard suggests that 'we should insist on no more significance tests with non-probability samples, including population data, convenience, opportunity or incomplete samples, or any data with measurement error or missing values' (p. 181).

The issues with NHST are not new and have been understood and discussed since the technique was first introduced. This is a complex area of analysis, which is – in too many cases – misunderstood and misapplied. The last word should go to the American Statistical Association, which notes that, 'Statisticians and others have been sounding the alarm about these matters for decades, to little avail' (Wasserstein and Lazar, 2016: 130).

8.7 The problems with correlational statistics

Once you understand the problems with correlational statistics, you begin to see examples of misguided and incorrect conclusions almost everywhere. The biggest and most common misconception is so well known that it is most often summarised in the pithy truism that 'correlation does not imply causation'. Websites have been constructed gathering together correlated data sets which clearly have no causative effect, and books have been published showing how easily spurious correlations can be found, and yet people are still irresistibly drawn to conclusions based on little more than correlation.

To be absolutely clear about spurious correlations, we need to explain exactly what they are and how they are misinterpreted. It is also useful to look at typical misconceptions which many of us make when we look at statistics which are correlated.

As we explored in Chapter 7, data are said to be correlated when there is a pattern which seems to link two separate measurements. Positive correlations are those in which measurements rise or fall in both cases, and negative correlations are those in which one measurement descends as the other measurement rises. Bits of data which follow no pattern – those which result in a random scatter graph – have no correlation.

Those looking at data are frequently looking for explanations as to why correlations might arise. We are all drawn to the search for a cause to explain the phenomena we observe. Unfortunately, correlation on its own tells us very little about causation. Whilst it is possible to design experimental projects to identify causation, this has its limits, and in the field of educational research – as with much of social science – data is often noisy and difficult to interpret.

8.7.1 The problem with reverse causation

For those of us who live in temperate climates, rain is a feature of our everyday lives. We have many ways to deal with precipitation, and most of us do what we can to avoid the minor inconvenience which rain causes. But what causes rain? There are clear scientific explanations, of course, and the way that clouds form, condense and water falls as rain is well understood.

But what if you did not understand the science? Those who experience rainfall might notice the clouds, but they will spot many other phenomena too. When it rains, people start to carry and open umbrellas; vehicles start to use windscreen wipers; people's dress changes as they opt to don waterproof clothing.

Wet weather is clearly positively correlated with umbrellas, windscreen wiper use and the appearance of waterproofs. It is a simple step to then assume that these things cause the rain, especially if the data set we use to identify the correlation contains snapshots of different periods of time which do not capture the transition between episodes of wet and dry weather. This simple fallacy is labelled 'reverse causation' and is the misconception that, because A and B are correlated, A must cause B. This is, of course, not necessarily the case.

Reverse causation is so widespread it has become known as part of 'the halo effect', which author Phil Rosenzweig summarises in *The Halo Effect* (2007: 64) by saying that 'so many of the things that we – managers, journalists, professors, and consultants – commonly think contribute to company performance are often attributions based on performance'.

Rosenzweig called reverse causation 'the delusion of the wrong end of the stick' and gives, as an example, the observation that, in recent years, successful companies have developed corporate social responsibility (CSR) policies. This has led many business analysts to recommend that companies that wish to become successful should introduce CSR policies. As Rosenzweig notes, companies which make excess profits are likely to have money to spend on CSR.

In education, there are countless examples of schools which are well-run, stable and successful, and therefore are able to introduce particular practices which are then interpreted as being the reason for the overall success of the school. For example, under then new head teacher Sir Anthony Seldon, Wellington College in Berkshire introduced a much-publicised wellbeing programme in 2005. This was then heralded as a key part of the school's success over the following decade, as it became an award-winning academic powerhouse. Wellbeing clearly caused better results, in the eyes of many observers, whereas the introduction and development of the wellbeing programme were equally likely to have been possible due to the better results the school was able to post.

Mistaken reverse causation can frequently arise due to a third factor which causes, or enables, both A and B. In the case of Wellington College, in 2006 the school moved from only admitting girls into its sixth form to becoming fully co-educational. As David Turner notes in *The Old Boys: The Decline and Rise of the Public School* (2015: 210), 'Girls improved boys' schools. They boosted academic results, since the boys' schools tended to pick the academically most distinguished girls. They changed the culture of the boys' schools forever'. This did not stop the wellbeing programme – rather than the wider pool of talent from which the academically selective school draws its pupils, allied to the general success of the school – being lauded, whilst the more able intake was quietly ignored.

8.7.2 The problem with bidirectional causation

In a competitive society, we frequently hear of research which attempts to isolate reasons for success. One of the key measures of success, for example, is earnings, and a second is general health. Both of these measures are strongly correlated. Wealthy people tend to live longer and those who live longer tend to be wealthy.

Of course, not all wealthy people are healthy, and vice versa. The overall pattern says little about any given individual within the distribution of a population. What the distribution does suggest, however, is that wealth and health are linked. Without a lot of further analysis and experimentation, we can't assign causality, however. It isn't immediately clear whether one variable causes the other.

In an educational context, we tend to find variations of the same pattern. Those who are wealthy tend to do better at school. Those who do well at school tend to be wealthy. But, once again, the causality is not a given. We don't quite know which variable, if either, directly influences the other. It is also well established that schools which are popular with parents tend to be those with better academic results. Schools with better academic results tend to be popular with parents. But we also know that more motivated parents tend to have children who get better grades in school. So do popular schools cause their intake to get better grades, or does a high-achieving intake make a school more popular? Without some kind of experimental data, the likelihood is that it will be impossible to separate correlation and causation.

8.7.3 The problem of confounding factor causation

Every year, sales of sun cream rise as sales of swimwear rise. When people stop buying swimwear, they tend to stop buying sun cream too. Whilst these two data sets are correlated, they are clearly being driven by a third factor, which is the annual weather cycle. As days get longer and warmer, people are more likely to want to spend time in the sun and in water. As winter approaches, both decrease. The confounding factor drives both sales of sun cream and sales of swimwear.

Educational statistics often bring together a number of variables, such as age, ethnicity, special educational needs status and proxies for wealth. It is generally harder to gather data on confounding factors such as neuroticism, conscientiousness, openness to experience, extraversion and agreeableness – the 'big five' personality traits which many psychologists consider to be the basic dimensions of personality. Where groups of children have high levels of 'positive' personality traits, their educational achievement is likely to be relatively high. They are likely to be successful in other areas of life such as arts and sports too. Anecdotally, one often finds that head boys and head girls tend to be captains of sports teams and leading figures in the arts, as well as being high academic achievers. In many cases, however, the confounding factors which underpin relative success or failure can be obscured.

8.7.4 The problems with lines of best fit

Many statistics attempt to summarise complicated data which is often difficult to interpret. Regression – the summary of correlations resulting in a single formula which describes a line of best fit – can be misleading, and we need to take care when interpreting results. Whilst it can be useful to use regression to make assumptions about patterns within data, reducing data in this way can be problematic.

Regression is used, for example, to estimate likely future grades based on prior attainment. Value Added models use regression to make assumptions about the progress which children make as they go through school. These models summarise vast and complicated data sets, and care needs to be taken not to be misled.

One of the best demonstrations of the problems of lines of best fit was produced by Francis Anscombe in the early 1970s. Anscombe wanted to show that graphing data before analysing it was extremely important, and that outliers can have a distorting effect on the statistical properties of data. He generated four sets of data which have identical means, sample variances, correlations and lines of regression, but which have very different distributions with graphs using scatterplots (Anscombe, 1973).

His data has the summary statistics given in Table 8.8.

Table 8.8   Anscombe's summary statistics

Property	Value	Accuracy
Mean of x	9	exact
Sample variance of x	11	exact
Mean of y	7.5	to 2 decimal places
Sample variance of y	4.125	plus/minus 0.003
Correlation between x and y	0.816	to 3 decimal places
Linear regression line	$y = 3.00 + 0.500x$	to 2 and 3 decimal places, respectively

The data on which the quartet are based is shown in Table 8.9.

Table 8.9   Anscombe's quartet

I		II		III		IV	
X	Y	x	Y	x	y	x	y
10	8.04	10	9.14	10	7.46	8	6.58
8	6.95	8	8.14	8	6.77	8	5.76
13	7.58	13	8.74	13	12.74	8	7.71
9	8.81	9	8.77	9	7.11	8	8.84
11	8.33	11	9.26	11	7.81	8	8.47
14	9.96	14	8.1	14	8.84	8	7.04
6	7.24	6	6.13	6	6.08	8	5.25
4	4.26	4	3.1	4	5.39	19	12.5

I		II		III		IV	
X	Y	x	Y	x	y	x	y
12	10.84	12	9.13	12	8.15	8	5.56
7	4.82	7	7.26	7	6.42	8	7.91
5	5.68	5	4.74	5	5.73	8	6.89

The graphs of Anscombe's quartet demonstrate how different the scatterplots of these data are.

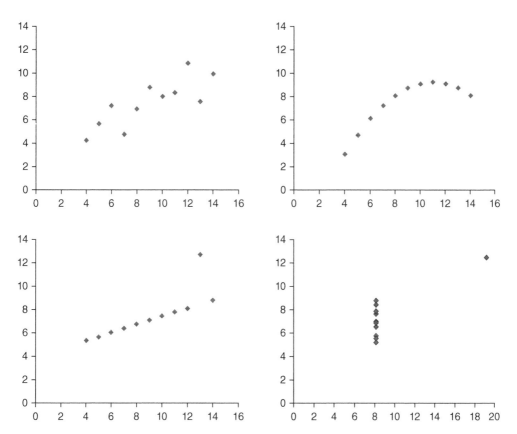

Figure 8.11 Anscombe's quartet

All of the scatter graphs have the same summary statistics, with the same line of best fit. The first graph appears to show a simple linear relationship, with data which is distributed normally. The second graph is clearly not normally distributed, although there is an obvious relationship between the variables. The third graph has been affected by a clear outlier, which has quite obviously influenced the line of best fit. The final graph shows that an outlier can produce a high correlation coefficient even though there is no linear relationship.

Anscombe's quartet is a clear call to use visualisations of data as well as summary statistics when attempting to summarise and interpret data sets, and a warning that lines of best fit can be highly misleading unless treated with care and a critical eye.

8.7.5 Problems with overfitting

So far, we have primarily looked at linear regression, in which a straight line is used to summarise the line of best fit between two variables. Some bits of data have non-linear relationships, however, and the mathematics required to summarise their relationships are a little more complicated. A graph of cumulative income against share of population, for example, looks more like Figure 8.12, in which the relationship is clearly a curve.

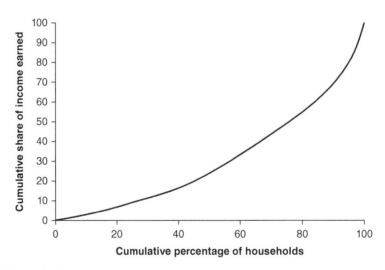

Figure 8.12 Lorentz Curve

Distributions of education data are often non-linear, as the graph of GCSE grades in Figure 8.13 shows.

It is possible to create a curved line of best fit which describes a mathematical relationship between variables. This can become a problem when sample data is 'overfitted' to the data, rather than providing an accurate model of the underlying population data. Data is said to be overfitted when the random error in any sample, rather than the underlying relationship, is described by a regression model.

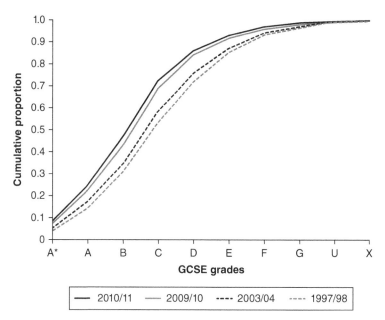

Figure 8.13   Cumulative proportion of GCSE grades

8.8 A framework for critically appraising research studies

Critical appraisal of a research study

Ben has been asked to review a study which has examined the efficacy of a particular approach to homework in secondary schools. The study seems persuasive and makes recommendations which would require a restructuring of Ben's school's homework policy. Ben is considering how to summarise what he has found in his reading of the paper. He is wondering how to present his findings.

In order to provide a clear critical appraisal of a study, Ben should use the following framework.

8.8.1 A critical appraisal framework

The critical appraisal framework has the following elements:

- a one-paragraph summary
- comments on the author, publisher, age of study
- a brief comment on the study design and main conclusion
- brief summaries of the paper
- introduction, including the objective, importance and relevance of the paper
- method, including the setting, subjects, method of sampling, controls (if any) and cases involved
- design – type of study and appropriateness, sample size and power
- data quality, including details of quality control, validity, data analysis appropriateness, response rate and missing data
- results – appropriate presentation, interpretation
- validity of the study, including whether results could be explained by chance, bias or are confounding; whether study is generalisable, whether results are relevant
- discussion of objectives, limitations, justification of conclusions, relevance and/or importance of results
- final comments on importance to school context, strengths and weaknesses.

8.9 Summary

Using data to provide information about real-world problems is clearly essential in much of the work we do in school. As numbers are frequently extremely abstract, we often find that data presented visually is much easier to interpret, and visual representations can help us to direct lines of enquiry which we might want to pursue. This chapter has given an introduction to the problems which may be encountered when interpreting data-based information, and should encourage you to read statistical representations critically.

A great deal of the more advanced statistics which you may encounter lean heavily on tests of significance, and you should now have the tools to view p-values and hypothesis testing with a critical eye. Whilst arguments about statistical significance are ongoing, you should understand the problems which misuse of statistics – either through design or misunderstanding – can lead to.

As you will now know, the phrase 'correlation does not imply causation' is paramount when considering conclusions based on data sets which correlate. You know some of the pitfalls which we can fall into when observing correlations, and the way in which very different data sets can generate surprisingly similar lines of best fit.

We concluded with a framework to critically appraise published studies, which should enable you to draw your own conclusions regarding a study's utility for you and your school.

References

American Statistical Association (ASA) (2016) 'American Statistical Association releases statement on statistical significance and p-values', *ASA News*, 7 March. Available at: www.amstat.org/asa/files/pdfs/P-ValueStatement.pdf. Accessed 29/1/18.

Anscombe, F.J. (1973) 'Graphs in statistical analysis', *The American Statistician,* 27(1): 17–21.

Department for Education (DfE) (2016) *RAISEonline Methodology Guidance*. London: DfE.

Fischer, R. (1935) *The Design of Experiments*. Edinburgh: Oliver and Boyd.

Goldacre, B. (2009) *Bad Science*. London: Fourth Estate.

Goldacre, B. (2013) *Building Evidence into Education*. London: DfE.

Gorard, S. (2013) *Research Design*. London: Sage Publications.

Greenland, S., Senn, S.J., Rothman, K.J., Carlin, J.B., Poole, C., Goodman, S.N. and Altman, D.G. (2016) 'Statistical tests, P values, confidence intervals, and power: a guide to misinterpretations', *European Journal of Epidemiology*, 31: 337–50.

Ioannidis, J.P.A. (2005) 'Why most published research findings are false', *PLoS Med*, 2(8): e124.

Machin, S., Telhaj, S. and Wilson, J. (2006) *The Mobility of English School Children*. London: Centre for the Economics of Education. Available at: http://cee.lse.ac.uk/ceedps/ceedp67.pdf

Organisation for Economic Co-operation and Development (OECD) (2004) *Learning for Tomorrow's World: First Results from PISA 2003*. Paris: OECD.

Rosenzweig, P. (2007) *The Halo Effect*. New York: Simon and Shuster.

Turner, D. (2015) *The Old Boys: The Decline and Rise of the Public School*. London: Yale University Press.

Wasserstein, R and Lazar, N. (2016) *The ASA's Statement on p-Values: Context, Process, and Purpose*. The American Statistician,70(2): 130.

9

DATA-BASED SCHOOL RESEARCH AND POLICY

USING DATA TO UNDERSTAND AND CHANGE EDUCATION

9.1 Introduction to the use of statistical data

This chapter will broaden out the discussion beyond the day-to-day work undertaken by teachers such as Kathryn and Ben and school governors such as Andrew and Samaya. It provides an extension of the ideas discussed in Chapter 2, in which we discussed the data currently generated within schools and the analysis provided by the government and other agencies. By the end of this chapter, you will have a much greater understanding of the development of the use of data in education, and a good sense of how we have got to where we currently are.

9.2 Development of the use of statistics in education

Statistics is, in origin, the collection and analysis of data about states; it is, in essence, data which is generated and collected by governments. Education statistics began to be collected in earnest in developed countries in the mid-19th century, in part due to the scientific congresses and great exhibitions of the Victorian period which were explicitly designed to share knowledge to enable further development both within and between countries. The USA created a government Department of Education in 1867; its main role was in the collection and dissemination of educational statistics, and the data which it was able to produce had an international impact:

> By the time of the Paris Exhibition in 1878, the United States was able to produce many reports and tables about its educational systems for display, and in doing so, began to shape the future of comparison through the exhibition medium. (Lawn, 2013: 13)

At this early stage, the data which individual US states produced was generated voluntarily and no state was compelled to collect or provide data. Much of the earliest education data was of low quality, relying on goodwill and leaving a wide interpretation of what was to be collected from and submitted to each state. Despite this, claims based on the information which was collected began to appear almost as soon as data was made available:

> It appears that a common school education adds fifty per cent, and such an additional education as can be obtained in most of our union schools and academies adds two hundred per cent to the productiveness of the ordinary unskilled labourer. (Bradley, 1879, cited in Lawn, 2013: 14)

The USA continued to innovate with its collection and use of statistics, and by the time of the World's Fair held in New York in 1939, a great deal of information about education was available to both the government and the general public.

Much of this early data concerned the numbers of teachers and of children in individual schools, and the buildings, equipment, and so on, which each school had at its disposal. The development of testing children's progress in school to create statistics which the government could use did not begin until the early 19th century.

The situation in the UK was markedly different. Central government did not collect much in the way of data in the early 19th century, and in the main any data which was collected was gathered by local education authorities. Collecting data centrally often caused political problems, as the central government Board of Education found when it collated data on the cost of elementary education per child in each English local area in the 1920s, and found wide variations in spending across the country.

The Scottish Education Department's 1948 report *Education in Scotland 1948* and the Ministry of Education's *Education in 1948* (covering England and Wales) greatly increased the data which was available, although this was generally concerned with costs and efficiency of the administration of the school system rather than the progress of the children being educated within it.

The post-Second World War period saw developments in the collection and analysis of education data as governments became more involved in the management and analysis of education itself. By 1961, the United Nations Educational, Scientific and Cultural Organisation (UNESCO) had published *A Manual of Educational Statistics*, and it began to issue an annual *Statistical Yearbook* in 1963.

Whilst the quality of data varied enormously from country to country, the rise in international data collection, comparison and development was inexorable and the use of data had become embedded within the business of education systems.

9.3 Edward Thorndike's influence

Much of modern thinking about education data has its roots in work pioneered by Edward Thorndike, whose three-volume *Educational Psychology*, published in 1913–14, was hugely influential in the USA and elsewhere. Over his long career, Thorndike's interests ranged from the practice of teaching to individual differences between students, and he was a driving force in the development of increasingly sophisticated tests of ability and aptitude in the USA. Thorndike was first and foremost interested in supporting those working in education by providing practical tools for use in day-to-day teaching, and his influence was widespread.

After completing an MA at Harvard in 1897, Thorndike's early work involved investigations into animal intelligence. He was critical of much of the thinking about intelligence which was then current, which he regarded as being based on anecdotal experience rather than scientific experimentation. Thorndike developed experiments to investigate the process of animal learning, and he was amongst the turn of the century pioneers who saw learning as a process of trial and error, response and reward, leading to neural adaptations which made appropriate responses to stimuli more likely in the future.

Thorndike was an influential figure in the field of psychometrics, the name given to the theory and technique of psychological measurement. Following the publication of Charles Darwin's *On the Origin of Species* in 1859, interest had increased massively in individual differences between humans, and in the difficulties inherent in measuring differences in populations. James McKeen Cattell, who supervised Thorndike's PhD at Columbia University, was one of a growing number of academics who helped to establish psychology as a legitimate science, largely by developing rigorous methods of measurement which enabled experimental psychology to flourish.

Cattell had worked in Germany and the UK, and his influence on Thorndike was clear. In order to move away from theorising based on anecdote, Thorndike needed to develop methods of measuring what had been learned. He published *An Introduction to the Theory of Mental and Social Measurements* (1904) which summarises much of what was then known about the complicated field of measuring individuals.

Thorndike's work on cognitive ability went hand in hand with his work on testing. Building on ideas developed by Alfred Binet in France, which introduced a scale of intelligence which the French government used to direct support to pupils who struggled to access the French school curriculum, Thorndike was a leading member of the committee commissioned to develop and administer tests which would help to classify US army recruits during the First World War.

In 1919, two million soldiers were assessed using the committee's tests, and three years later a million school children took similar assessments. Thorndike was, as with many psychometricians, always very careful to emphasise the limitations of the tests which were developed, and he continued to adapt and refine the tests which he had introduced.

As Thorndike's work on measurement progressed, he developed standardised achievement tests, using norms based on samples of students. Tests were created for students of all ages, from primary through to secondary school, and beyond into further and higher education. By 1921, two million American children had taken standardised tests of achievement and, in the USA, the testing of pupil achievement was widespread.

As Thorndike made clear in *An Introduction to the Theory of Mental and Social Measurements* (1904), even at this early stage, psychometricians understood that measuring ability is not straightforward. As he writes, when measuring, 'even so simple a thing as the spelling ability of ten-year-old boys, one is hampered at the start by the fact that there exist no units in which to measure' (1904: 5). The problems with measurement outlined in Chapter 3 were firmly established in Thorndike's time.

The solution to the lack of a unit of measurement was found in the use of relative position within a series of measures, which is the basis for much of the current more advanced use of numbers in education. Thorndike and a growing number of psychometricians postulated that assigning a rank order enabled advanced numerical analysis. Measures using relative positions are different to natural numbers, however. As Thorndike notes, 'ordinary arithmetic does not apply to them' (1904: 20).

Psychometricians like Thorndike built on the thinking about measurement which was being developed by statisticians such as Charles Spearman, and they understood that point estimates of variable traits were actually simply single observations drawn from a distribution of any given trait. In their work on measurement, psychometricians were always careful to detail the limitations of any measurements of individuals, whilst developing useful tools for interpreting measurements of groups of individuals.

What Thorndike and others did establish was that it was possible to construct tests which had high degrees of what came to be known as reliability and validity, and which could assign a rank to an individual within a population which could be used to draw conclusions about general performance in tests.

Box 9.1   Reliability and validity

If a student were to take any particular test on a number of different occasions, their score would not be the same on each occasion. Even if we assume that there is no additional learning between tests, and that the student forgets the experience of taking the test on other occasions, the scores will differ for a number of reasons: markers may interpret answers differently, the student might be well or poorly rested, motivated or fed, their handwriting might be more or less clear, and so on. Where a student takes just one test or set of tests, the particular choice of test items (the name given to questions selected to assess the student's knowledge of the knowledge domain which is being assessed) will affect the scores different students are given, since each child taking the test will have individual strengths and weaknesses in the subject being tested.

In Classical Test Theory (CTT), test **reliability** is based on the idea that a given student has a 'true score' for a given test. Any given test score will be unlikely to be equal to a student's true score, as any score will include a degree of measurement error, as detailed above. Sometimes a student will score more than their hypothetical true score, and sometimes they will score less.

Reliability is defined in CTT as the square of the correlation between observed and true scores. This has to be estimated, since the true scores are unknown. Fortunately, the mathematics required to do this is fairly simple. Using test scores from the same test on two different occasions, a reliability coefficient is calculated by finding the covariance between scores.

Covariance in this case is fairly straightforward. Simply record for each test item (the technical name for a test question) a 0 where there is no difference between answers on the two tests, and record a value of 1 if there is a difference. Summing the values and dividing by the total number of test items gives the covariance, and the square root the covariance gives you is the standard deviation of the measurement errors recorded by the two tests.

Where the scores are identical, and the standard deviation of errors is 0, the test is deemed perfectly reliable with a coefficient of 1. Where the scores are always different and the standard deviation of the errors is 0, the test is deemed to be entirely unreliable with a coefficient of 1.

It should be noted that there are problems with this interpretation of the reliability of a test, which were considered by later psychometricians. In CTT, however, reliability is a measure of whether scores on a test are in some way consistent.

The **validity** of a test concerns the question of whether a test tests something meaningful which its designers intended it to measure. All tests clearly test something. Validity is the question of whether what the test is testing – the 'construct', to use the technical term – is closely linked to the observed score on the test. An incredibly simple test may have high reliability, but may have little validity if it does not discriminate between test takers in a way which is useful, for example. Equally, an extremely difficult test may be equally reliable – test takers score 0 marks consistently – but will have as little validity as a test in which test takers get everything right every time.

As Dylan Wiliam notes in his (2001) article, 'Reliability, validity and all that jazz':

> It is sometimes said that validity is more important than reliability. In one sense this is true, since there is no point in measuring something reliably unless one knows what one is measuring. After all, that would be like saying 'I've measured something, and I know I'm doing it right, because I get the same reading consistently, although I don't know what I'm measuring'. On the other hand, reliability is a pre-requisite for validity – no assessment can have any validity at all if the mark a student gets varies

(Continued)

(Continued)

> radically from occasion to occasion, or depends on who does the marking. To confuse matters even further, it is often the case that reliability and validity are in tension, with attempts to increase reliability (e.g. by making the marking scheme stricter) having a negative effect on validity (e.g. because students with good answers not foreseen in the mark scheme cannot be given high marks). (Wiliam, 2001: 21)

By the 1950s, the field of educational measurement had made considerable advances, particularly in the USA. The psychometrician community had developed an advanced understanding of both the benefits and limitations of educational testing, as is made clear in *Educational Measurement* (1951), published by the American Council on Education (ACE):

> Achievement testing is in itself one of the major phases of instruction and in addition it helps the formulation of clear-cut educational objectives, it provides assistance in the selection of content and learning experiences, and it aids in the development of an effective organization of learning experiences. (American Council on Education, 1951: 59)

The ACE also noted that: 'Since comprehensive and systematic testing programs direct teaching procedures and learning toward the objectives measured, there is danger of warping the curriculum in the direction of measured objectives' (American Council on Education, 1951: 41).

Nevertheless, by the 1950s, in the USA, testing was a fundamental part of the educational landscape and much of the groundwork in understanding testing had been completed.

9.4 The Coleman report and the development of the use of theories of 'production functions'

Following the Civil Rights Act of 1964, the US government was mandated to conduct a survey 'concerning the lack of availability of equal educational opportunities for individuals by reason of race, color, religion, or national origin in public educational institutions at all levels in the United States' (Coleman et al., 1966: iii). The resulting report, *Equality of Educational Opportunity* (1966) by James Coleman and others, marked the next big step forward in the debate about the use of statistics in education.

Coleman had investigated whether there was any link between the funding of schools attended by different groups in the USA and the achievement of children attending particular schools. His findings were surprising to many of those who read them, not least because they did not support the prevailing view that 'poor and minority children performed poorly in school because their schools lacked resources' (Gamoran and Long, 2006: 3).

Coleman had an unusual background, having graduated in Chemical Engineering after serving in the US Navy in the Second World War, before turning to sociology which he taught at Stanford, the University of Chicago and John Hopkins University (Kilgore, 2016: 8). Much as pioneers like Edward Thorndike brought mathematical rigour to psychology, Coleman was amongst those who developed mathematical models using empirical data to explore social networks.

Introduction to Mathematical Sociology (1964) established Coleman's academic credentials, and with his team he analysed a huge amount of data in order to produce the Coleman report, as *Equality of Educational Opportunity* came to be known. The report used:

> Test scores and questionnaire responses obtained from first-, third-, sixth-, ninth-, and twelfth-grade students, and questionnaire responses from teachers and principals. These data were obtained from a national sample of schools in the United States. Data on students include age, gender, race and ethnic identity, socioeconomic background, attitudes toward learning, education and career goals, and racial attitudes. Scores on teacher-administered standardized academic tests are also included. These scores reflect performance on tests assessing ability and achievement in verbal skills, nonverbal associations, reading comprehension, and mathematics. Data on teachers and principals include academic discipline, assessment of verbal facility, salary, education and teaching experience, and attitudes toward race.

The Coleman report gathered together data from a nationwide sample of 600,000 pupils and thousands of teachers, principals and bureaucrats. As well as raw results, the report included a huge amount of advanced analysis of data. Much of this analysis would be familiar to Edward Thorndike and he would not have been surprised to read Coleman's finding that 'the variability between individual pupils within the same school … is roughly four times as large as the variability between schools' (Coleman et al., 1966: 296), a finding which psychometricians had long established by the 1960s.

What was new was the use Coleman was able to make of the additional information he had collected. Coleman broke new ground when he reported that:

> The first finding is that the schools are remarkably similar in the way they relate to the achievement of their pupils when the socio economic background of the students is taken into account. It is known that socio economic factors bear a strong relation to academic achievement. When these factors are statistically controlled, however it appears that differences between schools account for only a small fraction of differences in pupil achievement. (Coleman et al., 1966: 21–2)

Whereas psychometricians had developed the theory and use of standardised testing to the point where robust conclusions could be drawn from well-designed, well-administered tests, Coleman was able to use additional information about those who took the tests, and those who taught in schools, to make research-based observations which were entirely new.

In his report, Coleman pioneered the use of what are now known as 'education production functions'. This kind of analysis developed ideas which were being used in classical economics, in which researchers considered physical inputs to and outputs from production processes.

Education production functions, as developed by Coleman, use a number of sources of information, including funding, numbers of teachers, length of schooling, as well as extensive survey responses by students, teachers, school principals and others, to summarise what can be thought of as inputs into education. These inputs are then analysed in relation to measured school outputs, such as age on graduating from school, test scores, and so on. By analysing both inputs and outputs, Coleman was able to comment on those aspects of the inputs and outputs of schooling which appeared to be linked.

Box 9.2 — Accounting for difference – the use of variability in analysis

Educational researchers are frequently interested in accounting for the differences in educational outputs recorded by individuals and schools in relation to identified educational inputs. Coleman gives a clear explanation of the way in which he suggested this be done, using regression and the method of least squares.

Figure 9.1 shows a hypothetical set of data, based on Coleman's example.

The graph in Figure 9.1 plots a score from a pupil on a test (which, as Coleman makes clear using insights from psychometricians such as Edward Thorndike, could be affected by 'the pupil's ability and motivation, family interest and background, school characteristics, attitudes of the pupils peers, ... alertness on the day of the test, community attitudes which support education, and so on' (Coleman et al., 1966: 290)) against 'one factor out of many', from which Coleman selected a 'per pupil expenditure of the school which the pupil attends'.

The point marked 'c' represents a pupil with a score of 38 attending a school with an expenditure of $430 per pupil per year. Each of the other points represents pupils with their scores and school expenditure per pupil. As Coleman notes:

> the overall variability (or variance) of these scores is measured by drawing the horizontal line at their average value and using the distances of the scores from that average line. The common index of variability or variance is the sum of the squares of these distances. (Coleman et al., 1966: 292)

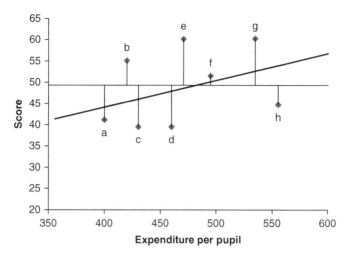

Figure 9.1   Coleman report: ordinary least squares illustration

The next step is to produce a regression line, or 'line of best fit', which reduces the sum of the squares to the smallest possible value. Whilst this is a tedious and complicated task to do by hand, Coleman had access to some of the best (admittedly very limited compared to what followed) computing power of the time. Calculating regressions in the modern era is made a trivial task by modern computing power.

Coleman then defined the difference between the variance – the simple sum of squares of the differences between points and the mean – and the sum of the squares of the differences between the points and the line of best fit – as the 'amount of variability' or the 'amount of variance' 'explained' or 'accounted for' by the factor.

This is a tricky idea to conceptualise, and it is worth considering exactly what is meant by these terms. As with so much of the terminology surrounding statistics, terms such as 'amount of variance accounted for' are not quite what they might seem to the casual reader.

As Coleman explained, if, in Figure 9.1, the squares of the differences between the slanted regression line for each point were 95% of the squares of the differences between the horizontal mean and each point, it would be possible to state that '5 per cent of the variance in pupils' scores is accounted for by the school's expenditure per pupil'.

This does not indicate a causal relationship, as might mistakenly be assumed. It does not mean that the school's per pupil expenditure 'causes' 5% of the pupils' test scores. It simply means that in the model which has been created of the relationship between the input and output factor, a certain percentage of the differences can be accounted for.

Using this terminology, Coleman was able to discuss those factors which could be said to account for certain amounts of the differences between inputs and outputs which he found in this research.

The methods Coleman used in his report were a huge step forward in the analysis of statistics in education. Using the data they gathered specifically for the report, his team constructed 103 input variables which were used in a massive regression analysis of 20 separate files, each with samples of records representing 1,000 individual students.

In addition to the 103 separate variables, Coleman combined selected variables to construct new variables which represented influences which his team examined. These included, for example, 'family economic level', 'student attitudes', 'teacher quality' and 'teacher attitudes'.

The regression analysis which Coleman and his team undertook was hugely complex, and required extensive use of the computers to which they had access. Prior to the Coleman report, whilst the ideas which Coleman used had been progressing, the time and effort required was simply beyond the education research community. As Blank notes, 'Much of the ground work was laid in the 1950s and 1960s; but it ran into a crippling limit. The computational power to analyse data on real networks simply didn't exist' (cited in Fielding et al., 2008: 546).

Coleman and his team, working on a US-government backed research project, were able to use a mainframe computer at the Educational Testing Service in Princeton, New Jersey. This enabled them to run repeated regressions to identify correlations within their data set. Their work was groundbreaking. Coleman 'invented much of the technology and methodology as he went along' (Dickinson, 2016: online). A new era of much more complex analysis of education data had begun.

9.5 The development of school effectiveness research

The Coleman report had a profound impact on the education landscape, changing the way in which researchers thought about the use of statistics in efforts to understand and analyse education. As Gamoran and Long (2006: 3) note in their review of the 40 years following the publication of Coleman's report in 1966, '*Equality of Educational Opportunity* ... inspired decades of research on school effects, on the impact of socioeconomic status (SES) on achievement, and on racial and ethnic disparities in academic achievement'.

As noted above, this was, in part, due to the many findings of the Coleman report being so unexpected and therefore subject to intense debate. As noted, prior to Coleman's research and analysis, is seems that many people had assumed that the reason why different groups of students achieved lower (and higher) results was due to the types of schools different groups attend, with their differing facilities and teaching staff. Coleman's suggestion – that the differences within schools were much greater than the differences between schools, and that factors external to a school had a much greater impact on student's academic achievement than those within a school's control – was not what he had been expected to conclude.

In addition, Coleman had produced extensive field data which was freely available for subsequent researchers to pore over, to reanalyse and to which to respond. Coleman also identified clear areas for further research, which were taken up following the report's publication. Furthermore, Coleman's use of an 'education production function' was to have a far-reaching impact, which informed much of the subsequent research into education, ushering in the era of school effectiveness research.

Production functions were first developed in the field of economics. In 1928, researchers Paul Douglas and Charles W. Cobb developed what became known as the Cobb-Douglas Production Function. This considered the inputs into and outputs from manufacturing processes, and developed equations to describe the relationship between the two. Cobb and Douglas worked on their ideas for the next 20 years, and by the 1950s production functions were a large area of research for economists across the world, who explored both the benefits and drawbacks of the concept.

Education production functions, as developed and used by Coleman and many others, built on those developed in economics. Both production functions used well-established multiple regression techniques. The concept of regression, in which a 'line of best fit' is developed for series of data, was discussed in Chapter 7. A typical education production function takes the following form:

$$A = f(X) + f(Y) + f(Z)$$

in which A is some measure of school output, $f(X)$ are the variables measuring school characteristics ('school effects'), $f(Y)$ are the variables representing external environment ('environmental effects') and $f(Z)$ are the variables representing the student's ability and level of prior attainment ('student effects'). In Coleman's case, he used a formulation which conceptualised a student's test score as being made up of an average for the student's group, an average for the student's group within their school and a component which is individual to the student.

Coleman acknowledged that his data was limited inasmuch as it was a snapshot taken at one particular time. It did not follow students through their schooling, and he was not able to take into account the differences schools – and teaching – might make over time:

Had a number of years been available for this survey, a quite different way of assessing effects of school characteristics would have been possible; that is, examination of the educational growth over a period of time of children in schools with different characteristics. This is an alternative and in some ways preferable method of assessing the effects of school characteristics.

It, too, requires caution in interpretation, because the various factors that could account for differences in growth are usually themselves associated, and also because the rate of growth bears a complex relation to the initial state. It should be recognized that the results of such an analysis of growth might differ in some ways from the results of the present analysis. If the sources of variations in achievement were less complex, the results would not differ; but here, as for most matters of human behavior, relationships are complex. Thus, the present analysis should be complemented by others that explore changes in achievement over a large span of time. (Coleman et al., 1966: 292)

The 1970s saw researchers reanalysing Coleman's data, as academics reacted to the findings which Coleman had presented:

Many scholars have critiqued the Coleman report specifically and the production function literature more broadly. These critiques have included arguments that Coleman's cross-sectional study could not adequately capture causal effects, that Coleman assumed a linear and additive relation between resources and learning, that cross-sectional measures of reading achievement could not distinguish between learning that occurs at home and learning that occurs at school, and that Coleman's estimation of school effects by measures of percent of variance explained were sensitive to assumptions about causal ordering. (Gamoran and Long, 2006: 7)

One of the more prominent names in the field of school effectiveness research is Erik Hanushek, who published extensively throughout the 1970s, '80s and '90s. Hanushek, an economist, sought to establish whether it is possible to link student learning to individual teachers and schools. Despite limited empirical evidence, Hanushek has become well known for the concept of the 'bad teacher' in which he suggested that 'there is no doubt that teachers vary dramatically in effectiveness. The difference in student performance in a single academic year from having a good as opposed to a bad teacher can be more than one full year of standardised achievement' (Hanushek, 1992: 113).

This disputed claim comes from an article which Hanushek wrote in 1992, 'The trade-off between child quality and quantity', in which Hanushek examined whether the number of children in a family has any relationship to the academic outcome for a given child. The 'bad teacher' suggestion, derived from data from a sample of 'low income black students from Gary, Indiana' in 1972–75 which, Hanushek noted, 'is clearly not representative of the entire population', appears in the conclusion of Hanushek's report, which focuses on another area of interest entirely (Hanushek, 1992: 104).

As with much of the research and literature on education production functions and school effectiveness, there are well-established criticisms of the fundamental

 Databusting for schools

assumptions made by those working in the field. Goldstein and Woodhouse (2000: 354) summarised these as including the criticisms that school effectiveness (SE) research involves an 'oversimplification of the complex "causalities" associated with schooling', that '"theory" in SE work is little more than reification of empirical relationships' and that 'too much SE research is simply poor quality'.

As Goldstein and Woodhouse note (2000: 356-7),

> Coe and Fitz-Gibbon (1998) are particularly critical of the way in which much SE research identifies the 'unexplained' variation between schools, after adjusting for intake, as measuring 'effectiveness'. They point out that there may be other factors, outside the control of the school, which could explain such variation. In other words, the term 'effectiveness' needs to be treated tentatively when applied on the basis of models which may have omitted important factors.

Goldstein and Woodhouse's academic phrase 'that "theory" in SE work is little more than reification of empirical relationships' can be rephrased in everyday language as suggesting that much SE work simply creates a circular argument that effective schools are schools with desired observable variables, and schools with desired observable variables are schools which are effective.

This criticism has been levelled at a great deal of SE work, suggesting that there are many factors which influence measureable outcomes such as exam and test results, and that many of these factors are beyond the scope of school. Whilst SE has attempted to control for these factors, by using measures of prior attainment for example, little attempt has been made to account for individual differences between children who, in the words of Wood and Scott (2014: 15), 'differ at a physiological level in (their) capacity to learn, and in (their) capability to learn to learn'.

Goldstein and Woodhouse suggest that too much SE research conducted in the 1990s is of poor quality, which 'does not adjust for intake achievement', 'uses non-randomly selected samples of schools' or finds '"causal" conclusions derived from cross-sectional studies' (Goldstein and Woodhouse, 2000: 358). In their article, they identify political interference as a serious cause for concern as regards the quality of research into educational effectiveness, and they called for great rigour in future research.

In an overview, Scheerens (2004) considers economic studies on educational production functions, summarising this as 'the question of what manipulative inputs can increase outputs':

> The findings of this type of research have often been referred to as being disappointing. Review studies like those from Mosteller and Moynihan (1972), Averch et al. (1974), Glasman and Biniaminov (1981), Hanushek (1979 and 1986) always produce the same conclusions: inconsistent findings throughout the entire available research and scant effect at most from the relevant input variables. (Scheerens, 2004: 4)

9.6 The growth of international educational reporting

In the period since the Second World War, countries around the world have increased their investment in education dramatically. The UK, for example, increased its spending on education from 3% of gross domestic product (GDP) in 1946 to 6% in 2010, as did the USA which doubled its spending of 3% of GDP in 1947 to 6% in 2010. This growth in expenditure on education has enabled children to remain in education for more years than they had previously, as well as given many children access to education from an earlier age.

As expenditure on education has increased, politicians and those involved in educational policy have naturally taken a keen interest in the effectiveness of education funded by the state. As the scope of education has risen, those responsible for allocating expenditure have been increasingly interested in comparisons between educational systems in different countries, and there is currently wide-ranging literature examining education around the globe.

This interest has developed in parallel to the growth in school effectiveness research discussed earlier in this chapter, and the links between governments and academics have become more complex as governments have sought to find effective ways to develop their educational programmes, and academics have explored new ways to understand educational effectiveness.

At the same time, the period between the 1970s and the present day saw a significant change to the post-war political consensus in the developed world, as the global economic outlook developed and governments explored new theories of economics and political management. Whereas the period immediately after the Second World War largely saw settled economies with rising growth, the significant economic upheavals of the 1970s ushered in a new era, which in turn impacted on the way in which governments viewed education, and the way in which information about educational systems was gathered, analysed and shared.

9.6.1 IEA's TIMMS and PIRLS

The International Association for the Evaluation of Educational Achievement (IEA) was founded in 1958 at the UNESCO Institute for Education based in Hamburg. It has long conducted cross-national surveys of student achievement, first conducting a multi-country study in 1960. It began by surveying 13-year-olds and it has tended to maintain a focus on this age group throughout its long history.

IEA's surveys include International Mathematics Surveys, International Science Surveys as well as studies into the use of computers in education. In 1995, it conducted a Third International Mathematics and Science Survey (TIMSS) which became the first in a four-year cycle of surveys now known as the Trends in International Mathematics and Science Study (TIMSS). The survey involved 500,000 students in 46 countries.

Subsequent surveys were undertaken in 1999, 2003, 2007, 2011 and 2015, and students surveyed were either in 4th Grade (9 years old) or 8th Grade (13 years old). The mathematics and science surveys have been taken every four years since 1995; with the four-year difference between 4th Grade and 8th Grade, this enables countries to track changes in achievement across consecutive iterations of the survey programme.

The Progress in International Reading Literacy Study (PIRLS) programme was first undertaken in 2001, and has been repeated on a five-year cycle, with surveys being undertaken in 2006, 2011 and 2016. PIRLS studies reading in 4th Grade (Year 5 in England and Wales). The surveys are low stakes for students and schools, and, in contrast to high-stakes accountability-based testing, there is very little evidence of any specific preparation work undertaken by schools or students.

Both TIMSS and PIRLS scores are based on complicated calculations, which aim to provide an indication of reading literacy over time. In essence, they are scaled around a mean of 500 and a standard deviation of 100, and use a version of a Rasch model of Item Response Theory; suffice to say that this makes them very difficult to understand at anything other than a superficial level for most readers, which may explain why the majority of press reporting and political use is often simplistic at best.

Box 9.3   Item Response Theory

As discussed in Chapter 3, Classical Test Theory (CTT) assumes that each item (or question) in a test is equally difficult, or at least that test takers will tend to get the same types of questions right and the same types of questions wrong. When testing the reliability of a test using a measure such as Cronbach's alpha, which is often claimed to measure the internal consistency of a test with values between 0 (seen as extremely negative) and 1 (extremely positive), there is no distinction between the difficulty of any individual item. Where a test was taken by a group of children who all scored 10 out of 20, with one group getting the first ten questions right and the last ten wrong and a second group getting the first ten wrong and the last ten right, CTT would hold the test to be unreliable.

Item Response Theory (IRT) takes a different view of test reliability, focusing on each item rather than on the test as a whole. By modelling the responses of test takers of differing abilities, based on the probability of a student of a given ability answering a question correctly, IRT aims to remove some of the problems inherent in Classical Test Theory. IRT enables, for example, a much larger bank of items to be used than is possible in CTT, as well as enabling computerised adaptive testing (where earlier answers are used to select later questions, with the aim of fine tuning the outcome of the test).

(Continued)

(Continued)

Rasch models of IRT develop the idea of focusing on test items rather than the test itself. In essence, a model is developed based on the item responses, and then the model is tested using the further responses to the test. If the responses do not fit the model, further modelling is undertaken. This might mean including or excluding certain items, and requires human judgement to develop a model which is ultimately used to assess the ability of those who have taken the test.

Given the complexity of Rasch models, they are often held up for scrutiny and there continues to be healthy debate regarding CTT, IRT and Rasch models.

England and Wales have tended to score reasonably well in both the TIMSS surveys in mathematics and science in both 4th Grade (Year 5) and 8th Grade (Year 9), and in the PIRLS programme. The spread of results for individual countries are quite wide, and mean results need to be considered alongside spreads when looking at how children in different countries perform in the surveys.

The data gathered by TIMSS and PIRLS is made freely available, and the IEA publishes extensive analysis of the research which it has undertaken. With extensive data published for each cycle, the overall picture which emerges is extremely complex. For any country, there is a range of positives and negatives which can be taken from the results. High-performing Eastern countries, which tend to score highly on achievement, often see concern at children's attitude to, and enjoyment of, learning. Countries in Europe, which tend to have more middling results, tend to compare themselves negatively to the highest performing nations.

TIMSS and PIRLS have tended to be taken seriously by academics and politicians, and have built up a solid reputation amongst those who take an interest in their findings. They paint a comprehensive picture of the complexity of education across the globe.

9.6.2 OECD's PISA

The Organisation for Economic Co-operation and Development (OECD), which was founded in 1960 to stimulate economic progress and world trade, grew out of the Organisation for European Economic Co-operation founded in the wake of the Second World War. As an umbrella organisation focused on comparing and developing policy at governmental level, the OECD has from its inception taken an interest in educational policy, practice and outcomes.

In 1968 the Centre for Research and Innovation (CERI), which focused on education, was established within the OECD, and throughout the 1970s and 1980s CERI focused primarily on education's social and cultural purposes. As the international political narrative evolved in the 1980s, pressure came from both the USA and France for a greater focus on collecting data to assess the outcomes of education.

Whilst the USA had been generating some educational outcome data for most of the 20th century, its data was incomplete at best. The 1980s saw calls for more data to be generated on school outputs, as measured by student testing, and the USA made it clear to the OECD that it wanted the organisation to develop a programme to enable international comparisons of educational systems.

Whilst the OECD is based in Europe, and although it is separate from the European Union, it has been heavily influenced by policy directions at European level. The EU's Maastricht Treaty in 1992 formally recognised education as one of the central areas of responsibility of the EU, and in the same year the OECD published the first of its *Education at a Glance* series of reports.

Education at a Glance contained data on 30 indicators drawn from information supplied by each of the OECD countries. As this evolved through the 1990s, the OECD put in place the Programme for International Student Assessment (PISA), partly in response to the development of the IEA's TIMSS and PIRLS programmes.

PISA is a worldwide study of mathematics, science and reading, and it began by using much of the publicly available framework for international surveys of education developed by TIMSS and PIRLS. PISA uses data generated from tests administered to a sample of 15-year-olds (10th Grade, or Year 11). Whilst the majority of countries included within the survey are members of the OECD, many non-member countries have also opted to be part of the programme.

The first OECD PISA tests were administered in 2000, focusing on reading. These were followed by tests in mathematics (2003), science (2006), reading (2009), mathematics (2012) and science (2015). Whilst the methodology and interpretation of the PISA programme is complicated and often disputed, it has had a considerable effect on the development of education policy throughout the world as countries try to improve their standing compared to their competitors.

Like TIMSS and PIRLS, PISA scores are based on complicated calculations and are also scaled around a mean of 500 and a standard deviation of 100. As with the IEA surveys, interpreting PISA surveys is complicated. As with TIMSS and PIRLS, some headline measures are often reported as if they were single point measurements, and news outlets frequently draw up misleading 'league tables' based on complicated summary statistics.

The UK is reported as a single country in headline PISA data, and the results of each of the surveys indicate that the country is near the mean score of 500 in most subjects in most years. The highest scoring countries tend to be those, once again, in the Far East, although there is some controversy as China allows the survey to present results for Hong Kong and Macau, both semi-autonomous areas of the country, as separate entities, and both Singapore and Taiwan – which have very high scores – are highly unusual outliers in many non-educational comparator metrics.

Further criticism of PISA scores suggests that countries with relatively high levels of inequality such as the UK and the USA have lower overall scores than countries such as Singapore and Finland which have relatively low levels of poverty, and as with TIMSS and PIRLS there are concerns surrounding the way in which results are extrapolated and interpreted.

Part of the impetus for these criticisms is what has become known as 'PISA panic' or 'PISA shock', whereby governments are spurred on to make significant changes to their educational policies based on negative reaction to the headline findings of PISA surveys. PISA panic has been particularly noticeable in Germany, which introduced far-reaching reforms following the publication of the first PISA survey in 2000, and has been used to justify significant policy changes in many countries, including England, Wales and France (Baird et al., 2011).

PISA produces a great deal of analysis based on PISA results, from overviews of the international picture to highly detailed country-specific reports. In addition, PISA produces monthly 'PISA in focus' briefings, reports highlighting gender differences in education, subject overviews and much more.

9.7 Measuring progress in education

Much of the academic work in the recent past has established beyond doubt that there is a clear link between non-school factors and average raw attainment as measured by tests of children's knowledge. It is well known that, on average, those classified as coming from families with higher socio-economic status, for example, record higher marks on any given academic test. This holds from the time the children enter school until the time they leave higher education.

This clear link between raw attainment and non-school factors has caused academics and politicians to think differently about ways in which to try to measure the success – or otherwise – of school-based activity. One of the significant ways this has been approached is to consider the difference in measures of children's attainment between two different points. This is labelled 'progress' in the UK (or 'student growth' in the USA), and is used in a number of ways to measure success.

9.7.1 Value Added measures

Value Added models – which use regression analysis to model a child's progress in test scores – were introduced to education by Erik Hanushek in 1971, following one of the suggestions for further study recommended by Coleman. Using the assumptions underpinning education production functions pioneered in *Equality of Educational Opportunity* (Coleman et al., 1966), Hanushek attempted to measure the impact of individual teachers using measurements of educational attainment taken at two points in time:

For instance, it is possible to develop many measures of the output of the educational process, such as standardised test scores, juvenile delinquency rates, post-school income streams, occupational choice or level of education completed. Yet, the availability of data has restricted most past studies of education – and this analysis – to a single output. (Hanushek, 1971: 281)

The mathematical concepts underpinning Value Added analysis were mentioned briefly in Chapter 8, when we considered regression models to produce lines of best fit for correlated data. To recap, where we have two variables, it is possible to create summary statistics which show to what extent two variables are linked, and to create models which show how, on average, two variables vary in relation to each other. Some data sets have high correlations – as one value increases or decreases, so does another – and some have low or non-existent correlations – where there is no pattern linking to data points.

Regression analysis allows us to create a model which estimates a dependent variable, the value of which depends on the independent variables used to predict the dependent variable, as well as some degree of constant value and error. So, for example, the relationship between a child's height at age 4 and their height at age 8 might be modelled as follows:

$$H(8) = c + rH(4) + e$$

In this model, c is a constant value based on a typical child's height at birth, rH(4) is a multiple of the child's height at the age of 4 and e is an error term which contains the variability of the dependent variable (in this case, the height at age 8) which isn't accounted for by the independent variable (the child's height at age 4).

In Hanushek's 1971 article, test data was used for children in the 1st and 3rd Grades, and Hanushek created a regression model to summarise the difference in children's attainment over a two-year period. His model took Coleman's lead and incorporated measures of teachers' verbal ability and educational backgrounds, teacher and administrator attitudes, how teachers used their time during the school day, and the backgrounds of students in his study. Hanushek's model did not account for measurement error and seems to have made strong assumptions about the reliability and validity of the tests used to generate the measures' output variables.

The model which Hanushek introduced in his 1971 paper was as follows (written in layman's terms, rather than as a mathematical model): educational outputs, at a later point in time, are modelled by taking an independent variable constructed from a measure of achievement at an earlier point in time, an independent variable constructed from a measure of 'family inputs' between the earlier and later points in time, an independent variable constructed from a measure of 'peer influences' between the earlier and later points in time, an independent variable constructed from a measure of 'innate endowments of a student', and an independent variable constructed from 'school inputs' between the earlier and later points in time.

Hanushek used this formulation of Value Added in his 1971 article as a basis of further analysis which attempted to isolate a measure of teacher effectiveness. In his early analysis using the concept of Value Added in education, he used an F-test (a statistical procedure based on concepts developed by Ronald Fischer) which – in essence – compares the explained and unexplained variance in a statistical model.

Value Added concepts began to be used in England in the 1990s, as the UK government sought to develop and utilise newly available national end-of-key-stage test scores to make judgements about schools, and UK-based academics began to develop their own Value Added models. One of the pioneers in the UK was Carol Taylor Fitz-Gibbon, who was the director of the CEM Centre at Durham University from 1983 to 2003.

Fitz-Gibbon wrote the final report for the 'Value Added National Project' (1997) instigated by the UK government, titled 'Feasibility studies for a national system of value-added indicators', which was used as the basis for Value Added measures in England and Wales. In Fitz-Gibbon's formulation (1997: 3), Value Added was defined 'as the difference between a statistically-predicted performance (based on prior attainment and the general pattern in the data) and the actual performance. Thus, value-added for a key stage was essentially a measure of the pupil's relative progress during that key stage'.

In essence, Fitz-Gibbon's formulation used test data from an earlier key stage to predict likely test results at a later key stage; students' actual results at later key stages were then compared to the predicted outcomes, and a single 'Value Added' measure was produced for each child. The model was adjusted at a second stage to account for known issues, including unreliable small cohorts and intake factors such as atypical numbers of students with English as a second language, differences between male and female students, and so on.

Fitz-Gibbon was reacting to political pressure, exemplified by the publication in 1994 of a detailed report on 'Value-added performance indicators for schools' by a governmental body, which indicated that Value Added measures were being driven largely by political expediency, primarily by concerns raised by the academic community and others that newly released league tables based on raw results were misleading. As Thomas (1998: 92) notes:

> Neither the initially high achieving nor the initially low achieving school is assisted by the publication of raw league tables. In the former, the need for improvement may not be appreciated; in the latter, serious demoralization of staff may occur through no fault of their own.

The initial Value Added scores made available to schools were not for public consumption, but by 2002 Value Added scores were being published alongside attainment scores for secondary schools, followed by the addition of Value Added scores for primary schools in 2003.

The complexity of Value Added scores has made them controversial from their inception. As Sparkes (1999) puts it, 'The way (Value Added) is calculated is so complicated for most people that there is a tendency to accept it at face value (or just reject it)'. Concerns were raised about the use of a single number to represent Value Added, with no sense of the spread of outcomes within a given school. Parents, certainly, found Value Added confusing and often ignored it when looking at school outcomes, somewhat defeating the purpose of the development of the measures.

By 2004, the government had begun to develop a 'Contextualised Value Added' (CVA) model, which attempted to incorporate the second stage envisaged by Fitz-Gibbon, using pupil background factors. In 2010, the new Coalition government took the view that CVA set variable expectations of schools, and reverted to a Value Added model which did not take any pupil level factors into account when calculating Value Added, preferring to induce measures of Value Added for proxies for disadvantaged children such as eligibility for free school meals (FSM).

9.7.2 Multi-level regression analysis, the use of effect sizes and meta-analyses

As relatively new methods of analysis, multi-level regression analysis, the use of effect sizes and meta-analyses are controversial and the controversies surrounding them will be discussed in Chapter 10. It is useful to have an overview of each, which we look at here.

As computing power increased through the 1990s, Value Added models became much simpler to develop and the data within the models became much easier to compute. Multi-level regression techniques were developed as academics and researchers sought to explore data in greater depth.

Multi-level regression was developed by a number of statisticians, the leading British researcher being Harvey Goldstein (1999) based at the University of Bristol. Whereas traditional multiple regression techniques generally assume a single level of analysis, in which the variables are independent of one another, in multi-level analysis, groupings of individual cases (in educational terms, of children within schools, classes or with particular teachers) are taken into account within the overall analysis.

Whilst this makes for extremely complex analysis, its developers suggest that this can provide insight into multi-level environments such as school systems, in which children and teachers are not randomly assigned to classes and schools.

Effect sizes in education are, in essence, an attempt to provide a measure of how effective a period of teaching has been. They are calculated by finding the difference between two means and dividing the result by the standard deviation (Coe, 2002). This results in a value which essentially gives an indication of how big the difference between the two means actually is, taking into account how typical the mean is of the data which it summarises.

The concept of the size of an effect comes from mainstream statistics, which use the term to describe a process by which a researcher assesses whether an experiment will have enough data from which to draw valid conclusions before the experiment takes place.

As there are many variables which may affect an effect size in education, such as the accuracy of the samples which provided the initial means and standard deviations, and the time period over which the teaching took place, effect sizes should be treated with care. They appear in many academic papers, their use has been popularised by John Hattie and the Education Endowment Foundation, amongst others, and they have been used extensively in efforts to find out 'what works' in education. Hattie is well known for having claimed that an effect size of 0.4 or greater indicates that a particular teaching practice or activity has a greater than average impact on pupil progress.

Much of Hattie's work uses meta-analysis, in which a number of effect sizes are combined into a single effect size for a particular education practice or activity. The term 'meta-analysis' was popularised by Gene Glass (1976) at the University of Colorado, who used the phrase to refer to 'the analysis of analyses'. Whereas primary analysis refers to original studies, and secondary analysis refers to re-analysis of data using new techniques or exploring new hypotheses using old data, Glass defined meta-analysis as 'the statistical analysis of a large collection of analysis results from individual studies for the purpose of integrating the findings'.

Glass (1976: 4) cautioned researchers to ensure that any primary studies whose results were to be analysed in conjunction with other similar studies should be comparable, but was happy to combine studies of variable quality with the aim of producing an overview of available research, say, where he wondered whether 'well-designed and poorly designed experiments give very different findings'. Glass said that he believed the 'difference to be so small that to integrate research results by eliminating the "poorly done" studies is to discard a vast amount of important data'.

There is an element of 'the wisdom of crowds' in this approach, a concept dating at least as far back as Francis Galton, who noted in 1907 that a crowd at a country fair was surprisingly accurate when guessing the weight of an ox when their individual guesses were averaged. Glass suggested:

No educational problem admits a single answer. We study a system and a process too complex and too interactive to give up its secrets so easily. The variance in our findings of studies is essential, largely irreducible. It should be viewed as something to be studied in its own right, not something that can be eliminated with 'tighter' designs or sharper measures. When a hundred studies can be arranged to yield a half-dozen answers to a question, we can feel confident that we are nearer the truth. (Glass, 1976: 6)

Noting that research in non-educational social science often combined results of separate studies, Glass combined studies which reported effect sizes, producing a combined effect size for a particular type of study. In his 1976 paper, for example, Glass looked at studies of psychotherapy and reported that, on average, 'the therapy group mean was about two-thirds standard deviation above the control group mean on the outcome variable' (Glass, 1976: 7). He went on to look at a study which combined primary studies of the relationship between socio-economic status and school achievement, and suggested that similar studies which combined previously published results would provide useful further insight, providing impetus for the subsequent development of meta-analysis in educational research.

9.8 The What Works Clearinghouse and Education Endowment Foundation

The 2000s saw the development of two national organisations in the USA and England dedicated to collating research into education. In the USA, the Institute of Education Studies (IES) was founded in 2002 with funding from the US government. Its mission was to 'provide scientific evidence on which to ground education practice and policy and to share this information in formats that are useful and accessible to educators, parents, policymakers, researchers, and the public' (https://ies.ed.gov/aboutus). As part of its work, the IES funds the What Works Clearinghouse which aims to review:

> the existing research on different programs, products, practices, and policies in education. Our goal is to provide educators with the information they need to make evidence-based decisions. We focus on the results from high-quality research to answer the question 'What works in education?' (https://ies.ed.gov/aboutus)

The What Works Clearinghouse (WWC) produces intervention reports which summarise educational programmes using 'effectiveness ratings' and 'improvement indices'. WWC effectiveness ratings range from '– –' (negative) to '+ +' (positive), with four intermediate categories of effectiveness (potentially negative, mixed, no discernible effect or potentially positive). The WWC improvement index is an indicator of the size of effect of using the intervention, and it is not shown if the effectiveness rating is mixed or shows no discernible effect. Improvement indices range from –50 to +50. In addition to its intervention reports, WWC also publishes a range of practice guides, which rate research as having 'strong evidence', 'moderate evidence' or 'minimal evidence'.

In the UK, the Education Endowment Foundation (EEF) was founded in 2011 with funding from the UK government and is:

dedicated to breaking the link between family income and educational achievement, ensuring that children and young people from all backgrounds can fulfil their potential and make the most of their talents. We fund rigorous evaluations of innovative projects aiming to raise pupils' attainment. We do this to find out what's most likely to work effectively and cost-effectively, and to put that into action across the country. (https://educationendowmentfoundation.org.uk/about)

The EEF aims to tackle the attainment gap between children who are in receipt of free school meals (FSM), a proxy for those children from the poorest families in the country, and other children. The EEF publishes a 'Teaching and Learning Toolkit' which is described as 'an accessible summary of educational research on teaching 5–16 year olds'.

The EEF Toolkit produces summaries of educational interventions which group research into broad categories and summarise their effectiveness using 'cost', 'evidence strength' and 'months impact' ratings. EEF uses five categories for cost ratings and evidence strength, and 12-month progress categories (https://education endowmentfoundation.org.uk/our-work/about-the-toolkits/about-the-toolkits). Cost ratings range from 'very low' (less than £80 per pupil per year) to 'very high' (over £1,200 per pupil per year); evidence strength ranges from '1 padlock' (very limited, single studies and no reviews or meta-analyses) to '5 padlocks' (very extensive, at least five recent meta-analyses). Months' progress is based on effect sizes, ranging from 0.02 to greater than 1.0, with 1 or 2 months' progress summarised as having 'low impact', 3 to 5 months' progress having 'moderate impact', 6 to 8 months' progress having 'high impact' and 9 to 12 months having 'very high impact'.

9.9 Summary

In this chapter, we have looked at the way in which the testing of individuals developed in the early part of the 20th century, and the influence of psychometricians such as Edward Thorndike in the academic underpinning of achievement tests using what has become known as Classical Test Theory.

The Coleman report of 1966 was a major turning point in the development of research into education, introducing an economic take on education which has persisted into the present day. The use and development of education production functions, and the subsequent development of Value Added theories of education, have had a huge impact on education, particularly in their appeal to and use by government agencies.

We have looked at the development of international education analysis and comparison by UNESCO and the OECD, principally via their TIMSS/PIRLS and PISA programmes. We have looked at the development of Item Response Theory as an alternative to Classical Test Theory, and the way in which IRT has been used by supra-national organisations.

Finally, we have looked at the developing 'What Works' agenda in the USA and in the UK, and the work of the What Works Clearinghouse and the Educational Endowment Foundation in assessing and evaluating research into effective education, particularly in their use of effect sizes and meta-analyses.

Many of the developments in this chapter have generated robust discussion, and much of the theory on which developments of educational analysis rest has come in for healthy criticism. In the next and final chapter, we will consider some of the criticisms of the use of data in education and consider where schools, academics and politicians may go next.

References

American Council on Education (ACE) (1951) *Educational Measurement*. Washington, DC: ACE.

Baird, J.-A., Isaacs, T., Johnson, S., Stobart, G., Yu, G., Sprague, T. and Daugherty, R. (2011) *Policy Effects of PISA*. Oxford: Oxford University Centre for Educational Assessment.

Coe, R. (2002) 'It's the effect size, stupid', presented at the annual conference of the British Educational Research Association. University of Exeter, 12–14 September.

Coleman, J.S. (1964) *Introduction to Mathematical Sociology*. New York: The Free Press.

Coleman, J.S., Campbell, E.Q., Hobson, C.J., McPartland, J., Mood, A.M., Weinfeld, F.D. and York, R.L. (1966) *Equality of Educational Opportunity*. Washington, DC: National Center for Educational Statistics.

Darwin, C. (1859) *On the Origin of Species*. London: John Murray.

Dickinson, E.E. (2016) 'Coleman Report set the standard for the study of public education', *Johns Hopkins Magazine*, winter. Available at: https://hub.jhu.edu/magazine/2016/winter/coleman-report-public-education. Accessed 30/1/18.

Fielding, N.G., Lee, R.M. and Blank, G. (2008) *The SAGE Handbook of Online Research Methods*. London: Sage Publications.

Fitz-Gibbon, C. (1997) *The Value Added National Project Final Report*. Durham: Centre for Curriculum, Evaluation and Management.

Gamoran, A. and Long, D.A. (2006) *Equality of Educational Opportunity: A 40-Year Retrospective*. WCER Working Paper No. 2006–9. Madison, WI: University of Wisconsin–Madison.

Glass, G.V. (1976) 'Primary, secondary, and meta-analysis of research', *Educational Researcher*, 5(10): 3–8.

Goldstein, H. (1999) *Multi-Level Statistical Models*. London: Institute of Education.

Goldstein, H. and Woodhouse, G. (2000) 'School effectiveness research and educational policy', *Oxford Review of Education*, 26(3/4): 353–63.

Hanushek, E. (1971) 'Teacher characteristics and gains in student achievement: Estimation using micro data', *The American Economic Review*, 61(2): 280–8.

Hanushek, E. (1992) 'The trade-off between child quality and quantity', *The Journal of Political Economy*, 100(1): 84–117.

Kilgore, S.B. (2016) 'Life and times of James S. Coleman', *Education Next*, 16(2): 8–16.

Lawn, M. (2013) *The Rise of Data in Education Systems*. Oxford: Symposium Books.

Scheerens, J. (2004) 'Review of school and instructional effectiveness research', *Education for All Global Monitoring Report 2005*. Paris: UNESCO.

Sparkes, R.A. (1999) *'Lies, Damned Lies and School Performance Indicators'*, presented at the Scottish Educational Research Association Annual Conference, University of Dundee, 30 September–2 October.

Thomas, S. (1998) 'Value added measures of school effectiveness in the United Kingdom', *Prospects*, 28(1): 91–108.

Thorndike, E.L. (1904) *An Introduction to the Theory of Mental and Social Measurements*. New York: The Science Press.

Thorndike, E.L. (1913–14) *Educational Psychology*. New York: Teachers' College, Columbia University.

United Nations Educational, Scientific and Cultural Organisation (UNESCO) (1961) *A Manual of Educational Statistics*. Paris: UNESCO.

UNESCO (1963) *Statistical Yearbook*. Paris: UNESCO.

Wiliam, D. (2001) 'Reliability, validity and all that jazz', *Education 3–13*, 29(3): 17–21.

Wood, C. and Scott, R. (2014) *A Tale of Two Classrooms*. London: Demos.

What you will learn from this chapter:

How to take a critical look at the use of numbers in education

What has been learned from psychometrics

How testing has developed as a driver of education policy

The problems with using Value Added measures to summarise school and teacher effectiveness

The ongoing concerns with the use and frequent misinterpretation of pupil performance data in education

The unintended side-effects of the use and misuse of test data

How school leaders, teaching teams, school governors, parents, inspectors and others should work with education data

10.1 Taking a critical look at the use of numbers in education

Having looked at the development of the use of numerical data in education, our teachers and governors are now considering how best to approach the use of data in their schools. In this final chapter, we will consider the lessons which have been learned about attempting to summarise learning using numbers. We will look at the distinctions between summative and formative assessment, and the tensions which often arise between these two types of assessment in schools, particularly when numbers are used in accountability measures.

We will look at the issues facing academic research into learning, with a particular focus on the way in which school effectiveness research has affected the ongoing debate about education. We will look at the effect that the changing focus on attainment and progress measures has had on education, and consider the wider issues with Value Added measures used to summarise school and teacher effectiveness.

We will also look at concerns raised by academics and practitioners about the way in which numbers have been used in the education debate, and look at the effect of high stakes tests on school systems internationally.

We will conclude with some thoughts on the ways in which those working within education should respond to the changes chronicled in this book.

10.2 What we have learned from psychometrics

The past hundred years has seen an increased desire to use numbers to help to provide insight into education, whether in attempts to avoid bias in stratification or simply to make classifying students more efficient. Much of this use of numbers has been driven by the political desire to use hard data to support decisions; the modern era has also seen the social sciences attempt to adapt numerical analysis developed in the natural sciences to enable greater insight into human endeavour.

Early attempts to assess the differences between students using written tests made the many issues with achievement testing clear, and those working to develop accurate measurements of individuals and their learning have discovered a great deal about the many difficulties which written tests encounter.

The earlier chapters in this book have detailed many of the issues which arise when numbers are used to summarise any complex situation. Any summary naturally loses much of the fine detail which is evident in raw data, but the necessary compromises can often be accepted as worthwhile provided the limits of using summary data are clearly understood and taken into account.

We now know a great deal about using numbers to summarise complex data sets such as those which are increasingly available in education, and we can use samples of a wider population to make reasonably robust predictions about populations themselves. We know that point estimates simply provide information about the broad range of values which estimates themselves represent. We know that there is always some degree of measurement error whenever we try to use numbers to summarise individuals.

So what have we learned from the field of psychometrics so far?

1. Test results are necessarily limited in the information they provide.
2. Testing uses samples to provide estimates of wider domains.
3. Well-designed achievement tests can differentiate between higher and lower performing students to some degree.
4. Any analysis of test results must take into account the reliability and validity of the test.
5. Well-designed tests aim to minimise test bias and measurement error.
6. The results of any achievement test should be treated with the utmost caution.

All of those involved in the creation of achievement tests are fully aware of the limitations of testing, and understand that the process of designing an achievement test involves making a number of complex decisions, all of which introduce problems of one kind or another. Unfortunately, many of those who consume the outcomes of achievement tests – including many of those working in schools, on governing bodies and for government bodies which hold schools to account – often have little training in or understanding of the limitations of achievement tests.

Whilst there have been moves to develop greater awareness of the lessons of psychometrics in schools, the basics of rigorous achievement testing are worth reiterating. A written achievement test aims to shed light on what is known as the *domain* of interest. A domain is the full range of skills and knowledge which a student is studying. In general, the domain of interest is necessarily very large, as even very young children know a large amount of information about subjects which we want to test.

The achievement tests we use at the end of periods of study in school are generally created to provide information about children's mastery of large domains of interest. Testing the entire domain – if this were possible – would take a great deal of time and money. Even where the domain of interest is relatively limited – as it is in the phonics check currently administered in Year 1 – it is impractical to create a test which would assess a child's mastery of the entire domain.

The results of achievement tests are therefore used to provide an estimate of a child's skills and knowledge across the entire domain of interest. As with any sampling exercise, the accuracy of the estimate depends on the decisions made by those who create the sample. For end-of-key-stage assessment tests, the domain of interest has to be precisely specified, after which the test questions (which are known to psychometricians as test 'items', since a number of different response methods are used, not all of which are questions) have to be created, and rubric has to be developed to ensure that the test is administered following a standardised procedure.

This lends these tests the formal designation of 'standardised tests'; tests which require all those taking the test to answer the same questions in the same way, with all answers being marked – theoretically at least – in a standardised manner. Modern standardised tests tend to have reasonably high measures of reliability and validity (which we discussed in Chapter 9), although, of course, designing and administering standardised tests is a complicated process, and test scores have clearly identified limitations when considered closely.

Tests often contain a degree of bias, in that some test takers might have advantages which may not always be immediately apparent. Written tests are clearly biased towards those with greater mastery of the language used in the test, and certain groups of children – those for whom the language of the test is additional to their home language, for example – are often at a disadvantage compared to others taking the test. Tests of reading are frequently biased towards those with greater prior knowledge of the subject matter used in the test.

Additionally, tests of achievement which sample domain knowledge are subject to an inherent degree of measurement error. A standardised test is essentially a measurement tool and, as with all measuring tools, they include a margin of error. Just as a standard 30-centimetre ruler is limited in its accuracy – making measurements possible only to the nearest tenth of a centimetre or so – a standardised test has a limit to its measurement accuracy.

An observed test score represents a single point estimate of a child's 'true score', where a 'true score' is the theoretical score a child would attain if the test had no measurement error. In Classical Test Theory (CTT), any observed score is held to be the sum of the 'true score' and an 'error score'. What's more, CTT estimates of the reliability of a test are based on the ability to calculate a value of the ratio between the variance of the true scores and the variance of the true scores and error scores combined. This means that an estimate of reliability close to 1 indicates that there is almost no observed error, and a ratio close to 0 indicates that observed scores are made up of a substantial element of error.

Given that CTT holds that it is impossible to know a true score, there is no agreement as to what a 'correct' estimate of reliability should be. When estimates of reliability are above 0.9, many test items are simply sampling similar areas as other items. This reduces error, of course, but may narrow a test such that its validity is sharply reduced. If estimates of reliability drop below 0.8, then substantial error is introduced and scores may vary considerably for candidates with similar 'true scores'.

These measurement issues should give those who attempt to interpret raw test scores reason to treat any inferences with considerable caution. Even if the reliability of a test is known – and most consumers of test results are rarely party to these complex issues – the interpretation of standardised tests should be made with care.

Where standardised tests have high stakes attached to them – tests which have consequences for those who take them, for those who have taught those taking the test, or for those responsible for those teaching children who take the test – the likelihood that the scores are not accurate samples of the domain of knowledge increases.

It is worth reiterating the issues which undermine high stakes achievement tests. Achievement tests are generally designed to provide relative measures of achievement, and therefore children are generally competing for position against others. The higher the score, the better the result. Whilst achievement tests tend to be norm referenced rather than criterion referenced, the process involved in setting standards within end-of-key-stage tests is often an uneasy mixture of the two, and therefore schools are incentivised to ensure that children get the highest possible score on the test, rather than necessarily to ensure that tests provide benchmarks of learning.

Box 10.1 — Norm- and criterion-referenced tests

How should achievement on a test be judged? This is a tricky question with two main answers. The first is that achievement should be judged with reference to the achievement of peers (norm-referenced tests) and the second is that achievement should be judged with reference to a set of standards (criterion-referenced tests).

Databusting for schools

Norm-referenced tests are those which assess how well a student has done on the test compared to their peers. Typically, a sample group of students of the same age and year group as those who will sit the test is used to create a set of norm-referenced scores for the test. Norm-referenced scores are normally distributed and follow a bell curve. Rather than assessing whether students have met particular standards, test questions for norm-referenced tests have to be designed to differentiate between test takers.

Results on norm-referenced tests are usually reported as a percentile ranking or using a grading system, which indicates the level that a student has achieved compared to those in the sample group. Where grades are used, test producers often aim to limit the number of students who can be allocated each grade, i.e. the top 10% receive an A, for example, and the next 20% receive a B, and so on.

Creating norm-referenced sample groups is often complicated, and in many cases the results of the whole cohort which take the test are used to create the grade distribution for the test (often referred to as 'cohort referencing').

A major disadvantage of norm-referenced testing is that it is very difficult to know whether (and if so, how) absolute standards are changing over time. If each year the top 10% of exam takers, say, are always awarded an A, then it is not possible to say whether results are improving, declining or remaining constant. The knowledge required to record marks within any particular grade may change over time, and a student who is awarded a C grade in one year may have been awarded a B or a D had they been part of a different cohort. In addition, norm-referenced testing creates 'winners' and 'losers', as a certain percentage of students will always be judged to have failed to reach the higher levels in the test. This may be useful within the broader system of education: tests can be used to filter access to further study, and norm-referenced tests can be used to limit the numbers of children who are deemed to have been successful.

Criterion-based tests are those which assess whether a student has met a specified set of standards, regardless of the performance of their peers. If a student performs at or above a pre-specified level, they are deemed to be proficient, and to have achieved the desired level for the test. In theory, any student who has learned the specified curriculum content for a criterion-referenced test could achieve full marks on the test, as test items are chosen for competency, not their ability to differentiate between test takers, as with a norm-referenced test.

Results on criterion-referenced tests are usually reported as a level of proficiency, indicating the level that a student has achieved compared to a given set of standards. Students are often graded into categories such as 'below the expected level', 'at the expected level' or 'above the expected level'.

A major disadvantage of criterion-referenced testing is that setting the standards is always arbitrary, as a particular level has to be selected by those managing the test and does not directly relate to the levels of attainment of those whom the test is assessing. The selected level may be high or low depending on the motivations of those setting the standard. In addition, criterion-referenced tests often struggle to differentiate between those with the greatest knowledge and skills and the inherent ceiling effects are often substantial.

(Continued)

(Continued)

Norm-referenced and criterion-referenced tests attempt to achieve clearly different ends. In addition, it is possible to argue that there is no such thing as a purely norm-referenced or criterion-referenced test, and that, in effect, test results can simply be interpreted with reference to a particular framework. The broad categories help to understand the compromises which test designers have to make.

In lay terms, if a driving test was criterion referenced, all those achieving a specified level would pass the test. If it was norm referenced, only those achieving above a certain rank compared to their peers would be deemed to have passed the test. Which test is preferable depends on whether it is desirable that the vast majority of a population should be able to pass the test, or whether only those who have achieved well compared to their peers should do so.

Whilst attaining high test scores might seem laudable, any system which rewards high test scores above all else forces schools to make decisions which affect the quality and breadth of the education which children receive. First, there is a clear incentive to narrow the curriculum to only those areas which are subject to examination. This is especially so in Key Stage 2, as only reading, maths and some elements of written English are tested. Second, schools are incentivised to focus on teaching test-taking skills in the run up to external examinations; the length of time for which this extreme narrowing happens varies considerably, as schools begin test preparations at different points prior to the tests. Both of these issues can result in a tragedy of the commons, whereby all schools begin examination preparation at ever earlier points prior to examination in order to compete with the other schools in the system. Ongoing issues with test score inflation – in which test scores rise over time with little or no rise in standards – suggest that these issues are inherent within any system of high stakes testing.

Furthermore, test preparation means that many children are held in limbo for long periods of their education, wasting time in test-taking practice which would be better used to develop their intellect. For those external tests which have no consequence for the child, this seems particularly unfair.

Of the many other issues which have been identified with high-stakes testing, perhaps the most worrying is the incentive which is created to manipulate results unfairly. Schools and children have cheated in examinations in many ways, from schools providing unreasonable support during examinations, to direct manipulation of test answers post-test, to theft and illegal distribution of test papers prior to examination dates (e.g. BBC, 2017). When individuals are driven to these measures, results of system-wide testing have to be treated with the utmost caution.

In summary, the results of external tests should always be treated with care. The impact of test bias, measurement error, and so on, means that raw scores are always somewhat fuzzy and simply represent a point estimate of a spread of possible scores which a child might obtain when taking a sample-based achievement test. This is why test results are often reported with a grade which encompasses a range of raw scores, and why test scores are often standardised to indicate a position within the spread of typical results. Whilst there is clearly a difference between a child who scores an A and another who records a D, the difference between 34 out of 50 and 35 out of 50 is moot.

Estimates of the measurement error in tests make this clear. Dylan Wiliam (2000: 3), for example, has estimated that 32% of pupils could be given the wrong National Curriculum level, and that 'we must be aware that the results of even the best tests can be wildly inaccurate for individual students, and that high-stakes decisions should never be based on the results of individual tests'.

Even those tests which are not external high-stakes end-of-key-stage tests are often distorted, as schools introduce perverse incentives for teaching teams to maximise results on internal tests. As Daisy Christodoulou has noted in her influential book, *Making Good Progress?* (2016: 129), summative tests (designed to estimate a child's achievement within a domain) are 'blunt and insensitive instruments when it comes to measuring progress over smaller domains and spans of time'. As Christodoulou says, the risk is that teachers will 'end up prioritising activities which don't lead to significant long-term learning but which do lead to quick, yet misleading, short-term gains' (p. 129).

There are further issues with the conflation of formative assessment and summative assessment, as discussed in *Making Good Progress?*, and Christodoulou's book clearly articulates the problems which schools have faced while struggling to track children's progress using numbers.

Whilst numbers are often defended as 'a signpost, not a destination' (Ofsted, 2017), those who use data in schools should be aware of the uncertainty surrounding the numbers which are generated by tests. This is particularly acute in schools with small cohorts, or when looking at groups with small numbers, but all numerical summaries of children's learning should be treated with the utmost caution by anyone seeking to understand progress and attainment in school.

10.3 The rise of testing as a driver of education policy

The field of school effectiveness research (SER) was discussed in Chapter 9, along with some of the major criticisms levelled at SER. Following the Coleman report in 1966, a growing number of policy researchers in education began to use students' test results in their efforts to explore ways in which education might be improved.

Much of this work is controversial, however. SER rests on a fundamental assumption that state education is broken in some way, and that it needs to be fixed. This is not an uncommon point of view, and discussions about the ongoing need to improve state schools are not new. As Gene Glass, professor at Arizona State University says in *Fertilisers, Pills, and Magnetic Strips* (2008: 4) – which draws on a 40-year long career as a psychometrician, statistician and influential member of the American Education Research Association – 'Debates about reforming schools are as old as public education itself'.

The way in which measurements and numerical data are used by SER researchers is relatively new, however, as is the amount of test data which has been generated within different school systems around the world. Before Coleman, very little test data was available, and what was available was not often matched to schools and teachers. By collecting data on students' test results, matching these to schools and teachers, over multiple school years, early SER advocates believed that it would be relatively simple to identify what makes some schools and teachers 'good' and some schools and teachers 'bad'. Policy makers – particularly those in the USA and the UK – have encouraged this line of enquiry, mandating the use of tests across a wide age range, which has enabled further research and analysis which utilises test data, which in turn has encouraged researchers to lobby for yet more test data to be generated and made available to them.

Whilst ever more ingenious ways are found to differentiate between schools which are held to be similar in some way (either because the proportion of children with particular socio-economic backgrounds is similar, or with similar levels of attainment at some stage, for example), SER researchers have been unable to find very much which would allow policy makers to identify 'good' schools a priori, that is, to identify in advance those factors which might transform schools which are not currently 'good'.

This is partly because test results have proved themselves to be an extremely noisy measure. School test results frequently tend to rise and fall in ways which have been shown to be unpredictable. Outliers within school cohorts often have disproportional effects on the production functions which researchers create, and managing complex data sets regularly proves to be extremely problematic. Schools tend to be dynamic organisations and many cohorts are not particularly stable over time. Children enter and leave school systems randomly, and maintaining accurate data is difficult. Matching data to children and teachers has proven to be complicated. Where education policy decisions are influenced by interpretations of test results, the pressures brought to bear on the system frequently result in perverse incentives for schools and teachers, which in turn often result in undesired outcomes within the school system.

Much of this has been tested to destruction in the USA, which has seen some of the most extreme test-based education policy decisions in the world. Within two decades of the publication of the Coleman report, the Reagan administration had issued an alarmingly titled report on US schooling which ushered in a radical SER-based policy era. *A Nation at Risk* (US NCEE, 1983) was every bit as hysterical as its title suggests, and it laid the foundations for the SER-based experimentation to come.

The authors of *A Nation at Risk* pulled no punches, claiming in the report's introduction that 'the educational foundations of our society are presently being eroded by a rising tide of mediocrity that threatens our very future as a Nation and a people' (US NCEE, 1983: 7). The report drew on test results over the previous 50 years, and based this claim on data showing that average SAT results had dropped between 1963 and 1980.

As others pointed out, the same period had seen a huge change in the numbers – and in particular the numbers within different subgroups of the population – of children taking the SAT. Whereas in 1963 the vast majority of American children were simply not entered into the SAT examinations, by 1980 a much wider cross-section of US society was taking the tests. Whereas previously only rich white children had taken the test, over time more and more less affluent children were doing so.

One well-established positive correlation in education is that between wealth and attainment (Cook, 2012). The increase in numbers of SAT takers in the USA came primarily from groups who were less affluent than those who had previously taken the tests. The reality was that every demographic group had increased its average score on the SAT over time; an example of Simpson's paradox, in which a mean can drop, even though every subgroup's results are increasing, because of changes in the underlying proportions in each subgroup.

This detail did not stop the USA's infatuation with SER-based policy solutions, and the febrile atmosphere created by *A Nation at Risk* enabled George W. Bush to introduce his controversial 'No Child Left Behind' (NCLB) policy in 2001. This tied federal funding to strict data-based conditions and saw large numbers of schools subject to brutal decision making based on test results.

Schools were required to test children in Grade 3 to Grade 8 (aged 9 to 14) in reading and mathematics. Test scores had to be reported by race, ethnicity, low-income status, disability status and proficiency in English. Any school which did not meet its annual targets would be subject to intervention by the state. This might mean that staff would be fired, or the school might be closed or handed to a third party.

By 2014, the point by which the Bush administration had decided that all students should achieve proficiency on state tests, the experiment had failed. As Diane Ravitch, a Washington insider turned critic, noted in her book *Reign of Error*, 'as 2014 approached, the majority of public schools in the nation had been declared failures, including some excellent, highly regarded schools' (2014: 11).

Ravitch summarised the rise of data: 'As 2014 neared, states were spending hundreds of millions of dollars each year on testing and on test preparation materials; the schools in some districts were allocating 20 percent of the school year to preparing for tests' (2014: 13). And this data was being generated at a clear cost to the schooling which children were experiencing:

This unnatural focus on testing produced perverse but predictable results: it narrowed the curriculum; many districts scaled back time for the arts, history, civics, physical education, science, foreign language, and whatever was not tested. Cheating scandals occurred in Atlanta, Washington, D.C., and other districts. States like New York manipulated the passing score on state tests to inflate the results and bring them closer to Washington's unrealistic goal. Teaching to the test, once considered unprofessional and unethical, became common practice. (Ravitch, 2014: 13–4)

Once it became clear that the NCLB and its successor, the Obama administration's Race to the Top programme, had failed in their goals to ensure that every child reached proficiency, a new consensus helped to introduce the Every Student Succeeds Act of 2015. Whilst this continued to require schools to test children in Grades 3 to 8 as before, the act gave individual states much more flexibility in the way they held schools to account.

The UK was not immune to the pressures which SER advocates had brought to bear. The current system of educational testing in England is outlined in Chapter 2. When national testing was introduced in the 1990s, written tests of children aged 7, 11 and 14 joined a revised system of testing of 16-year-olds. Prior to this, the government did not have comprehensive test results for those under 16, as no national system of testing had existed. As per the American model, tests of those under 16 focused on English and mathematics. Tests at age 14 were abandoned altogether in 2008 after various marking scandals. Science was initially tested at age 11, until these tests were abandoned in 2009.

The English system was specifically designed to allow government officials to compare test results over time, so that numerical measures of progress could be created with which to hold schools to account. Subsequent UK governments have continued to place test data at the heart of school accountability processes. By the early 21st century, despite the many problematic issues which had become clear, testing had taken its place as a significant driver of education policy.

10.4 The problems with using Value Added measures to summarise school and teacher effectiveness

School effectiveness researchers have developed and promoted the use of systems which attempt to measure 'value added' by schools and teachers. This concept, borrowed from economics, is essentially fairly simple: measure value prior to a process, then undertake the process and measure the value of the final output. The difference between the output and the initial input is the value added by the process.

One of the main proponents of using what have become known as Value Added Measures (VAMs) in education was William Sanders, who helped to develop the

Tennessee Value-Added Assessment System (TVAAS) in the 1990s. An agricultural statistician whose main expertise was developed whilst working for the University of Tennessee's Institute of Agricultural Studies, Sanders developed a system which compared expected test scores (which were modelled using a form of an education production function, as popularised by James Coleman) with actual scores recorded by children on tests.

Sanders' system was based on monitoring student progress over a single school year, and he asserted that he could produce a numerical summary of the value added by whoever taught a particular child. This idea was taken up enthusiastically by SER proponents, who were keen to identify 'good' and 'bad' teachers and schools, based on test results.

As a result of the TVAAS, and systems which were similar to it, policy makers began to rank teachers and schools. In many US states, those teachers who were held to be poorly performing were either threatened with the loss of their job if scores did not improve, or, in some extreme cases, were simply fired. Some US policy makers took up the reins of VAMs, claiming that 'deselecting' teachers (i.e. removing those whose VAM figures placed them at the bottom of the rankings) would improve outcomes, and suggested that policies which implemented these kinds of measures should be pursued urgently.

In *Rethinking Value-Added Models in Education* (2014), Professor Audrey Amrein-Beardsley of Arizona State University refers to policy based on VAMs as a 'Measure and Punish' (M & P) Theory of Change.

> The M & P Theory of Change is based on a paucity of empirical research evidence, however. Very few scientific studies have evidenced that this theory of change works. Rather countless scientific studies have evidenced that the numerous educational policies based on this theory of change have caused unintended consequences. In addition, numerous academic researchers suggest that the negative side effects altogether outweigh the few positive benefits that may have been realised, if at all, post policy. (Amrein-Beardsley, 2014: xiv)

Writing in 2012, Professor Linda Darling-Hammond of Stanford University said that she

> was once bullish on the idea of using 'value-added methods' for assessing teacher effectiveness. I have since realized that these measures, while valuable for large-scale studies, are seriously flawed for evaluating individual teachers, and that rigorous, ongoing assessment by teaching experts serves everyone better. (2012: 24)

Having reviewed the evidence, Hammond changed her view. 'These test scores largely reflect whom a teacher teaches, not how well they teach', she wrote. 'In particular, teachers show lower gains when they have large numbers of new

English-learners and students with disabilities than when they teach other students. This is true even when statistical methods are used to "control" for student characteristics' (2012: 32).

The rush to evaluate the outcomes of schooling via VAMs in the USA, and the increasing concerns voiced by the academic community, became so great that by 2014 the American Statistical Association (ASA) was moved to issue a statement on the use of Value-Added Models for educational assessment. Whilst the ASA naturally supported the use of data and statistical models to improve education, it urged caution, noting the statistical complexity of VAMs, the limitations and sensitivity of different models, and that 'most VAM studies find that teachers account for about 1% to 14% of the variability in test scores' (ASA, 2014: 2).

In plain English, the ASA encouraged data analysis in education, encouraged policy makers to beware unqualified users of complex statistics, noted that VAMs are highly sensitive to assumptions made in the modelling process, and pointed out that teachers account for extremely small levels of variability in test scores. This is not to say that teachers do not matter. As the ASA noted:

> This is not saying that teachers have little effect on students, but that variation among teachers accounts for a small part of the variation in scores. The majority of the variation in test scores is attributable to factors outside of the teacher's control such as student and family background, poverty, curriculum, and unmeasured influences. (ASA, 2014: 7)

Teachers clearly make a difference; the effect of most teachers is of similar magnitude.

As the ASA explained, VAMs typically capture correlations, not causations. Given the fact that the majority of the variability in test scores is accounted for by factors beyond the control of the school, using VAMs to measure teachers (and, by extension, schools) is clearly not justified. The signal is simply swamped by the noise in any set of measures.

As Diane Ravitch (2014: 113) summarised somewhat more bluntly, 'Stated as politely as possible, value-added assessment is bad science. It may even be junk science. It is inaccurate, unstable, and unreliable'.

The UK has not been immune to the use of Value Added measures. The introduction of end-of-key-stage tests and assessments in the 1990s were explicitly designed to provide data which could then be used to hold schools to account. Following concerns raised by the academic community that the use of raw test scores to judge school effectiveness would simply reflect non-school factors influencing educational outcomes, the government instructed a team of academics to provide a method of using Value Added measures, mandating that they develop 'a national system of value added reporting for schools based on prior attainment, which will be statistically valid and readily understood' (Fitz-Gibbon, 1997: 3).

The final report to the government, written by Carol Taylor Fitz-Gibbon (1997) of Durham University, made it clear that there were many concerns about the potential misuse and misunderstanding of the Value Added measures which were proposed, but also recommended, as the government mandated, that a system of Value Added measures should be introduced. Whilst the academic report suggested that any publication of Value Added information should be limited – due to potential misinterpretation by non-experts – the government simply went ahead and published Value Added scores for all schools.

Whilst the Fitz-Gibbon recommendations suggested that only the top 10% of schools for Value Added in each major subject be published (with minimum cohort sizes of '30 to 40' being recommended), at least three years' data should be used in any analysis and, tellingly, they listed ways in which the school system would be negatively affected by the publication of performance data. This was ignored as the UK government developed its version of Value Added measures for schools over the coming years.

Value Added scores for schools in England were first published in 2002. They proved controversial, as schools with high raw results inevitably had linked high Value Added scores. As a result, a system of 'Contextual Value Added' (CVA) scores was published from 2006 to 2010. CVA scores were:

> calculated as a flexible function of not only their KS2 test scores when they started secondary schooling, but also on their age, gender, ethnicity, socio-economic status (as proxied by free school meal eligibility), and various other pupil and school characteristics. (Leckie and Goldstein, 2016: 5)

These, in turn, were controversial, with the government claiming that 'by adjusting for school differences in pupils' socioeconomic and demographic backgrounds CVA entrenched low education aspirations in disadvantaged pupils groups' (Leckie and Goldstein, 2016: 5). CVA was superseded by a return to the Value Added measure used from 2002 to 2005.

From 2016, secondary schools were evaluated using a new measure, Progress 8, using a Value Added approach with certain limitations as to which subjects can be included in calculations. These are still biased, however, and 'schools with the most able intakes, whether they are overtly selective or not, tend to achieve an above average Progress 8 score', as EducationDatalab, an influential education think tank, pointed out in 2016 (Thompson, 2016).

The situation in English primary schools has been similar, with a range of Value Added measures being used. Measuring children as they begin primary school has proved to be difficult for a number of reasons, not least because formal school begins in Year 1, at a point when children have usually had an initial year of teaching (in Reception classes which take children aged 4, who turn 5 during the academic year). Whilst (at the time of writing) there are moves to introduce a 'Reception baseline' assessment which could be used to generate VAMs, the government has struggled to create a suitable measure which could be used.

VAMs in elementary schooling have employed test scores at the end of Year 2 (the end of Key Stage 1) and the end of Year 6 (the end of Key Stage 2). This has introduced incentives for primary schools to suppress KS1 scores (which are internally generated by teaching teams) and to maximise scores at KS2 (which are externally assessed). In addition, infant schools (which cater for children up to the end of Year 2) have tended to report high KS1 scores relative to primary schools, and junior schools (which teach children in Key Stage 2) have complained that they inherit children with inflated scores, which makes generating high progress scores difficult.

Unlike the USA, Value Added has not been created at teacher level by the UK government, and the impact of Value Added has been somewhat different to the extremes in the American experience. Ofsted have used VAMs extensively, however, and the predictions about the negative effects of VAM-based accountability have largely come true. Whilst this has to be balanced against the pressure which VAMs have placed on the school system as a whole, the net result has meant that individual schools have had to work hard to ensure that those both managing and overseeing them understand the wider picture of each school's academic performance, and the many limitations of Value Added measures.

10.5 Ongoing concerns with the use and frequent misinterpretation of pupil performance data in education

One prominent critic of the way in which pupil performance data has been used to judge schools and teachers in the UK is Harvey Goldstein of the University of Bristol. As early as 2001, Goldstein expressed concern that 'an important foundation for … accountability measures in the eyes of government is the notion that assessments based upon centrally controlled tests are "objective" and also reliable enough to provide acceptable criteria for comparisons; both these assumptions are questionable' (Goldstein, 2001: 434).

As well as concerns about the accuracy and utility of measures of pupil performance over time, Goldstein identified further issues which arose with the governmental use of the data being generated by government-mandated testing of pupils. As politicians began to use test data to drive change in schools, teachers came under pressure via the use of annual performance reviews which were required to place, as Goldstein notes, 'considerable emphasis upon pupil progress as a means of judging the performance of teachers' (2001: 436).

Goldstein was very clear that there were multiple issues with the way in which pupil performance data was being used within the schooling system as a result of government policy. He made clear the serious concern that the non-school drivers of pupil performance were often ignored, and the direction of travel in attempting to link teachers to pupil performance was likely to cause problems in future:

> Throughout these documents there is the implicit assumption that teachers and schools alone are what influence the achievements of their pupils. Yet, not only is prior attainment important, so is the education at any previous schools attended, mobility, special needs etc. Moreover, especially in secondary schools, it is very difficult to ascribe the progress of any one pupil in a given subject to the teacher of that subject. Pupil progress will be affected by other teachers and features of schooling and background – perhaps to an even greater extent – and the attempt to associate progress for a pupil with a single teacher is not only divisive, it is also likely to be misleading. (Goldstein, 2001: 437)

Goldstein's concern with the misleading use of pupil performance data pre-dates the introduction of end-of-key-stage testing, and as early as 1996 he was expressing alarm about the way in which data was beginning to be used to hold schools to account. In an article written with David Spiegelhalter, another prominent voice in discussions about the use of statistical techniques in education, Goldstein notes that 'current official support for output league tables, even adjusted, is misplaced and governments should be concerned that potential users are properly informed of their shortcomings' (Goldstein and Spiegelhalter, 1996: 405).

School league tables were beginning to be published in the 1990s and Goldstein became one of their most trenchant critics. In their most simplistic form, league tables simply list schools by rank of an output measure, such as average examination score at age 11, 16 or 18. Over time, GCSE scores began to be reported by slightly more specific measures, such as the percentage of students achieving five or more grades at A to C.

Encouraged by the availability of student data, news media outlets reported these results in simple league tables. These league tables took no account of the intakes of different schools, and, as a result, those schools with high attaining children on entry naturally recorded higher exit grades. Goldstein was particularly concerned that parents were being encouraged to use GCSE results as a measure of a school's performance, arguing that the time span between children entering and leaving secondary school was so great that any data was out of date, and that the data simply reflected average intake in any given school.

Following the concerns expressed by Goldstein and others, official statistics attempted to provide some indication of the uncertainty in the data which was being published. This led to schools being treated as if they were random samples of the wider population, and official statistics began to use techniques developed to manage standard errors to present results with confidence intervals.

Thus, by 2011, school performance tables were being published by the government, which presented 'statistical-model-based estimates of the educational effectiveness of schools, together with 95 per cent confidence intervals to communicate their statistical uncertainty'. As Goldstein notes, however, 'this information, particularly the notion of statistical uncertainty, is hard for users to understand' (Leckie and Goldstein, 2011: 207).

Government data reported schools as a Value Added score with a lower and upper limit to a confidence interval, which Goldstein summarised as: 'loosely speaking, each 95 per cent confidence interval gives the range of scores within which we are 95 per cent certain that the true CVA score for that school lies' (Leckie and Goldstein, 2011: 209). News outlets simply ignored this attempt to represent uncertainty about school effectiveness data, and reported schools in rank order of raw Value Added scores.

Elsewhere, the rise of the use of performance data meant that schools were increasingly being judged using complex statistics which also relied heavily on ideas derived from methods for interpreting standard errors. Official statistics used for school accountability (such as annual RAISE reports used extensively from the early 2000s) included confidence intervals, which encouraged those who used the data to consider whether results were 'significant', and to assume that any unusual data implied that a school was either 'better' or 'worse' than average.

Whilst Goldstein's concern about the misuse of school league tables was laudable, others were concerned that the underlying assumptions being made were questionable, and that the use of confidence intervals was not justified, either within school league tables or in statistics used for the purpose of accountability in general.

Stephen Gorard, Professor of Education and Public Policy at Durham University, has long argued that the use of standard errors in educational contexts is unjustified: 'All work based on standard errors – significance testing, confidence intervals, power calculations, multilevel modelling, and so on – requires complete random samples/groups as a mathematical necessity' (Gorard, 2015: 72).

Since schools are not random samples of the population, it makes no sense, in Gorard's view, to present any kind of confidence interval of the sort recommended by Goldstein, and used with much of the pupil performance statistics which have been used for purposes of accountability. It can be argued that using measures of uncertainty when summarising school pupil performance data simply muddies an already confusing picture.

Certainly, official interpretations of statistical significance and confidence intervals are often highly misleading. Part of the confusion arises from the frequent conflation of statistical significance and what might be termed 'educational significance'. Even where government statisticians have attempted to help users of statistics understand the nuances involved, the underlying problems in interpretation become apparent. In official guidance published in RAISEonline Summary Reports in 2015, examples of which can be found on the Databusting for Schools website, the DfE explained that 'in RAISEonline, green and blue shading are used to demonstrate a statistically significant difference between the school data for a particular group and national data for the same group. This does not necessarily correlate with being educationally significant'.

A key issue with this type of statement is not only that it implies that using a confidence interval (which is largely what the green and blue shading in these reports was used for) is justified when presenting the underlying data, but that it also recognises that misinterpretation of confidence intervals is widespread.

Gorard goes as far as suggesting that all statistics based on standard error are fundamentally unsound:

> Anything predicated on a standard error does not make sense – it cannot exist mathematically – unless it involves true random sampling. Significance tests, p-values, confidence intervals, power calculations and some complex statistical models such as multilevel modelling, are all clearly predicated on working with a random sample(s). This means that all such techniques are useless in practice for the simple reason that random samples generally do not exist in real research. (Gorard, 2015: 79)

Criticism of the use of standard errors has increased in recent years, and the misunderstanding and misuse of p-values appear to be widespread. Multiple problems with research which relies on p-values in particular have been discussed widely since the turn of the century. As early as 2005, John Ioannidis published an enormously influential study entitled, 'Why most published research findings are false', which expanded on issues raised by 'the convenient, yet ill-founded strategy of claiming conclusive research findings solely on the basis of a single study assessed by formal statistical significance, typically for a p-value less than 0.05' (Ioannidis, 2005: online). The problems have become so well established they are now known as the 'reproducibility crisis', in that the results of many studies are difficult or impossible to replicate.

The concern regarding the use of p-values led the American Statistical Association to publish a statement on p-values in 2016 (Wasserstein and Lazar, 2016), which acknowledged the longstanding issues which had been raised by the statistical community, and attempted to provide some clarity on the acceptable limits to the use of statistical significance.

The debate about the use of p-values, standard errors, confidence intervals and statistical significance continues. It is clear, however, that anyone using complex statistics to shed light on school performance should be aware that there will always be considerable controversy about their interpretation. Academics like Goldstein have rightly worried about the over-simplification of summaries of pupil performance data, and have attempted to suggest ways to improve public understanding of the uncertainty involved. Gorard and others have argued that many of the fundamental assumptions made by those analysing pupil data are not warranted, and lead to incorrect and misleading conclusions.

This ongoing debate about the use and interpretation of complex statistics should give anyone working with school data cause for concern. Over and above the issues we have touched on here – from problems inherent in attempting to rank schools by their effectiveness, through questionable attempts to understand uncertainty and randomness within data, to the dubious use of statistics based on standard errors – are the unintended side-effects of systems which elevate numbers above the people they attempt to summarise.

10.6 The unintended side-effects of the use and misuse of test data

The consequences of reducing aspects of schooling to simplistic numerical measures have become increasingly clear as educational systems have become gradually more fixated on pupil performance data. Whilst a degree of pressure on schools to strive for ongoing improvement is clearly necessary, data-related pressures have caused some systems to buckle under the weight of accountability measures which are increasingly data-led.

The demands of the USA's No Child Left Behind policy led to a widespread campaign of civil disobedience, as parents began to resist the testing regimes which were being imposed on schools. Parents raised concerns that school time was being dominated by test preparation rather than being focused on teaching and learning. Many parents were concerned that test results were being used in ways which actively discriminated against certain groups of pupils, such as English-language learners, children with disabilities and those from lower-income backgrounds.

Groups such as National Center for Fair & Open Testing (FairTest) began campaigning for parents to opt out of testing regimes, which led to widespread boycotts of testing. In 2012, Reuters reported that a 'backlash against high-stakes standardized testing is sweeping through U.S. school districts as parents, teachers, and administrators protest that the exams are unfair, unreliable and unnecessarily punitive' (Simon, 2012: online). By 2017, local newspapers in New York were reporting that, in some areas, 20% of local children were being withdrawn from standardised testing (Campbell, 2017).

In England, the focus of discontent has been on Key Stage 2 tests, taken when most children end their primary school education. The earliest protests came in 2010, when the BBC reported that a quarter of schools had boycotted the Key Stage 2 SATs (BBC, 2010). These protests were led by teaching unions, and the decision to boycott tests was made by head teachers, rather than by parents and families, as in the USA.

The 2010 boycott, coupled with a change of government, saw a government review of Key Stage 2 testing, which reported that 'the main concern is that the current system is too "high stakes" for schools due to the publication of test results and their use for holding schools accountable for their performance, which leads to unintended consequences such as over-rehearsal and "teaching to the test'" (Bew, 2011: 22–23). Whilst minor tweaks to the testing regime at Key Stage 2 were recommended, many of the complaints made by the teaching unions were disregarded.

The success of parent-led campaigning against standardised testing in the USA led to similar campaigns (often supported and fuelled by teaching unions) being developed in England. 2016 saw the founding of the *Let The Kids Be Kids* pressure group, which campaigned for parents to boycott both Key Stage 1 and Key Stage 2 tests from 2016 onwards, partly as a result of changes in the way in which children were being assessed at the end of these key stages.

All of this came during a period of intense criticism of the way in which reform of primary assessment, in particular, was being implemented. The UK parliament's Select Committee on Education conducted its own review in 2016–17, which criticised the way that reforms to primary end-of-key-stage assessments had been managed since 2010, and made recommendations for ways to improve the system of national testing in primary school. The Department of Education conducted its own consultation of primary assessment in 2017, which introduced yet further recommendations for the future of assessment in primary school.

Changes to secondary assessment were also under close scrutiny, as reform of both Key Stage 4 and Key Stage 5 (GCSE and A Level) examinations took place. Most political discussion of secondary assessment was held at governmental level, and a lively debate continues about the most effective methods of grading pupils nearing the end of compulsory education.

Whilst ongoing reform of state education is clearly desirable as governments and the teaching profession strive to improve the effectiveness of schooling, the increased focus on data based on pupil performance in assessments has clearly had an impact beyond the classroom. The tension between the benefits of accurate measurement and the negative effects of systems of measurement has proven to be difficult to resolve, and those within education are likely to struggle with the inherent dilemmas for some time to come.

10.7 So what should we do?

It is clear that there is no settled consensus on the way in which numerical data based on pupil performance in assessments is gathered, analysed and used. For every measure developed, and every interpretation of the resulting data, there are justified concerns about the validity of claims which are made based on pupil performance data.

Whilst this is particularly true of performance data generated by younger children for whom the outcomes of tests have no direct consequence or meaning, the drivers of test results in older children also mean that misinterpretation of test data is, unfortunately, all too common. For example, whilst school clearly has an important role to play in enabling children to learn, extensive evidence suggests that the main drivers of outcomes in school are external to school themselves. Whilst cautious politicians are careful to distinguish between school effects and pupil effects, this subtlety is easily lost in the hubbub of educational debate.

We also know that using pupil performance data to judge schools by attainment benefits some schools and disadvantages others. The focus on pupil progress rather than pupil attainment recognises the fact that there is a clear relationship between different groups of children – and by extension the schools in which they are educated – and the outcomes those children record in assessments. Put bluntly, those who start schools at higher (or lower) levels of attainment tend to record higher (or lower) levels of attainment at later points in their education.

Whilst a focus on the progress different children make from similar starting points is welcome, it does not remove the underlying issues with using measures of attainment to judge schools and children. The simple fact is that those who make the most progress in education are also, by definition, those who achieve the highest levels of attainment. The idea that progress is a better guide than raw attainment makes a number of assumptions about the accuracy and validity of earlier measurements of attainment used to measure progress, as well as making assumptions about the way in which children develop as they progress through education.

Reducing the effectiveness of schooling to pupil performance data leads to other perverse incentives. Schools have clear motivations to seek out only those students whose test results add to overall results, and to avoid those children who do not. Those who struggle to show above-average progress and attainment through difficult personal circumstances, special educational needs or any of the many factors which affect children's educational progress, have found themselves subtly (and not so subtly) excluded from certain schools. When the easiest way to improve a school is to change its intake, it is not surprising to see schools pursuing policies which do just that.

Even where schools are acting honourably, and educating a representative cross-section of the population which applies to attend them, wider factors influence the intake of schools. In the UK and the USA, the majority of schooling is non-selective, inasmuch as schools do not select the children who attend them. Using strict admissions criteria based on distance from home to school is the most common method of allocating pupils to particular schools.

This gives parents some choice over schooling, as families can, to a certain extent, select where they live and therefore which schools their children attend. This selection by families changes the intake of schools, such that the population local to a school is different to the national population of school-aged children.

This clustering effect is well known and understood in academic education circles, but often ignored by (or simply outside the knowledge of) politicians and others.

As a result of these issues and more, academics such as Harvey Goldstein and Stephen Gorard in the UK, and Linda Darling-Hammond and Audrey Amrein-Beardsley in the USA, have cautioned against the over-interpretation of complex statistics. Whilst their criticisms are often difficult for lay people to follow, their voices are important in the debate about the use of pupil performance data in discussions regarding school improvement and accountability.

This suggests, once again, that those assessing schools should be extremely cautious in their use of pupil performance data to judge those schools. Numbers may not mean what people take them to mean, and, rather than being 'a signpost not a direction', data may actually direct decisions rather than start conversations about schools. Some data may actually be harmful to good decision making, providing a false sense of security when the situation is much more unclear than might be assumed.

10.7.1 What should school leaders do?

Those who manage schools will be well aware of the sheer volume of data which is available to decision makers in education. This in itself makes the task of managing education data almost impossible, as the sheer weight of numbers is frequently overwhelming.

There are a few broad principles for school leaders, however:

1. Be extremely selective.
2. Use visual representations of key data sets.
3. Avoid internal misconceptions.
4. Prepare for external scrutiny.

Rather than being overwhelmed by the sheer volume of data, choose to focus on key areas which you have identified. Endless discussion about subgroups of subgroups is unnecessary. Look at key areas which match your school improvement plan.

Numbers are difficult to interpret. Use visual representations of data. Ensure that any graph is not misleading, and do not be tempted to present data selectively.

Ensure that you have a good data team. If you find sifting data difficult, find a member of staff who can help, or make use of an external data analyst. Several pairs of eyes are always better than one, and ensure that key members of staff do not over-interpret data.

You are accountable for your school, and external agencies will make assumptions about your school based on the available data. Work with your data team to anticipate potential misconceptions and prepare your response to any lines of enquiry.

10.7.2 What should teaching teams do?

Broadly, you will have two distinct sets of data: that required by school managers, and that you use to assist in your teaching. For mandated school data, make sure that you work as a critical friend to your school managers. Many schools make extensive demands of their teaching teams' time to collect data which is either unusable or simply ignored. Ensure that managers have reduced the burden of data as much as possible, whilst allowing for a reasonable monitoring of standards.

In your own work, consider how data gathering can assist you to support all of your pupils. Use age data to monitor children's progress relative to their peers. Use rankings to identify and investigate unexpected movements over time.

10.7.3 What should school governors do?

Be aware of the measurement errors inherent in pupil attainment and progress data. Ensure that your school management team is focused on reducing the data burden on teaching teams, and that the school is prepared to manage lines of enquiry which may come from the accountability system.

10.7.4 What should parents, inspectors and others do?

If you are an expert user of data, ensure that you share your expertise. If you are not, listen carefully to those who can explain the common misconceptions about school data, and treat claims based on data with cautious scepticism.

10.7.5 What should everyone involved with schools do?

Accept that large amounts of complex data are overwhelming. Whilst there are many excellent ways of summarising numbers, every statistic loses some definition of the bigger picture. As we summarise numbers, we move into bands of uncertainty, and we use numbers in ways which might not be immediately apparent. Even a simple statistic such as a mean can hide a huge variety of possible underlying data and, in the wrong circumstances, can mislead to an extraordinary extent. We owe it to our students and ourselves not to be misled.

10.8 Summary

In this final chapter, we have taken a critical look at the use of numbers in education, considering what has been learned from psychometrics to help us to understand the possibilities and limitations of the data we generate in schools.

We have explored how testing has developed as a driver of education policy, and how Value Added measures, in particular, have become an increasingly contentious part of the current educational policy framework. We have considered the problems with using Value Added measures to summarise school and teacher effectiveness, and looked at the ongoing concerns with the use and frequent misinterpretation of pupil performance data in education, and the potential harm this can cause, particularly in light of the unintended side-effects of the use and misuse of test data.

Finally, we have considered how school leaders, teaching teams, school governors, parents, inspectors and others should work with education data, recognising the many benefits which rigorously developed data can bring whilst ensuring that data is not used in ways which may cause more harm than good. As the examples discussed in the opening chapter clearly demonstrate, it is easy to jump to simple conclusions when looking at seemingly conclusive data-based evidence. Databusting requires further careful analysis before decisions are made.

References

American Statistical Association (ASA) (2014) *ASA Statement on Using Value-Added Models for Educational Assessment*. Alexandria, VA: ASA.

Amrein-Beardsley, A. (2014) *Rethinking Value-Added Models in Education*. New York: Routledge.

BBC (2010) '"A quarter of schools" boycotted Sats tests', *BBC News*, 6 July. Available at: www.bbc.co.uk/news/10521289. Accessed 20/2/2018.

BBC (2017) Eton College teacher 'breached exam security'. *BBC News*, 26 August. Available at: www.bbc.co.uk/news/uk-england-berkshire-41060011. Accessed 20/2/2018.

Bew (2011) *Independent Review of Key Stage 2 Testing, Assessment and Accountability*. London: Department for Education.

Campbell, J. (2017) 'Opt-out movement remains strong across New York'. *Democrat & Chronicle*, 2 March. Available at: www.democratandchronicle.com/story/news/politics/albany/2017/03/02/opt-out-movement-new-york/98608956. Accessed 20/2/2018.

Christodoulou, D. (2016) *Making Good Progress? The Future of Assessment for Learning*. Oxford: Oxford University Press.

Cook, C. (2012) 'The social mobility challenge for school reformers', *The Financial Times*, 12 February.

Darling-Hammond, L. (2012) 'Value-added evaluation hurts teaching', *Education Week*, 31(24): 24–32.

Department for Education (DfE) (2015) [add full details]

Fitz-Gibbon, C. (1997) *The Value Added National Project Final Report*. Durham: Centre for Curriculum, Evaluation and Management.

Glass, G.V. (2008) *Fertilizers, Pills, and Magnetic Strips: The Fate of Public Education in America*. Charlotte, NC: Information Age Publishing.

Goldstein, H. (2001) *Using Pupil Performance Data for Judging Schools and Teachers: Scope and Limitations*. London: Institute of Education.

Goldstein, H. and Spiegelhalter, D.J. (1996) 'League tables and their limitations: Statistical issues in comparisons of institutional performance', *Journal of the Royal Statistical Society: Series A (Statistics in Society)*, 159(3): 385–443.

Gorard, S. (2015) 'Rethinking "quantitative" methods and the development of new researchers', *Review of Education*, 3(1): 72–96.

Ioannidis, J.P.A. (2005) 'Why most published research findings are false', *PLoS Med*, 2(8): e124.

Leckie, G. and Goldstein, H. (2011) 'Understanding uncertainty in school league tables', *Fiscal Studies*, 32(2):207–224.

Leckie, G. and Goldstein, H. (2016) *The Evolution of School League Tables in England 1992–2016: 'Contextual Value Added', 'Expected Progress' and 'Progress 8'*. Bristol: University of Bristol.

Ofsted (2017) *Inspection and the Use of Grade Predictions*. Available at: https://education inspection.blog.gov.uk/2017/03/02/inspection-and-the-use-of-grade-predictions. Accessed 20/2/2018.

Ravitch, D. (2014) *Reign of Error: The Hoax of the Privatization Movement and the Danger to America's Public Schools*. New York: Vintage.

Simon, S. (2012) 'Parents protest surge in standardized testing'. *Reuters*, 12 June. Available at: www.reuters.com/article/us-usa-education-testing/parents-protest-surge-in-standard-ized-testing-idUSBRE85B0EO20120612. Accessed 20/2/2018.

Thompson, D. (2016) 'Why do pupils at schools with the most able intakes tend to make the most progress?' Available at: http://educationdatalab.org.uk/2015/05/why-do-pupils-at-schools-with-the-most-able-intakes-tend-to-make-the-most-progress/2. Accessed 20/2/2018.

United States National Commission on Excellence in Education (US NCEE) (1983) *A Nation at Risk*. Washington, DC: United States National Commission on Excellence in Education.

Wasserstein, R.L. and Lazar, N.A. (2016) 'The ASA's statement on p-values: Context, process, and purpose', *The American Statistician*, 70(2): 129–33.

Wiliam, D. (2000) *Reliability, Validity, and all that Jazz*. London: King's College London.

Index